Soul Journeys:

Past and Future Lives

Soul Journeys:

Past and Future Lives

Rosemary Ellen Guiley

Visionary Living, Inc.
New Milford, Connecticut
Copyright Visionary Living, Inc., 2013

Soul Journeys: Past and Future Lives
By Rosemary Ellen Guiley
Copyright Visionary Living, Inc. 2011, 2013

This book is a revised and updated edition of *Tales of Reincarnation* by Rosemary Ellen Guiley, copyright Visionary Living, Inc., 1989.

All rights reserved.
No part of this book may be reproduced without permission.

Cover art designed by Raúl DaSilva

ISBN 978-0-9857243-7-5 (pbk.)

Contents

Introduction	vii
1. Reincarnation in the Age of New Consciousness	1
2. Spontaneous Recall of Past Lives	18
3. Induced Recall of Past Lives	29
4. Patterns in Past Lives	45
5. Slain in the Viet Nam and Civil Wars	60
6. The New Atlanteans	66
7. Karmic Ties with Others	79
8. Keeper of the Jim Morrison Flame	95
9. The Karma and Grace of Love and Hate	106
10. Phobias and Physical Karma	127
11. Skills and Talents	145
12. The Traveling Interplanetary Musician	157
13. The Past-Life Muse	168
14. Marion Zimmer Bradley's Mirror to the Past	180
15. Lessons and Missions	189
16. A Pagan Priestess Finds Her Roots	205
17. The Healer Within	218
18. New Horizons in Reincarnation Research	228
About the Author	237
Bibliography	239

Introduction

I believe in reincarnation. Since childhood I have had inklings of other lives in other places, and by my early teens I decided I could not accept the prevailing Western view that each soul has but one life on Earth followed by eternity in either a heaven or a hell. Even the prospect of eternity in heaven did not seem pleasing, and it reduced life on Earth to little more than a pass-fail entrance exam. One life followed by eternity in heaven or hell did not explain the inequities of life I saw around me.

As I grew older I researched reincarnation, and absorbed it into my increasingly eclectic spiritual belief system. I also had more personal experiences that validated for me that I have lived before. Some of the experiences came in past-life regressions, but the most convincing came in spontaneous experiences such as lucid dreams.

Soul Journeys: Past Lives & Reincarnation discusses a cross-cultural history of our beliefs about reincarnation, and presents dramatic true stories about the past-life discoveries of individuals around the world. The stories are full of surprises, drama, tragedy, happiness, discovery and revelation. Most of them are drawn from contemporary people from all walks of life. I draw on cases reported in the reincarnation literature, and also tell original stories, some of the first time, from people I interviewed.

Among those who granted exclusive interviews to me on their reincarnation experiences and research were noted authors Marion Zimmer Bradley, Michael Talbot and Barbara Hand Clow; Danny Sugerman, manager of The Doors and a close friend of Jim Morrison; psychic Laurie McQuary; regressionist Sandee Mac; Pagan leader Selena Fox; and interdisciplinary cosmologist Paul von Ward. Of those, Bradley, Talbot and Sugerman have passed on—and perhaps into new lives.

In addition, I have added a new section, the final chapter, on psychophysical research of reincarnation, and the potential of Electronic Voice Phenomena and spirit communications.

I am not attempting to prove reincarnation, but to allow readers to draw their own conclusions from the experiences and evidence. The past-life experiencers express a range of attitudes toward reincarnation, from skepticism to acceptance to passionate belief. Rather than trying to prove reincarnation, we gain more benefit from the examination of past lives and their impact upon the present life. When confronted with information or memories related to another life in another time, how does one's perspective of self, the world and the cosmos change? As the stories here demonstrate, the change is often positive, from a shift in attitude to complete transformation of lifestyle and vision of one's purpose in life.

Over the course of time, my own views have expanded, changed, and, most importantly, become much more fluid. We live within overlapping dimensional realities, and that the fullness of our being is beyond our present comprehension. I think that some of our "past life memories" are time/dimension slips, in which we get a glimpse of our multi-dimensional self having an experience simultaneous to the life we are living in this particular reality. Other recollections may be dips into a cosmic pool of human experiences, accumulated throughout history, which might explain why multiple people can feel they were the same person in the past. Yet other recollections may be distinct and unique to the individual.

Some people believe reincarnation is a series of lives that moves a soul personality through time and growth. I believe the progress of the soul involves also concurrent lives rather than a single march through linear time.

The important thing is to integrate our experiences in meaningful ways that help us make sense of life, purpose, and connection to the whole of creation. Our explorations of our memories of other lives may lead us to profoundly change what we believe about reincarnation, and survival after death.

Learning about our other incarnations is like finding a treasure chest of information. We are enriched in wonderful ways about who we are, and our journeys through this amazing cosmos.

— Rosemary Ellen Guiley

1

Reincarnation in the Age of New Consciousness

THE DOOR TO THE PAST sometimes swings open unexpectedly. When it does, strange winds blow through our lives. The winds bring bits and pieces from unknown lands in unknown times swirling round us, teasing us and mystifying us. Oddly, we know these bits and pieces belong to us. Looking through the open door into an endless dark, we are suddenly aware that the immediate physical world in which we are rooted no longer is All There Is. We feel extensions of ourselves out there in the dark, shapes waiting to take on more form.

A glimpse through the door to the past can challenge our fundamental beliefs about life, death and the fate of the soul upon death. If we have not believed in reincarnation and are confronted with an experience that convinces us we have lived before, then we must reevaluate our view of our role in the scheme of the cosmos. If the experience has any meaning for us at all, our lives invariably change, and usually for the better.

The interest in exploring past lives is part of the New Age, or more aptly, the Age of New Consciousness, the movement which began in the

1960s to explore metaphysical, spiritual, religious and holistic systems and concepts. Those who are influenced by the New Age are searching for ways to expand and uplift our consciousness, to see the cosmos and our role in it in new perspectives. Looking at past lives is one of those ways.

Since the 1960s, an increasing number of Westerners have embarked upon past-life journeys for self-discovery or to solve problems, by undergoing regression by hypnosis. Many persons have sought past-life therapy, a relatively new profession.

For some individuals, however, the journey into the past begins unexpectedly, when the door to the past swings suddenly open and they dare to step through to the other side:

From Masada you can see forever
The ruins of Masada, the ancient fortress where the Jews made their final and desperate stand against the invading Romans in 70, sit atop a dry, boat-shaped mountain in southeast Israel. More than 1400 feet below is the southeast shore of the Dead Sea. Masada, which may have been settled as early as 900 B.C.E., reached its peak in glory under the rule of Herod the Great, king of Judaea under the Romans from 37-4 B.C.E. Herod built palaces, huge walls, aqueducts and water cisterns there. Following his death in 4 B.C.E., the Romans took Masada, but lost it in 66 to Jewish Zealots who opposed Roman dominion. The Romans attacked again, and in 70 destroyed the Temple. The city of Jerusalem fell.

A band of 1,000 Zealots refused to surrender. The men, women and children took refuge in Masada, and held off 15,000 Roman soldiers for more than two years. The Romans finally breached the fortress by building a slope to the wooden walls and setting them afire. Inside, they found that the Zealots had committed mass suicide rather than be taken captive. Only seven women and children, who hid in an aqueduct, survived.

For Pamela Glasser, a young musician from Texas, the first inkling that she had lived before came in a startling *deja vu* experience at Masada in

May 1986 during Passover. Glasser, a French horn player, was spending a year with an orchestra in Israel. Of mixed ancestry and raised a Catholic, she did not consider herself particularly religious and knew only a little about Judaism and the history of the Hebrew people. Yet she felt strangely at home in Israel, as though she had returned to familiar and comfortable surroundings. During her visit to Masada, a popular tourist attraction, that feeling of familiarity became a catalyst for a journey into the past. Here is Glasser's account:

> *I was climbing the Snake Path of Masada. When I was about halfway up, I had a strong, visual flash of a covered earthen vase. It was a simple clay pot with a top. Immediately after I turned a curve in the path, I saw a niche in the rock with a flat shelf, and I knew that the vase had been there at one time, and that it had held water. The niche was a water stop. It was an eerie feeling.*
>
> *I continued up the path. When I got to the top, I looked out over the ruins. It was a pretty, bright day, and everything looked sparkly. I went to the edge farthest from the Dead Sea, and as I looked down the slope that the Romans had built, I felt a great tightness in my entire abdomen area, and strong anger. I had a flash of soldiers swarming up the slope. I felt both anger and grief. I felt that I had been up there in the fortress and had taken my own life and the lives of my family. It was quite an unexpected and very emotional experience.*

Glasser mentioned her experience to several persons, but was dismayed when they failed to grasp the emotional significance of it for her. "Interesting," they commented. Nonetheless, the memory of it burned in her mind. It was still fresh when she returned home to the States a few months later.

She wondered if there was truth to reincarnation, a concept about which she knew little. Her Catholic faith certainly did not endorse it. Some of her friends believed in it. She felt ambivalent about it.

The *deja vu* at Masada was like an itch that refused to go away until scratched. The opportunity to scratch it came when Glasser mentioned her experience to her horn instructor, who in turn referred her to Sandee Mac, a past-life hypnotherapist then living in Houston. Glasser undertook a series of hypnotic regressions that, as she described it, "turned up a lot of surprises." Each life had a lesson for her to apply to her present life.

In the first session, she returned to that life that ended at Masada, and saw herself as a forty-year-old man, a Zealot soldier named "Ilan." Ilan and his two sons, ages nineteen and twenty, fought fiercely against the Romans and sacrificed themselves when they saw the end was at hand. She said:

> *The important lesson for me to learn from this life was that I was still carrying a lot of anger that had to be resolved. I also had to learn to forgive myself for committing suicide and forgive the Romans for what they did. I had to be able to take a higher view of the whole situation, see the sweep of history. That was far more important than my personal feelings of anger. As a result, I resolved a lot of resentment that I had in this lifetime for authority figures, which I think related to that life.*
>
> *Since then, it's been easier for me to work with others, especially if they're giving me instructions. I used to resist taking directions. Now when I work with a conductor, it's much easier for me to accept what the conductor says and just do it.*

Because of Glasser's affinity with Israel, Mac suggested looking at other past lives in that part of the world. One life that surfaced struck Glasser as "bizarre," but left a tremendous impact upon her and shifted her professional focus:

> *I was a person called "Aella," a female, and I lived in Atlantis near the end before it sank. I worked in a pyramid-shaped healing center to help people who had deformities, like missing or extra limbs. Inside the healing temple were huge granite baths that had grills or*

grates inside them. The water was filled to just above the grate line. Under the water below the grates were amethyst clusters. Patients would lie in the water on top of the grates and go into a meditative state. I would either sing or play a type of stringed instrument which somehow vibrated the grate and the water. Incredible cures happened. People who were missing limbs would grow new ones after several treatments.

Before Atlantis sank, I moved on into Egypt, where I did not feel at home at all in the culture. I went off with some followers into the Sinai area, where we found a valley with a subterranean cavern. There were four entrances to the cavern, which was almost pyramid in shape. We reconstructed pretty much what had been in the Atlantean healing temple. I felt we had some help from alien beings in doing the grate work, which was made out of a strange metal, something like titanium.

The life was bizarre to me because I didn't know very much about Atlantis and didn't even know what amethyst was, other than a crystal. I knew that pyramids supposedly have some kind of power, although I didn't necessarily believe it at that time.

I feel very strongly that the cavern is still in existence somewhere in the Sinai. The entrances are probably under sand, but I think they could be excavated.

Aella's lifetime also is affecting my lifetime now. I've become more interested in healing, especially in techniques to combine sound and crystals. It also opened up a chakra point, a sensitivity, in my hands, and I have stopped headaches and such. I've never been trained in massage therapy, but now, using my hands, I can locate points on the body, including the feet, that throb and pulsate. I work with these spots, and then the headache or whatever is gone. People say my hands get very hot, but I don't feel the heat myself.

Glasser said she did not intend to become a touch healer, however, because the direction of her healing work lies in music and crystals. She began a study of how music and sound affect the mind and body, and the use of music and sound in healing. She discovered, for example, that Baroque pieces, especially played on the flute or recorder, stimulate the intellect. Various instruments seem to affect different chakras, she said: the flute stimulates the crown chakra while the French horn stimulates the heart.

Glasser also has pursued study of "crystal energetics," the healing properties of crystals, and the mysterious power of pyramids. With others, she began work on construction of a small pyramid healing chamber, built to the scale of the Great Pyramid and with a gold capstone. Glasser's role was to develop crystal gridworks and select a music library for use in the chamber.

Other past lifetimes explored by Glasser revealed her karmic ties to family members and other persons in her present. Glasser had suffered a traumatic childhood and the early death of her father. One past life helped her to heal old wounds:

> *When I was two [in the present life], my father died of cancer. My mother told me later that she took me to see him right before he died and that I had a fit in the hospital. I was emotionally scarred by his death. I had a pretty rough childhood, problems with thumb sucking until I was six and bedwetting until I was nine. My mother remarried, but I don't have any recollections of getting along with my stepfather.*
>
> *[As an adult] I've had a lot of relations with men and none of them seemed to work out very well. I've often looked for a father figure. I thought it would be a good idea to check this out in past lives.*
>
> *I found out that I've been connected to my father in many, many lifetimes. The most important one was in Druid times, a long time ago in Britain, in an area that is now northwestern England. We lived out in the woods. My father was a religious leader of our group. I played a flute and worked closely with him. I got so involved in going off on my own into the woods to play the flute and converse*

with birds that I had a hard time getting along with people. I was very close to my father

too close, probably, that was the lesson there—and when he died I completely withdrew. I had married someone because I was instructed that I had to. He was somebody I used to be involved with romantically in this lifetime. In this life, he withdrew from me the way I had withdrawn from him in that life. I saw the karmic relationship there, and it helped to understand what had happened between us.

I also realized that when I was born in this lifetime, I expected to have once again that real good closeness with my father. My lesson was to learn to live without him and get more involved with people. Seeing the Druid life also helped me get back in touch with my love of nature, and I'm really grateful for that. I'm getting involved in saving trees and critters, as well as learning to like people again. It's been a real beneficial thing to go through.

The other past lives I saw dealt with karmic issues concerning family and boyfriends. What I'd like to say about them is they have brought a great deal of healing, and have helped me get along much better with my mother. I have not had a past life that I can recall with my stepfather, but I get along better with him, having learned that he did not replace my father and put him out of my life. I now have a boyfriend with whom I'm getting along quite well. We are learning a lot from each other and having a good time doing it.

Overall, going through these past-life regressions has opened me up. My music means a lot more to me. I've always loved music but it's been a selfish love. Now I'm learning that it helps others. Performing has become more important to me, not for my own sake but for the sake of the audience as well. Formerly, I just wanted to play and make money doing it. Money is still important—I have bills to pay, of course—but I do more for free and more for children. Reaching children is a beautiful experience. I joined a woodwind quintet that does concerts for young audiences. And, I teach private-

ly and I'm enjoying that much more. Even if none of them become horn players professionally, the experience is great.

The experience in Israel made me start thinking that reincarnation is real. If not, maybe there exists some kind of collective unconscious, as Jung put it, and somehow our minds can tie into it and see these experiences. I'm comfortable with either explanation. I see the value of doing regression work, because it has helped me in this lifetime. It probably could help others as well.

Glasser's experience is not an uncommon one. An experience, such as a flash of *deja vu*, a vivid dream, a conversation with a friend, or the reading of a book, stimulates the desire to find out if and how we lived in lives before. The exploration is never dull. Rather, it is full of surprises, revelations, intense emotions and insights that lead to change and growth. There is something rich to be learned from even the most humdrum past life.

Who believes in reincarnation?
Most of the world's population believes in some form of reincarnation or rebirth, in which the soul returns to earth to inhabit another body as part of a spiritual evolution or ongoing cosmic cycle. In the predominantly Christian West, belief in reincarnation is low, but there are indications that it is rising, as least in some parts.

A 1969 Gallup poll of twelve nations found belief among the adult populations to range from a low of 10 percent in The Netherlands to a high of 26 percent in Canada; Great Britain and the United States fell in the upper two-thirds at 18 percent and 20 percent respectively. In 1981, a Gallup survey limited to the United States showed that reincarnation believers had risen to 23 percent, nearly one-fourth of all adults in the country. More women were believers (25 percent of those polled) than men (21 percent). In terms of Christian denominations, Methodists ranked the highest with 26 percent, followed by Catholics at 25 percent, Lutherans at 22 percent and Protestants and 21 percent.

It is likely that the number of reincarnation believers continues to rise. The New Age, which flowered in the 1960s, came into full bloom by the 1980s, bringing many persons into contact with a wide range of metaphysical and spiritual doctrines and concepts. Past-life regressions, the act of examining past lives under hypnosis, became more commonplace, and also gained acceptance as an alternative therapy tool.

The 1980s also were witness to the success of actress Shirley MacLaine in her revelations about her personal past-life odysseys. MacLaine made it acceptable to millions not only to explore and speak of such concepts, but consider them as possible truths. Other individuals who have brought reincarnation to large audiences is Dick Sutphen of California, who began giving regression seminars in the 1970s, and author Ruth Montgomery.

All these individuals have built upon the work of Madame Helena P. Blavatsky, who introduced Eastern thought to the West through theosophy beginning in the late nineteenth century, and upon the work of Edgar Cayce, one of America's best-known psychics, who could accurately diagnose illness and prescribe remedies while in trance. Cayce, who died in 1945, began talking about karma and the influence of past lives as early as 1923. His thousands of readings continue to be cited as authoritative sources on reincarnation and a wide range of other subjects.

Reincarnation in Eastern thought
Reincarnation is a complex doctrine with many variations and subtleties and a long history. A brief summary is given here. Readers who wish to explore the subject in more depth will find excellent sources in the bibliography.

The modern West derives its concept of reincarnation from the Hindu and Buddhist religions. The Buddhist concepts of reincarnation are derived from Hinduism, though there are some significant differences between the two faiths.

According to the doctrine, the soul is imperfect when it first comes into the world, and perfects itself through a series of incarnations, beginning with the mineral kingdom and moving up through the plant kingdom, animal kingdom and finally the human realm. In each kingdom, the soul begins at the lowest level of consciousness and must advance to the highest level possible in that realm before it can graduate to the next kingdom.

In the human kingdom, the soul begins in the bodies of persons preoccupied with gratifying the senses. It then advances to intellectual levels, and finally to spiritual levels, where the personality is more interested with the pursuit of enlightenment through meditation, study and contemplation than in lower material ways. In Hinduism, the goal of the soul is to be reunited with Brahman, the ultimate reality of the universe. When that happens, the need to reincarnate ceases.

Dharma is the law or truth which governs the operation of the entire universe. In terms of the physical world, the most important aspects of dharma are *samsara*, or reincarnation; karma, the law of cause and effect, and *moksha*, or spiritual liberation. Reincarnation is governed by karma, which says in essence that we reap what we sow. One's pain and joy, success and failure, beauty and ugliness, indeed, all aspects of life, are the result of karma. Good thoughts and acts are rewarded in future lives with spiritual advancement; evil thoughts and acts are punished by regression, including incarnations in lower forms of life.

Moksha is the release of the soul from reincarnation through realization of the self, which is the merging with Brahman. In the Hindu view, the personality remains intact throughout its many lives. In the Hindu sacred writings, there are merely inferences of rebirth or reincarnation in the oldest works, the Vedas (Sanskrit for "knowledge"), most of which date to circa 1200 B.C.E. and which consist of four collections of mantras, chants, hymns, rituals and prayers.

The Upanishads ("Sitting at the Master's Feet"), a collection of philosophical scriptures composed around 800-700 B.C.E., elaborate upon the

Vedas and deal primarily with self-realization. They contain references to reincarnation. The doctrines of reincarnation and karma are explained in the Bhagavad-Gita ("The Lord's Song"), part of the epic poem, the Mahabharata ("Great Bharata"), circa 400 B.C.E.–200 C.E. (according to some scholars, it is pre-Buddhist and dates to the sixth century B.C.E.)

In Buddhism, the soul also goes through a series of lives, the circumstances of which are governed by the law of karma. The Pali Canon, the early Buddhist scriptures, show that Buddha taught that the individual has a lesser self which dies with the body, and a greater self, which survives. However, modern Buddhists believe that the personality does not remain intact from life to life. Instead, they embrace the concept of *anatta*, or "no-self" or "non-self." At death, the personality disintegrates into sparks or pieces, mix with other pieces and coalesce into a new personality: it is the life-force, the will to live, which survives. An analogy is the lighting of one candle with another.

Furthermore, Buddhists do not view the concept of Brahman as the ultimate reality. The end goal of reincarnation is nirvana, or enlightenment. The highest level of nirvana is Buddhahood, in which all ego, desire and ignorance are extinguished; nirvana itself means "extinction." Nirvana is a state of ineffable happiness and peace, free of reincarnation. There is disagreement between the two major schools of Buddhism, Theravada and Mahayana, as to whether Buddha himself attained nirvana. In the Theravada view he did; the Mahayana view asserts that at the threshold of nirvana, Buddha vowed never to cross it as long as there were suffering beings on the earth still in the wheel of rebirth.

Both the Hindus and Buddhists view reincarnation as misery, suffering, sorrow and illusion. All acts of bad karma bind one to the wheel of rebirth, which means more misery. Reincarnation is something from which to escape.

There are different kinds of karma. Karma of the body includes one's gestures and physical acts, such as hugs, blows, building, destroying, nurturing, killing. Karma of the mouth concerns one's words. Karma of the mind concerns one's thoughts. Thus, with each thought, word and deed, we create karma. The Mahabharata states, "Just as a calf finds out its mother among a thousand cows, so also an action that was performed in a previous birth follows the doer." Both Hindu and Buddhist faiths teach that the individual is his or her own master, and is completely responsible for his or her karma.

Both Hindus and Buddhists believe that humans may reincarnate in non-human form, such as animals. Transmigration, as it is called, is dictated by karma. In Buddhism, reincarnation occurs in a wheel of rebirth that has six regions: *devas* (gods); *asuras* (elemental forces); humans; animals; *pretas* (hungry ghosts)—a purgatory of unsatisfied desires); and hell, another temporary state of purgatory. Only the human realm offers the opportunity for awareness and enlightenment. Reincarnation revolves around the wheel, governed by karma, until ignorance and earthly cravings are overcome.

In Eastern doctrine, karma is literal in cause and effect, that is, an eye for an eye. It also is immutable and inescapable: once committed, karma must be balanced. According to some Eastern schools of thought, however, karma may be "worked off" through meditation, chanting mantras and the like.

Reincarnation in the Middle East and West
The ancient Egyptians believed in reincarnation, and in the transmigration of human souls into animal bodies, concepts probably learned from ancient India. The Egyptians at one time held that a soul might remain in an animal form for as long as 3,000 years before being able to return to human form. The earlier Egyptians believed reincarnation applied only to rulers; the doctrine eventually was extended to the masses.

The ancient Greeks had a concept called metempsychosis, which is the passage of a soul at death into another body, human or animal. The concept was passed from the Egyptians into the Orphic mysteries prior to the

time of Pythagoras (c. 582–507 B.C.E.). Pythagoras, and later Plato (c. 427–347 B.C.E.) were among the Greek philosophers and mystery initiates who taught reincarnation; Pythagoras is said to have remembered his previous lives and his times between lives. There is disagreement among scholars as to whether the two philosophers also taught metempsychosis in a literal sense.

Some Platonists said that if a soul regressed to animal form, it did not actually become the soul of the animal, but rather took the animal over much like a daemon, which, in modern terms, is the approximate equivalent of a spirit guide or inner voice.

The Romans absorbed Greek thought and culture into their own, including the concept reincarnation, but belief in it reached a low point by 44 B.C.E., when Julius Caesar was murdered.

Reincarnation is not officially part of Islam, Judaism or Christianity, though sects of each religion do believe in it. The Sufis, the mystics of Islam who claim to pre-date the prophet Muhammad (570–632) by several thousand years, believe in it. In Judaism, reincarnation is the concept of *gilgul*, which has had various interpretations over the centuries. Reincarnation does not appear in the Torah, but does in the Kabbalah, the mystical teachings, which were first published in the thirteenth century but attributed to first century authorship. According to the Kabbalah, early Jews believed great prophets reincarnated, that Adam became David, who was to be the Messiah. The suffering of Job is interpreted by some as karma. From about the thirteenth century through the eighteenth century, one dominant concept held that Adams's soul scattered into sparks, which were being reassembled through reincarnation. The idea is very similar to the Buddhist concept.

Reincarnation is not taught by the three main branches of Judaism, Reform, Conservative and Orthodox, but is by the Hasidim, a sect which teaches the mysteries of the Kabbalah.

The presence of reincarnation in Christianity has been the subject of great debate. Cayce perhaps summed it up best when he once commented, "I can read reincarnation into the Bible, and you can read it right out again!" Reincarnationists interpret numerous passages from the Bible as evidence of the concept, while opponents take the same passages and disagree. Reincarnation was taught by the Essenes, a sect with which Jesus had contact. The Gnostics believed in a concept of karma and reincarnation.

Origen (185-254), a Christian theologian with Gnostic leanings, believed in pre-existence of the soul and reincarnation in a succession of bodies determined by the soul's merits and demerits. Origen's teachings were condemned as anathema in 553 by Emperor Justinian, the head of the Christian Church. From that time on, reincarnation withered in orthodox Christianity, but was kept alive by sects, mystery schools and secret societies. Today, no mainstream denomination of Christianity teaches reincarnation. The Unity Church, whose metaphysical teachings attract many New Age followers, endorses the concept.

Reincarnation in the West received renewed attention in the nineteenth century with the rise of the Spiritualist movement and the Theosophical movement. The Spiritualist movement was concerned largely with proving survival after death through mediumistic communications with the dead, and as the movement grew, it split on the issue of reincarnation. Most modern Spiritualists believe in pre-existence of the soul; some believe in an Eastern-like law of return, while others feel free will is a determining factor in whether or not a soul reincarnates.

The Theosophical Society, founded in 1875 by Blavatsky, a Russian mystic, and Colonel H.S. Olcott, William Q. Judge and a small group of others, was instrumental in bringing reincarnation to a wider Western audience. In the Theosophists' view, however, reincarnation is endless, for the universe is endless.

Reincarnation among tribal societies
Beliefs in reincarnation are widespread in tribal societies in the North,

Central and South Americas. Medicine men, shamans, seers and the like, who are initiated into the mysteries of death and birth, are the most likely individuals to hold reincarnation beliefs.

In North America, the Eskimo and Tlingit have strong reincarnation beliefs and customs. The Tlingit expect reincarnating souls to announce themselves beforehand in dreams, usually to the mother, but possibly to other family members. This act serves to identify the incoming spirit, usually a deceased member of the family, so that the child can be named appropriately. The Eskimo believe that some souls may inhabit either human or animal bodies, while others inhabit only human forms.

The Dakota hold that medicine men may be reborn four times. In between times, they live in the spirit realm where the gods give them instruction in healing and magic. When they reincarnate, they remember these times. The Algonquin east of the Mississippi have a curious "reincarnation" rite in which outsiders may be adopted by families to replaced deceased members of the household. The adoptee takes the dead person's name and is considered the reincarnation of that individual. Reincarnation beliefs also exist among the Winnebago (a Sioux tribe), Creek, Hopi, Mohave, Montagnais (an Algonquin tribe), Haida, Athabaskan, Aleut (an Eskimo tribe), Kiowa, Aht and Gitskan. The Iroquois believe in reincarnation of human as animals.

Since some of the North American tribes are descended from the Aztec, Toltec and Maya cultures of Central America, it may be inferred that these Central American cultures also believed in reincarnation. In South America, reincarnation is widely believed among numerous tribes, as well as the Patagonia of Argentina and the Jivaro of Ecuador. The Jivaro believe humans reincarnate as animals and birds.

Elsewhere, reincarnation beliefs are held by tribal societies throughout Africa, Australia and the Pacific Islands. In parts of Africa, is it believed that one perpetuates oneself by reincarnating on through family lineage; childlessness is considered a curse because it hinders an ancestor from returning. Reincarnation prevails universally among the Australian aborigines, the central tribes of whom believe they will come back as whites.

Beliefs vary among Pacific Islanders; Okinawans, for example, believe the soul lingers in its former home for forty-nine days, then enters the spirit realm, where it spends an indeterminate time before re-entering a new human form. The Huna system of Hawaii embraces an evolutionary spiral from the mineral kingdom up to the human kingdom.

Tribal reincarnation beliefs vary greatly around the world, and have more differences than similarities. Some societies believe that humans return only as humans, and some restrict this even further to reincarnation only within families. Others believe humans return only in non-human form, such as animals, birds, insects, reptiles, fish, flowers, trees and rocks. Still others believe humans reincarnate in either human or non-human form.

Modern views of reincarnation
Westerners who believe in reincarnation have adapted the concept to fit prevailing beliefs in society. Perhaps most significantly, Westerners look at reincarnation optimistically and do not view it as a wheel of misery, but as a wheel of growth, with the end result being reunion with God, or enlightenment in a spirit state, dimension or plane of existence. Westerners believe strongly in free will and self-determinism. Therefore, the law of karma is not entirely immutable, but may be affected by choices. It is believed that the individual plans the next life and chooses the circumstances in order to balance certain karma. The planning is done by the Higher Self, which is the sum total of the soul, with the assistance of spirit guides and other highly evolved beings.

Westerners resist the idea that humans can reincarnate in non-human forms, or that non-human forms may move up to human bodies. While some persons do claim to regress to non-human life forms under hypnosis, they are in a very small minority. Such recollections are virtually impossible to prove.

A strong Western belief is that karma is not immutable, but may be mitigated by forgiveness and a change in consciousness, and by the concept of grace. Grace is God's mercy offered through Christ, salvation for those who cannot or will not save themselves. There are differences of theological opinion as to whether grace alone is sufficient for salvation, or must be augmented with ethics, work and worship ritual. In mainstream Christianity, grace applies to salvation in terms of heaven, but reincarnationists apply it to reincarnation.

Grace figures significantly in the readings of Cayce, who characterized it as both a state of mind and as a gift from God. Grace comes into play when one contemplates an evil act and then has a change of heart because one realizes the act is evil and should not be committed. It comes into play when one forgives others for wrongs. Grace, it is believed, has the power to supersede karma because it necessitates a growth in spirit. Otherwise, the lessons of karma may be lost. Grace assumes that God does not wish to punish people for their sins, but to help them learn from the mistakes.

In interpreting the Cayce readings, author Lynn Elwell Sparrow, in *Reincarnation: Claiming Your Past, Creating Your Future*, provides an excellent example of karma versus grace. A woman abandons a child to an unknown fate in order to preserve herself. Under the law of karma, she returns as an orphan. Under the law of grace, she returns as a social worker who serves children.

Grace must not be misinterpreted as an "out" for transgressions. To knowingly commit a wrong and then be "sorry" for it is not grace.

In the New Age, reincarnation has become a means of transformation. Through an understanding of both karma and grace, one can examine oneself in various roles and situations, to learn from them and grow spiritually.

2

Spontaneous Recall of Past Lives

JUST BEFORE WE ARE REBORN, the veil of forgetfulness descends to block our remembrance of our past lives. We come into life with a karmic history and a purpose, yet we have conscious access to neither. According to Eastern doctrine, forgetfulness is a blessing and enables the soul to make a fresh start in each incarnation. Otherwise, life would be made extremely complicated and confusing, perhaps even paralyzing. Nonetheless, we catch glimpses the past in certain moments. Fragments and fleeting impressions and feelings bubble to the surface, only to be passed off as imagination in many instances. In some cases, a person may be swept into an incredible vision that unfolds before the eyes.

There are many ways to experience past lives spontaneously:

Deja vu
Deja vu is an unexpected and unexplained feeling of familiarity in relation to places, events, people, dreams and all manner of experiences. A French term for which there is no exact English equivalent, *deja vu* generally

means "already seen." It is a common experience: you meet someone for the first time, yet feel you have known them before; you visit a strange place for the first time and feel oddly at home. *Deja vu* varies in intensity, from vague feelings of familiarity to specific knowledge, such as how to get around a strange city, or the location of hidden objects in a strange place.

Many scientific theories have been advanced since the latter nineteenth century to explain the phenomenon, yet none has been adequate. Perhaps the best explanation is that *deja vu* is the surfacing of fragments of past-life memories. Carl G. Jung once had a powerful *deja vu* experience. During his first trip to Africa, he traveled by train along the rugged coastline from Mobassa to Nairobi. Looking out the window one dawn morning, he saw a steep red cliff on which a lone black man stood, leaning on his spear, watching the train. Jung felt an intense *deja vu*.

He wrote in his memoir, *Memories, Dreams, Reflections*, "I had the feeling that I had already experienced this moment and had always known this world which was separated from me only by distance in time. It was as if I were this moment returning to the land of my youth, and as if I knew that dark-skinned man who had been waiting for me for five thousand years." The curious sensation of familiarity lasted with Jung throughout the rest of his journey through Africa. He called the feeling a "recognition of the immemorially known."

Waking visions and intuitive flashes
Visions and flashes of past lives can arise during waking consciousness, triggered by *deja vu*, meeting someone which whom one has a karmic tie, visiting a place tied to a past life, hearing music or even seeing art that has a past-life meaning for the individual.

The visions may flash quickly across the mind's eye or may appear as hallucinations, in which the present surroundings disappear and are replaced by scenes from the past, and the viewer literally feels transported to another time and place. All the senses are engaged, and for a few brief moments, they relive the past.

Sometimes the past-life connection is sensed merely as an intuitive "knowing." Intuition, the power to know without conscious reasoning, plays an ancillary role in past-life recall, reinforcing what one experiences through other forms mentioned here. Intuitive flashes can provide supplemental details to a recall and insight into karmic situations.

In his book *Lifetimes*, Frederick Lenz formulated a model for a waking vision recall, based on his interviews with 127 persons. A person is engaged in a normal activity, and becomes aware of a high-pitched ringing or buzzing in one or both ears. The noise escalates until all other noises are blocked out. His body becomes light. His surroundings begin to change, becoming hazy and wavy as though everything around him is vibrating. Colored lights may pass before his eyes. He feels ecstatic. Strange scenes begin to appear, as though he is watching a movie. At some point, he realizes he is no longer watching the movie, but participating in it. His consciousness may alternate back and forth between that of viewer and participant. Eventually, the scenes fade and he become aware of his body once again.

Lesser phenomena associated with waking visions include an awareness of being out-of-body during the experience, and being guided by a voice or angelic being. In a nonjudgmental fashion, the guide presents an overview of the past.

In some cases, individuals see more than one life. The guide presents an overview of many lifetimes, from a few to hundreds. The lives are laid out like a string of beads or pearly globes, or are strung out like photographs. They flash by quickly yet are completely understood by the witness, who feels an amazing capacity to absorb tremendous amounts of "knowing" in some sort of telepathic fashion. It becomes instantly clear what has and has not been learned through a series of lives. While witnesses can see the positive things, more often than not the review serves as a helpful prod to quit wasting time mired in hate, jealousy, greed, apathy and other negative conditions and get on with spiritual development.

Dreams

Some investigators of reincarnation have found dreams to comprise one of the most common sources of past-life recall. Jung was skeptical about reincarnation yet investigated it, looking for empirical evidence which would prove the doctrine to him. He found nothing—*deja vu* was not empirical—until he had a series of dreams "which would seem to describe the process of reincarnation in a deceased person of my acquaintance," as he wrote in *Memories*. "But I have never come across any such dreams in other persons, and therefore have no basis for comparison... I must confess, however, that after this experience I view the problem of reincarnation with somewhat different eyes..."

Past-life dreams may occur once in a great while or with great frequency. Distinguishing past-life dreams from ordinary ones is not always easy. Individuals who have experienced many past-life dreams learn to recognize them by the impressions they create. Such dreams usually are extremely vivid and clear, and remain sharp in the memory for a long time. Many are lucid, in which the dreamer is aware he or she is dreaming, perhaps even knowing the dream is a past life. Recurring dreams often have past-life connections. Interpreting such dreams often requires the help of a therapist who specializes in past-life recall. Dreams should be recorded in a notebook or journal immediately upon awakening.

Past-life information also can surface in the twilight periods at either end of the sleep cycle: the hypnagogic state, which occurs as we drop off to sleep, and the hypnopompic state, which occurs as we rise back to wakefulness. In these states, when the brainwaves are drifting down through theta toward the delta levels of sleep, we experience reveries of snatches of images and voices. They usually seem like a jumble, and perhaps are the conscious mind clearing itself for sleep. Some of the reveries may contain psychic or past-life information which is not filtered out by the conscious mind.

Spontaneous memories

The ability to remember a past life spontaneously, as though it were just another memory like yesterday or the day before, is rare, but from a scientist's point of view, is quite significant. Spontaneous recall almost always occurs in children between the ages of about two and four. By age three, children have learned enough vocabulary skills to describe, even in rough fashion, what they remember. By age eight, the past-life memories begin to fade or are already obliterated by the memories accumulated in the present life.

Scientists view spontaneous recall as significant because in many such cases, children talk about places, things and people they have no way of knowing; they exhibit knowledge and skills they have not been taught; and they often can identify people, places and things from the deceased personality's life. In the eyes of science, these cases constitute the strongest evidence in support of reincarnation, but do not necessarily prove reincarnation.

In contrast, an adult who experiences spontaneous recall might possibly be drawing subconsciously upon dozens of sources "forgotten" by the conscious mind, such as old memories of experiences, books and movies. In addition, scientists posit that extrasensory skills might also come into play, including picking up information through clairvoyance or telepathy.

Ian Stevenson, one of the world's leading experts on reincarnation and former chair of psychiatry at the University of Virginia in Charlottesville, investigated reincarnation cases from the 1960s until his death in 2007. He collected more than 2,000 cases. Not surprisingly, most of them are in Eastern countries where religious beliefs support reincarnation or rebirth.

Stevenson said that Western cases are few because parents typically ignore or discourage a child's utterances about a previous existence, or chalk them up to imagination. To verify a claim, Stevenson undertook a lengthy and painstaking investigation, visiting the child and his family, the family of the deceased, and others who could verify the claim. A case was "solved" when Stevenson and his associates were satisfied that a child's statements did refer to an identifiable dead person.

A high incidence of Stevenson's cases involved violent death. The children often remembered quite well how they died. They may have had birthmarks coinciding with the place of the death wound, and phobias related to the means of death, such as a fear of water due to drowning.

In such cases, the intense emotional and trauma generated by a violent death probably makes it easier for such memories to surface. The interval between the death and the reincarnation often is short, sometimes less than the gestation period of nine months, perhaps indicating that the soul is not necessarily inhabiting a fetus from conception. In Eastern belief, individuals who suffer violent death are granted the opportunity to be reborn quickly, in order to finish out their karma.

The Resonance Method

A resonance is a sound which continues in the ear or memory; we say that something is resonant if it has a prolonged, subtle or stimulating effect beyond the initial impact. The same may be said for past lives: they continue to resonate into the present in a multitude of ways both dramatic and subtle.

A means for discovering these resonances, the Resonance Method, was developed by author Michael Talbot. In his book *Your Past Lives: A Reincarnation Handbook*, Talbot defined past-life resonances as "an inexplicable tugging at your heart strings, a special draw that you feel toward some things and not others when there is no logical reason in this life for you to feel the way you do." Resonances occur in natural affinities for places, things, cultures, races, periods in history, foods, hobbies, occupations, styles of music and art, clothing, religions, languages and climates. Resonances also surface in dreams, daydreams, inspired thoughts, *deja vu* and what Talbot called an innate "bedrock knowing." They may be discovered in personality traits and relationships with animals and people. Even dislikes and aversions are resonances. In an interview for this book, Talbot explained:

> We have enormous contact with our past-life memories, but they are separated from us by a thin film, so we don't know they are memories. They surface in the form of resonances. I think most resonances have past life echoes to them. You can't take a single resonance and say, 'This is a past life memory,' but they do piece together if you keep lists of them. It's like putting together a giant jigsaw puzzle on a table—none of the pieces makes any sense until all of them come together in a larger constellation of information. When I started developing the Resonance Method, it was astonishing to me how well this works.
>
> The Resonance Method was itself a kind of resonance. I think I always knew it. I was thinking about what I felt resonances for, and the question occurred to me, 'I wonder if I've ever lived in Berlin?' I immediately had this feeling, not really. I was startled that I knew the answer just like that. So, I started asking myself questions and realized there were lots of things in me that I had always known...
>
> When you ask yourself questions about resonances, you don't try to intellectually answer them. We are all incredibly psychic. There is a knowing within us that is below all the chatter in our head, and it will give us answers to questions. Just ask and listen.
>
> One method I use a great deal is I tell myself I am going to remember. The way we process our earth memories is through contact with our unconscious, and one of the most powerful ways we have that contact is through habit. You establish the habit of remembering... Ian Stevenson said that when you investigate [reincarnation] you have to be a lawyer, an historian and a psychologist. That is what I always recommend to people. You have to be all those three things, and you cannot jump to conclusions.

Talbot recommended recording resonances in past-life journals or on index cards. Jot them down when they occur to you. Ask yourself questions about places, things, etc., and note down the answers that automatically arise. Besides their spontaneous occurrence, resonances may be coaxed through a variety of ways, including divination, psychic readings, hypnosis, guided meditation and other forms of enhanced recall.

Before he died in 1992, resonances helped Talbot discover at least twenty past lives in varying detail. His own resonances began early in childhood, when he became aware that he possessed memories that were part of other lives. Up until age five, he refused to call his parents "father" and "mother" but addressed them by their first names instead. He was strongly drawn to the Asian culture, including a fondness for strong black tea and sitting cross-legged on the floor. Before going to bed, he recited the traditional child's prayer, "Now I lay me down to sleep..." but added a Buddhist ending, asking God "to release the suffering of all conscious beings."

When Talbot was older, he explored fragments of memories and his resonances with the Far East and, with the help of a psychic, discovered past lives as a Buddhist monk. One involved death by drowning:

> *One of my earliest memories was drowning. I remember drowning twice. In one memory, I was out in the open sea and there was a ship involved. In the other, land was in sight where I drowned. In the second memory, I looked up, knowing I was drowning, and saw the surface of the water without being able to reach it. I could see the faces of men looking down at me through the water. They were dark complected and had on orange robes, and they were bald. As I grew older, I realized they were monks of some kind. I was puzzled. Who were these men? For a while, I thought I had been ritualistically drowned. I was always looking for some account of ritualized drowning in different cultures and never found it. I was angry towards that memory. Why did they let me drown?*
>
> *When I had my first reading with [psychic] Jim Gordon, I told*

him I thought I had drowned before. He said I had drowned twice. One time I was on a ship. It didn't seem to be significant, and it didn't have that much emotional or psychological impact for me. The second time did. I was a monk in India. I knew I'd lived in India before and that I'd been very religious, if not a monk, because I have such a strong feeling for Hinduism and Buddhism and for India in general.

In this past life I was a Buddhist monk. There was a storm, a terrible monsoon, and I sought refuge in a Hindu ashram. They would not let me in because I was Buddhist. I kept walking and got lost in the storm. I fell off of a precipice into the ocean and drowned. Gordon said I have held a great deal of resentment toward those monks even in this life, and this is why I held onto the image of them in my mind as I died...

One could make the argument that a psychic is just telepathically picking up on your fantasies. But Gordon took a story that I had in my mind, had a different interpretation and made it make more sense. If he was merely telepathic, at the very least it would mean that I myself did not know all the story. It was something spun by my unconscious mind that he had to bring out for me.

Resonances act as powerful triggers to past-life memories. Past lives which have the greatest resonance with the present life, in terms of emotions, events and circumstances, are the most likely to be recalled.

Illness and accident

Severe illness, especially involving high fever, delirium and coma, sometimes induce past-life recall. Accidents involving severe trauma, especially to the head as in concussions, also jar loose past-life memories. In 1907, three-year-old Dorothy Eady of London tumbled down a flight of stairs and was pronounced dead by a doctor. An hour later, the child was revived completely and seemed to suffer no injuries or ill effects from her terrible fall.

However, Eady soon began having strange dreams of a large building with columns and an exotic garden. She cried that she was not "home," but didn't know where "home" was. On a visit to the British Museum, the child was excited by Egyptian artifacts, and declared she had found her people. By age seven, she identified the building in her dreams as the temple of Sety the First, pharaoh of Egypt in the Nineteenth Dynasty, who lived from 1306-1290 B.C.E. As she grew older, she pursued an intense study of Egyptian history. Her story is chronicled in the book, *The Story of Omm Sety* by Jonathan Cott.

In 1918, she awoke one night to see a face bending over her—the face of the mummy of Sety. The hands and arms of the figure moved, but it said nothing. After that, she began having a recurring dream in which she was a young Egyptian girl who was beaten with a stick for refusing to answers questions. Gradually, she discovered that she and the pharaoh, who was in his early fifties, had been passionate lovers. She was a fourteen-year-old orphan, Bentreshyt ("Harp-of-Joy"), who served as priestess of Isis in Sety's temple at Abydos, the building she had seen so often in her dreams. At age twelve, she took vows to remain a virgin and be temple property. She fell in love with Sety, however, and became pregnant by him. The temple high priest tried to beat the truth out of her, but rather than reveal it, she took her own life.

Eady instinctively knew that in order to contact the spirit of Sety, she would have to move to Egypt. At the age of twenty-nine, she married an Egyptian man and went to live in Cairo. She had visions and saw ghosts at many Egyptian ruins. She worshipped the ancient Egyptian gods. More remarkably, she was able to resume her 3,000-year-old love affair with the spirit of Sety. At first, she could just feel his presence.

Then one night he sent the spirit of an ancient Egyptian priest to fetch her in her astral body. She awoke and grew very light, and followed the priest through a black fog until they arrived at Sety's palace at Amenti. Inside was Sety, who proposed that from then on, he materialize to her in solid form as he had appeared when they were lovers, as a vigorous man in his early fifties. She consented and he did so, appearing often and making tender and passionate love to her. He told her he intended to marry her at Amenti; apparently, however, it could not happen until she left her life as Eady.

Eady, who had become known as Omm Sety, desired to return to the temple of Abydos, even though it meant she would once again become "temple property." The opportunity to do so presented itself in 1956. When she informed her ghostly lover, Sety told her that he would continue to visit her, but they would never more make love. If they resisted temptation during the rest of her life at the temple, their original crime would be forgiven and they could be together for eternity.

In the village of Arabet Abydos, Eady worked at a low-paying job as a draftswoman and helped in the restoration of her beloved temple. The strange Western woman who seemed so at home in the antiquities of Egypt mystified the locals, who feared her as a witch or adept of Egyptian magic. Living conditions were primitive—she lived in a mud-brick hut with no running water, plumbing or electricity—but she was infinitely happy. Sety visited her and they spent nights in each other's arms, but refrained from making love. Eady rarely spoke of her secret life to anyone, even close friends. She kept her confidences in her diaries.

Eady died on April 21, 1981. She was buried facing west, toward the Land of the Dead, in the desert north of the Sety and Ramesses temples. Undoubtedly her freed soul headed straight for the palace at Amenti, for the long-awaited reunion with Sety, her soul mate and lover.

3

Induced Past-Life Recall

WITH OR WITHOUT spontaneous recall, past lives may be remembered through methods of induced recall, some of them ancient and some modern:

Hypnosis
The concept of reincarnation didn't really have much attention in the West until the 1950s, when a Colorado housewife's recollections under hypnosis of a past life as "Bridey Murphy" in eighteenth-century Ireland was publicized in the press and in the book *The Search for Bridey Murphy* by Morey Bernstein. The case created a maelstrom of controversy in which it was alternately denounced as a hoax and hailed as proof of life after death.

The case began in 1952 when Bernstein, a business executive and skilled amateur hypnotist in Pueblo, Colorado, tried an experiment to find out if human memory could be regressed to a period before birth. His subject was twenty-nine-year-old Ruth Simmons (a pseudonym), whom he had discovered had the ability to enter an "uncommonly deep" trance.

Simmons went back to the life of a little girl in Cork, Ireland, Bridget (Bridey) Murphy.

In regressions over a period of time, Bridey's story emerged. She had lived between 1798 and 1864. She had married a man named Brian MacCarthy, and had died at age sixty-six, withering away after falling down stairs and breaking bones in her hip. She gave specific descriptions of her world, and used archaic Irish slang. Despite shrill denunciations and attempts to discredit it, the case remains one of the most convincing on record for reincarnation.

While the Bridey Murphy case brought reincarnation to modern public attention, it was by no means the first regression recall. At the turn of the twentieth century, Colonel Albert de Rochas, a French psychical investigator, undertook a systematic study of past-life regressions. A hypnotist in the style of Mesmer (placing patients in trance by making hand passes in front of the body), Rochas regressed nineteen French men and women beginning in 1904. The subjects regressed easily and gave descriptions of varying detail, including a young Frenchwoman who said she had lived before as "Lina," daughter of a fisherman in Brittany, and had killed herself by throwing herself off a cliff into the sea after her husband had been killed in a shipwreck. In going through the death experience, the subject gasped and writhed as she "drowned." Rochas attempted to verify his cases but met with little success; the information simply couldn't be found or, in some cases, contradicted what had been reported.

In the 1960s and 1970s, past-life recall under hypnosis gained popularity as a psychotherapy tool. Psychotherapists discovered that going back to past lives to confront traumas often speeds the patient's healing. Hypnosis is now the most common means of induced past-life recall. Beginning in the 1970s, hypnotist Dick Sutphen brought past-life regression to the general public, in group seminars around the country.

There are three levels of hypnotic trance. The first is light trance, in which the patient feels very relaxed and probably does not realize he or she is hypnotized. The patient remains aware of what is going on, internally and externally. An estimated 95 to 98 percent of the adult population can be put in this altered state. According to Dr. Bruce Goldberg in *Past Lives Future Lives*, information obtained in a light trance often is sketchy, but is adequate for working with phobias, habits, anxiety and depression. Light trance is also known as "guided meditation," "alpha-state meditation," "guided visualization" and "guided imagery," among other terms, which seem less intimidating than "hypnosis."

The second level is medium trance, which can be achieved by an estimated 70 percent of the adult population. In this state, the patient may be aware of outside noises but is not distracted by them. It is considered ideal for most regressions, for the patient can relive and feel the experience, and the information is much more detailed. The third state is deep trance, accessible to only about 5 percent of adults. The patient is not aware of the experience and will remember what transpired only if given the instruction to do so. Some therapists prefer to work at this level. While some individuals have learned how to hypnotize themselves, most persons prefer to work with another person. Because hypnosis and past-life regression can stir up potentially troubling material, it is very important to undertake regression only with a skilled therapist.

Reasons for trying hypnotic regression usually revolve around conditions, issues and problems in the present life, such as phobias, physical complaints which have resisted medical diagnosis, obesity, problems in relationships, and feelings of being off-track in career or overall life purpose. Some persons merely want to explore past lives out of curiosity or to learn more about themselves. Alice T., a past-life regressionist in Manhattan, has a clientele comprised predominantly of creative and performing arts professionals, physicians, psychiatrists, attorneys, stockbrokers, academics and others in white collar occupations. "Information received during a regression often brings the root of a problem into focus, acting as a catalyst for them to seek out other forms of self-exploration or therapy," she said. The Higher Self and/or spirit guides select the past lives which are most relevant to each situation.

Hypnotic regressions may be done individually, in couples or in groups. Individuals and couples can set their own agendas and pace, while those in groups cannot. Group regressions usually are theme-oriented, such as periods of history, lives as the opposite sex, lives of power, and so on.

A regression begins with physical relaxation. The viewer lies down or reclines and is led to relax with background music and suggestion. The eyes remain closed. To deepen the altered state of consciousness, practitioners usually have clients mentally walk down stairs or enter a tunnel, where, at the bottom or the end, they are asked to visualize a light. When the client reaches the light, he or she will then step out into a past-life scene. The therapist then "grounds" them by having them look at their feet and then the rest of their bodies to describe what they are wearing.

What else is encountered in that scene varies greatly according to the individual. "The large majority of persons get some sort of visual images," said Alice. "For some, it is like watching a three-dimensional movie, while others see scenes only in still photographs. Some see in color while others only in black and white, and a few see things in silhouettes. Some just get a flash or intuitive impression. Other senses may be involved as well. Some people hear voices, conversations and music, and can smell, taste and feel touch. Emotions may come through. Many people experience combinations of sensory impressions that vary from life to life."

One example of vivid, nonvisual sensations comes from a young American woman who viewed numerous lives in which she was not very intelligent, and one in which she was a primitive man with no language skills. The nonvisual phenomena accompanied visual images:

> *I was a wench in England who was knocked up by a soldier. When I got into this past life, I felt my mental capacity close down.*

Everything I looked at was filtered through the eyes of a very simple, unintelligent woman. I could feel her personality very strongly.

[In another session] I wanted to see my very first life on this planet. I was a cave man. I was hairy but not animal-like. I lived in a commune and hunted. I saw myself standing outdoors looking up at the stars. They were amazing because [in this life] I had never seen stars like that—they were bigger and cruder in shape. They didn't seem as far away as they do now. I had a frustrated feeling because I couldn't speak—there wasn't any language. I had thoughts I wanted to communicate, but I couldn't gather them and give them form. As I was looking up to the stars, I was uncomfortable in my body, trying to put into words what I was feeling. It was like being in jail in my own body.

I communicated with the other humans with drawings. Also, we seem to have had a crude sign language that was almost telepathic. We couldn't communicate concepts, but simple things like meals being ready.

Some individuals see or sense their surroundings quickly and clearly, while others have difficulty at first. The therapist keeps the regression moving by asking objective questions and giving directions, such as "go to the next significant scene in this life" or "go to your last moments in this life." Part of a regression involves going through the death of a life; the viewer is instructed at the beginning to feel detached from the death and to play the role of observer. Nonetheless, some deaths, especially violent ones, can be extremely traumatic, which is why it is so important to work with a competent therapist.

Overall, good therapists will not plant suggestions or interpret what the viewer is experiencing, but will allow the viewer to make his or her own discoveries. The information that is revealed is chosen by the Higher Self or one's guides as that which is needed for growth.

Sandee Mac, a hypnotherapist and spiritual counselor, began regressing clients in the late 1970s. At the end of a regression, Mac invited present and past self to meet each other and exchange gifts and information. A gift could be a hug, a beam of light, or whatever seems fitting to the individual. The exchange of information enabled lessons and solutions to crystallize for the client, who saw a karmic balance sheet from the past and the effect it has on the present. The positive energies released from such an inner journey carry on into daily life, often inspiring fresh ideas, an expanded sense of self-awareness and understanding and confidence, and renewed energy.

Hypnotic "progressions" may be taken into the future. These tend to be hazier than past lives, perhaps because of uncertainty or apprehension on the part of the viewer, or perhaps because the future is ever changing in response to circumstance and free will. Perhaps more than anything, future progressions help crystalize hope and desire, and when hope and desire take shape, action follows.

Psychic readings and consultations
Past-life information may be accessed with the help of psychics and channelers, some of whom specialize in past lives. Their techniques vary. Some psychics get past-life information about clients through their own dreams, while others use retrocognition, a type of clairvoyance in which one sees into the past. Channels communicate with their clients' Higher Self or spirit guides to obtain past-life information.

In a psychic reading, past-life information is given to the client without the client undergoing hypnosis. The disadvantage for the client is that he or she does not actually see the images. However, the information may click with fragments already known to the client, who can then put pieces into a whole.

Past lives often surface spontaneously in psychic readings, even when the client is not seeking information on them. The reason for the reading may involve unknown, unresolved issues from the past. Laurie McQuary, a psychic consultant in Oregon, often gets flashes of her clients' past lives when she conducts readings. "If I feel the person is open to it, I will give the information," she said. "Sometimes it doesn't apply to the reading, so I don't bring it up. I don't ever do a reading that is all devoted to past lives unless I feel that the person can look at them objectively and can benefit from the experience."

Although examining past lives can prove to be beneficial and therapeutic, McQuary advises her clients to do so with prudence: "I like people to balance themselves. I don't like people getting so involved in the past that they forget the present, or want to blame the past and not live for today. Frankly, there are things you wouldn't want to look at in your past lives. Certainly we're always learning, but we don't need to have *everything* from the past at a conscious level."

In reading for clients, McQuary occasionally gets glimpses of her own past lives as well. She told of one amusing incident: "I have a former associate, whom I met the first time at a reading. I said, 'You know, we've had a past life together.' She said, 'Yes, I can feel that.' I could see it clearly. We were in Pompeii. I was a cantina dancer, or whatever they called a cantina. I said, 'You and I never lived for anything but the moment. We were having a glass of wine when they were hollering *Volcano!* and the lava was rolling down and everyone else was running. We said, 'Oh no, we've got time for one more.' We laughed about that."

Meditation and yoga
Past-life recall during meditation can be either a spontaneous by-product or a means to induce recall. In meditation, the body is relaxed and the mind is in an altered state of consciousness, in which brain waves range from alpha, which is akin to taking a light nap, to the much slower theta, the stage just before sleep. In such an altered state, the mind is much more attuned to information which flows along psychic channels, which usually is blotted out by the noise of conscious thought. It also is more recep-

tive to information floating up from the unconscious, where past-life memories lie buried.

Patanjali (c. 400), the compiler of the Yoga Sutras, or truths, stated that memories of past lives may be awakened by a special method of Yoga meditation. The memories, including all details of past lives and all impressions of karma, reside in the *chitta,* or subconscious mind.

Trance and enhanced recall

Some persons develop their own customized methods of tuning into past lives with combinations of altered state, meditation, psychic and astral projection skills. Edgar Cayce, who became famous for his trances in which he could diagnose illnesses and prescribe cures, found the root of most physical and emotional ailments in past-life karma. Cayce said he got his past-life information from the Akashic Records, which are said to be the master records of every thought, deed and emotion of everything in the universe since its beginning. The records exist as impressions upon the astral plane; Cayce described them as travelling on waves of light. Those who learn how to access them may view past lives, much like looking up a biography in a library.

While in trance, Cayce would feel himself leave his body and begin moving through a shaft of light. In misty realms beyond the light, he saw other beings that pleaded for his help or tried to wave him aside, but he ignored them. The beings gradually took on more form and began helping him along his way. His destination was a hill, where there was a mount and a huge temple. It seemed to be a cosmic library, filled with books on every life since time immemorial. Cayce found the book on his particular client and looked up the answers to the client's questions.

British novelist Joan Grant, called her enhanced recall technique "far memory." Since childhood, Grant had numerous psychic experiences, and eventually taught herself how to shift her consciousness to her past-life personalities so that she could look out through their eyes and relive their lives. During her altered states, she dictated what she saw, did and felt. Grant published seven of her past lives as novels. She believes she first learned "far memory" as a female priest and ruler in ancient Egypt.

Grace Cooke, British Spiritualist who founded the White Eagle Lodge, a Spiritualist organization, was skilled in meditation. An Eastern adept taught her a meditation technique that enabled her to rise through her crown chakra to the astral plane, where she read the Akashic records. She learned of her past lives as a Mayan priestess and an Egyptian priestess, the stories of which she recorded in her book *The Illumined Ones*. She said the Mayan priestess, Minesta, lived about 10,000 years ago in the Andean foothills of South America. Her civilization had been seeded by extraterrestrials who had first established Atlantis.

Archaeologists place the Maya only in Central America and not earlier than about 1500 B.C.E., which did not dissuade Cooke about the reality of Minesta's world. It is not uncommon in past-life recall to encounter information that runs contrary to the history books. The accuracy often is impossible to judge, for if no surviving records have been found, there is no way to verify it. Yet most persons, like Cooke, feel an intuitive certainty about their own versions. When Peruvian remains discovered in 1965 showed a Central American influence, Cooke took it as evidence in support of her past life.

Minesta received spiritual training under the tutelage of Hah-Wah-Tah and was initiated into a circle of adepts, the Plumed Serpent, the Brotherhood of the White Magic. She married her brother, T. When she died, Hah-Wah-Tah, who had died before her, became her guide in the afterlife, and prepared her for her next incarnation as Ra-min-ati in Egypt. Hah-Wah-Tah reincarnated as Is-Ra and became a high priest. In that role, he trained and initiated Ra-min-ati into the Osirian mysteries. Ra-min-ati married Ra-hotep, and the two became pharaohs of the Two-Lands.

Cooke, who died in 1979, was aided throughout her life by a the spirit of a Native American Indian, White Eagle, a member of the Great White

Brotherhood, the Brotherhood of the Cross of Light within the Circle of Light. White Eagle and other Indian spirit guides appeared to her as a child, and took her on journeys to the astral plane. White Eagle directed Cooke in her spiritual work. From the enhanced recall of her past lives, she learned that White Eagle had been her tutelary Maya and Egyptian priests, Hah-Wah-Tah and Is-Ra. She also believed he had incarnated as the legendary Hiawatha, though White Eagle never confirmed nor denied it. He told her he had lived as White Eagle, a Mohawk chief and head of the League of Six Nations of the Iroquois.

In her incarnation as Grace Cooke, she continued the spiritual work of her lives before, this time as a teacher herself, guiding others who sought to be "channels of light."

Mirrors

Mirrors have had reputed magical powers since antiquity. They are believed to reveal the future and to reflect the soul. They also can reveal the past by giving fleeting glimpses of the faces of persons one has been before. The visions of past-life faces may appear unexpectedly. Some individuals see their own past by gazing into a mirror, much as one would gaze into it for divination of the future. By looking steadily into a mirror in dim light or candle light, one's face seems to undergo changes. Is it a trick of the eye? Many believe not.

Craig Junjulus, a psychic consultant in New York, has used mirrors extensively in exploring his own past lives, as he explained:

> *I would look into my eyes, and then my entire face would start to change. I'd see flashes of different faces go by very quickly. Then they would slow down until a single face remained for me to look at. The more I practiced it, the more relaxed I became, and the more I learned—the face telepathically told me about itself.*

Among the past lives revealed by the mirror were an Oriental man, a

Native American Indian medicine man, a Viking warrior, a Neanderthal and a pirate. Each past life presented a different aspect of himself.

> *The first time I saw a female face looking back at me, I had a hard time accepting it. In this life, I was raised in a very macho way. Learning that I had lived as a woman shook me up at first, but made a good impact. Immediately afterwards, I started becoming softer in my approach to people.*

Junjulas advised that watching facial changes in a mirror can be unsettling, and one should look away or discontinue the procedure if results are disturbing.

Astrology
Your natal chart, or horoscope, won't tell you that you were a tailor in Ireland in your previous life, but it can reveal the karmic lessons created by past lives, according to professional astrologers.

According to the tenets of astrology, one's life and destiny is influenced by the positions of the planets at the moment of birth. These positions are depicted in a horoscope. A horoscope is divided into twelve houses, each of which governs a different aspect of life. Beginning with the first house, they are: self; finance; communications; home life; romance, children and creativity; health, work and service; marriage and partnership; needs; recognition; career; friendship; and the subconscious.

Each house is related to a sign of the Zodiac, which in turn is ruled by a planet; both are ascribed certain characteristics. Other planets may be placed in various houses, depending on where they are in the heavens at the birth moment. In addition to determining the placement of planets, astrologers also consider aspects, which are the mathematical relationships of one planet to another.

In her book *Astrology and Your Past Lives*, astrologer Jeanne Avery writes that Saturn, the planet of suffering, karmic burdens and higher consciousness, provides one of the greatest clues to an individual's past: "The placement of Saturn [in a house] indicates the specific area of life in which the most severe lessons are to be learned, the areas of responsibility are the most pronounced and restrictions are most likely to occur." For example, Saturn placed in the first house, Self, indicates deep insecurity coupled with a deep sense of responsibility, resulting in the need to control and be judgmental. Past-life regression, perhaps through hypnosis or guided meditation, can explain why those innate conditions exist.

Bodywork
Therapies that involve manipulation of the body's energy fields frequently trigger snatches of past-life recall, both on the part of the patient and the therapist. The physical body is surrounded by an envelope of energy, the aura. At various points, called chakras in yoga, for example, the universal life force permeates the aura and enters the body. In Chinese acupuncture, the Life Force runs along fourteen meridians in the body, which may be accessed at various points. This force is called by many names, such as *prana, chi,* and *ki*; it is believed to be essential to health. An imbalance in the life force in the body causes disease.

Past-life flashes do not always accompany holistic and alternative therapies to restore balance in the life force. They are not uncommon in acupuncture and massage therapies, such as polarity, shiatsu and Rolfing; the latter is a hard manipulation of deep facial tissue designed to release psychological blockages, which possibly could be karmic blocks as well.

Shirley MacLaine, who brought the subject of reincarnation home to millions with her accounts of her own past-life discoveries, received special past-life acupuncture treatments given by Chris Griscom, founder of The Light Institute in Galisteo, New Mexico. Griscom had learned an ancient form of acupuncture using gold needles to open the "windows to the sky," thus accelerating energy from higher dimensions into the body, and releasing past-life energy relevant to the present life. MacLaine, who described her experiences in *Dancing in the Light*, had been told about previous lives by channeled entities, but wanted to experience them herself.

Griscom worked with her own spirit guides and those of her patients to determine where to place the needles. The guides, she told MacLaine, could see the patterns of past-life memories being held in the body's cells. By remembering certain past lives associated with the memory patterns, traumatic energy could be released, resulting in spiritual growth and enlightenment.

As MacLaine lay on the table with gold needles quivering in her, she felt her consciousness shift so that she became both participant and observer of her past lives. Images came in the form of motion pictures, accompanied by emotions and tactile sensations. She viewed dozens of lives, some of which flashed by quickly while others, involving greater lessons, were shown in more detail.

MacLaine relived a remarkable life in India, in which she saw herself as a girl aged twelve named Asana who could commune telepathically with elephants. Her father in that life had once been kind to a bull elephant. Her father died when Asana was an infant, and for some reason, her life was in danger. The bull elephant took her away from her village to live with his herd. She grew up in complete rapport with the giant and gentle creatures. She taught them to dance and they in turn taught her to live in the moment, and to live without judging others.

Then a tragedy occurred which transformed the relationship between the villagers and the elephants. One of the male villagers killed a friend of Asana's in an argument. Picking up on Asana's thoughts, the elephants understood who the killer was, and the males in the herd wanted to seek revenge. Asana communicated with the female elephants to restrain the males, who agreed not to kill the murderer, but demonstrated their wrath by stampeding through the village and encircling his hut. The villagers, understanding the elephants had the power to destroy them, established a covenant in which the humans agreed to maintain peace with one another. Disputes were mediated telepathically with the elephants.

Asana's life explained to MacLaine why she felt an inexplicable fascination with, and love for, elephants. Her New York apartment was decorated with elephant paintings and figurines. From her Higher Self, MacLaine learned that Asana's life was a crucial one in her spiritual development, for she learned how to communicate on a collective level with animals, which respecting each animal individually.

Her Higher Self told her that the lesson was that humans should never forget their ability to connect with the collective spirit of animals. MacLaine quoted her Higher Self: "Their [the animals'] energy is essential to our future growth. The animals are on the earth for a reason and our disrespect for them has become alarming. They are totally without ego. Animals would teach us if we would listen. Pulsating in their collective consciousness are the lessons of the past."

Griscom and her colleagues at the Light Institute since have use techniques of esoteric healing designed to clear the emotional body. The physical body is surrounded by an aura of energy, which is layered in envelopes, or bodies. The envelopes are the etheric body (overall health and well-being); the emotional body; the mental body; the causal body (the Higher Self), and the astral body. According to Griscom, the emotional body absorbs anger, guilt and fear generated in life after life, the accumulations, like layers of grease, in turn clogging up the physical body. The release of negativity from the emotional body facilitates healing.

Another bodywork technique in past-life recall is the Christos Technique, the origins of which are obscure and are attributed to different sources. It was popularized in the mid-1970s by author G.M. Glaskin in his book *Windows of the Mind*. Glaskin said he learned the technique from an article in an Australian magazine. The Christos Technique requires three individuals. The subject lies down and relaxes, while one helper massages his feet and ankles and the second helper uses the outer edge of a clenched hand to massage the third eye area, which is located in the center of the brows. The third eye, the seat of the brow chakra, governs psychic faculties, and stimulating it can activate one's Clear Vision into the past or future. After the massages come a series of mental exercises in which the subject is guided to imagine himself growing in length and then shrinking. The ultimate goal is to expand the consciousness beyond the body to visit the past. In variations, ointments are used in the massage.

Rhythmic activities

Activities which induce an altered state of consciousness, such as chanting, ecstatic dancing or rhythmic aerobic exercise, such as running, can be conducive to past-life recall. Writing in the *Journal of the Association for Past Life Research and Therapy*, Marshall F. Gilula, M.D., recounted how chanting a Tibetan mantra while running opened access to a past life as a Tibetan monk. For years, he had seen a "tall, headless-appearing male spirit figure" within his peripheral vision during meditation. In 1983, shortly after he had begun to chant the mantra during his runs, his voice changed and became more guttural, and suddenly he realized he was the figure he had so often seen while meditating. It came to him that he had been a Tibetan monk or scholar. Over several days, the monk's story unfolded during Gilula's runs.

The monk was viciously tortured, apparently due to fear of some ability of his. He was suspended on some type of rack or wheel while his eyes were torn out, his flesh ripped, and his hands, feet and genitals mutilated and then cut off. He was then buried alive but exhumed before death. He was again tortured and cut, and finally stuffed into a brine-filled cask, where he drowned.

Gilula connected the drowning to recurring respiratory problems he had experienced. Almost as if in reaction to the recall, he suffered a severe cold. Over a period of time in which he reviewed the recall, Gilula passed a "sticking point" and felt the life forces flowing more freely through his body. After a spiritual consultation that included a past lives reading, he felt improvements in his breathing during meditation, and in his ability to channel a higher energy for healing.

Drugs
Hallucinogenic drugs such as LSD might stimulate past-life recall; LSD brings to vivid life memories from the present. However, since hallucinogenics distort reality, visions which seem to be past-life might not be reliable. It must be stated here that LSD and other hallucinogenics are not recommended as a means to recall past lives. Hallucinogenics can have profound, and sometimes disturbing, psychological after-effects.

The importance of intuition
Past lives can be revisited in various combinations of both spontaneous and induced recall. A hypnotic regression, for example, may be augmented with psychic consultations, channeling, and insights from dreams, *deja vu* and intuitive flashes.

The stronger your intuition, the more receptive you will be to past-life memories floating below the surface of your mind. Intuition is a right-brain phenomenon, associated with creativity and inspiration. One way to strengthen intuition is to pay attention to your gut feelings; that's your intuition talking to you. More often than not, gut feelings are rationalized away by a busy left brain. In any profession or occupation, the most successful persons usually are those who listen closely to their intuition.

The stories in the following chapters demonstrate how varied, rich and stimulating past-life recall can be. In many cases, the experience served as a catalyst for change and sometimes profound transformation.

4

Patterns in Past Lives

In 1966, Helen Wambach, an American psychologist and clinical psychiatrist, visited a Quaker memorial in Holly, New Jersey, and suddenly found herself in an altered state of consciousness, and a feeling of being in another time and place came over her.

> *As I entered the small library room, I saw myself going automatically to the shelf of books and taking one down. I seemed to 'know' that this had been my book, and as I looked at the pages, a scene came before my inner eye. I was riding on a mule across a stubbled field, and this book was propped up on the saddle in front of me. The sun was hot on my back, and my clothes were scratchy. I could feel the horse moving under me while I sat in the saddle, deeply absorbed in reading the book propped before me. The book I was reading was a report of a minister's experience of the between-life state while he was in a coma. I seemed to know the book's contents before I turned the pages.*

Wambach's experience took her by surprise, and led her to investigate reincarnation through hypnotic regression. After ten years and regression sessions with 1,088 subjects, she had amassed considerable data concerning patterns in past-life regressions, which she published in her first book *Reliving Past Lives*. As she pursued her study, she understood some of the odd cases she had encountered as a psychotherapist since 1955—like Peter, a five-year-old black boy who told her about his life as a rookie policeman who smoked. Peter wanted to smoke and could not understand why he was forbidden to do so. The boy's mother, who said he had talked about the policeman from age three, had discouraged him from "making up stories."

Wambach divided her regressions into time periods from 2000 B.C.E. to the twentieth century; not all subjects, of course, had lives in each period. She regressed her subjects to a time period and asked them about their sex, race, social class, clothing and footwear, utensils and their death experience. Among her more significant findings were:

—49.4 percent of past lives were as females and 50.6 percent as men, which matches true biological balance.

—The large majority of lives fell into the lower class in all time periods, from just under 70 percent in 2000 B.C.E. to a high of nearly 80 percent around 500 to nearly 70 percent again in the 1900s. Throughout all time periods, upper class lives constituted fewer than 10 percent. The middle class reached peaks of between 30 and 40 percent around 1000 B.C.E. and in the eighteenth century.

—World population figures, extrapolated from the numbers of lives reported in each time period matched historical population growth.

Wambach also found consistent descriptions of clothing, footwear and utensils in given time periods. Of her 1,088 subjects, only eleven gave reports which showed "clear discrepancies" from historical record.

In terms of race, Wambach found that again, the recalls conformed to history. From 2000 B.C.E. to about 500, black and Near Eastern (including Egyptian) lives predominated, followed by Asian and Indian. Caucasian lives fell third, except around the time of the birth of Christ, when they surpassed the Asian/Indian but not the black/Near Eastern. Most early white lives were in the Mediterranean area, with some throughout Central Asia.

Around 400, the three racial types were nearly evenly distributed; the Caucasian rate rose steadily to a peak of about 69 percent in 1850, then dropped sharply, while the other two groups rose sharply. Wambach confessed to being most perplexed that one-third of the lives reported from 1900-1945 were Asian, and others were black.

Overall, her findings ruled out the theory that fantasy or genetic memory accounted for past-life recall.

The following is the story given to me by a Caucasian man who regressed to a primitive life as a black man:

He healed the lepers

Doug Hobart, a film location scout in Oregon, shares interests in reincarnation, parapsychology and psychic phenomena with his wife, Sue, an editor for *The Oregonian*. When a friend of theirs went through a past-life regression with a psychic, the Hobarts were intrigued and decided to try it, too. It sounded like fun: you lay down, relaxed in a light altered state of consciousness, and watched your past lives unfold.

The regressions were conducted individually. Of all possible past lives Hobart might have fantasized, he was astonished at the one that materialized. He found himself in the body of a black man, in a primitive setting that appeared to be the Middle East in pre-Christian times. Hobart described his experience:

> *I met with the psychic [Marsha] in her apartment. It all seemed so ordinary. I sat and watched a football game with her husband while she finished the dishes in the kitchen. After about five minutes, she was done, and then she led me upstairs to a bedroom. I lay down on the bed. She turned on a tape recorder and sat in a chair next to me.*

She said, 'I'm not going to tell you that this is a past life. I want you to ask yourself why your imagination sees these images.' I felt very comfortable with that.

Then she started the relaxation process. I became very, very relaxed. She asked me to focus on a black spot on a white screen, and to enlarge that black spot and enter it, like I was coming into a tunnel. I looked down that tunnel and saw a light at the end. Marsha said to imagine large stone steps, and to step down until I could move into the light. As I moved into the light, she said, 'Can you see anything around you?' I said, 'No, just a white light.' She said, 'Look down at your feet.' When I looked down—and this was extremely vivid—I saw I had thin, black legs. I laughed and said, 'My legs are black!'

I could describe in great detail my legs, the type of sandals I was wearing. The hair on my legs was very dark and wiry. The sandals were leather, with thongs wrapped around my feet. Marsha asked me to look around me. It was hazy, I couldn't see that much. Whenever I had trouble seeing things around me, she would have me look back at my feet and then out again. I laughed every time I looked at my feet. I could wiggle the toes. They weren't my feet but they responded to my movements. That was fun.

As I kept describing a little more detail about my sandals or the hair on my legs—it was real stubbly, coarse hair—I began to notice what the ground looked like, and things started to get clearer. I could describe the stony ground around me, and the hillside, which had a kind of a sage growing on it. The earth was white, light and dusty. There was sand, but it was not a desert area. The hills had lot of shale rock and huge granite rocks. I saw a crow sitting in a madrona-like tree with red, peeling bark. The scene grew like a painting in my mind, and once it was complete, I could see anywhere.

There was a trail, and Marsha had me walk along it and describe what I saw. I could smell goats. I never saw them, but I could smell them very distinctly. It was a strange sensation. I wanted to know what direction I was going, but I could not figure out my direction or the time of day. The light never varied.

As I walked along, I came to a wall made of stacked stones. It was higher than my head. She told me to float up and see what was on the other side. I laughed and said, 'I can't do that.' She said, 'Go up on your tiptoes and you'll just float up.' I tried it and it worked. I floated up very high, to where I could see the entire village, including the central well with water jugs around it. There were maybe eight or ten square houses, built into the sides of the hills, and all facing the central well. The houses had thatched roofs. The thatching looked more like coarse bundles of sticks, not grass. There was no furniture that I could see, everything was rather primitive. I didn't see any people, although I could hear people. I couldn't discern whether they were speaking a foreign language.

After floating down, I went back to walking the trail. I would be walking along, and suddenly the scene in front of me would be different. A young girl was suddenly running in front of me. She was about six or seven, with long, straight, dark brown hair, and almond brown skin. She was wearing the same type of short, brown, coarsely woven sack that I was wearing. She was smiling and laughing and pointing at me, taunting me to chase her in some kind of game. She was saying my name, but I couldn't get it.

When I saw this little girl, I started to cry. I loved her. I still get goose bumps when I think about it, because I loved her so much, but I didn't know what my relationship was to her. I felt this tremendous yearning—it was overwhelming. I was so surprised. Here I was, lying on this bed in tears, supposedly 'imagining' these things, and the tears were streaming down my face! At the same time, I had this feeling of joy. I wanted to know her name or get more details about her, but for some reason, I couldn't, and that frustrated me. She ran on ahead, and I continued walking and never saw her again. I haven't a clue as to who she was. She doesn't seem to be anyone in my present life.

An odd thing was, as I moved along, I got older. I was walking along the trail at what seemed to be the same speed all the time, but *suddenly I would be in a different place, and there would be a change in me. I'd started out wearing this burlap sack that came down to just above my knees. As I got older, I noticed I was wearing the same kind of sack, but just below the knees. I became more aware of the heat as I grew older, because my clothes seemed to be heavier and stickier. The leather sandals also changed a little. My feet got flatter and there were more striations on the light bottoms. I also became aware that I now carried a leather bag. I didn't know what the bag was, just that it was there. It was made of leather and had drawstrings, so that it would close up like a purse. This strap was across my chest and the bag sat against my right hip. It was bulky and uncomfortable.*

I found myself in a fairly wide gully, a canyon that looked like high water had gone through it. There were trees and big rocks on each side. I saw two people coming at me, but I had the feeling they were 'things,' not people. When they saw me, they cowered away. I said, 'I don't like this, I want to get away. Marsha said, 'You can't get away. There's nothing to be afraid of. You must face this and see what it is.' I repeated, 'No, I don't like this, I want to get away.' She said, 'You're relaxed. This is something you should look at.'

Then I saw that these people were lepers. They were all wrapped up and covered with grungy burlap. They cowered, and I had to grab them and turn them around. The next thing I realized, I was kneeling down next to one of them, grinding herbs in a crucible. I put leaves in with these dried herbs and made a paste, and put the paste on the skin of the lepers. I could see the cracks and the black, dead portions of their skin. I didn't notice what their skin color was—all I saw were the sores.

I must have been a healer. I used the bag to carry the herbs and the little crucible, which looked like a round river rock. I would get fresh green leaves and add them to the dried herbs, and that made the paste because there wasn't any water.

The next thing I realized was that I was in a leper colony and I had the same black patches on my arms. The first sore appeared on the top of my forearm. I was still grinding herbs and putting the paste on the arms and thighs of people. The lepers lived in caves which were undercuts in these huge slab rocks. It was cooler in these undercuts. There were depressions, all smoothed out, where people had slept. There were cooking utensils, bowls, made out of clay. The lepers just wandered around, waiting to die. I had the impression that I had gone there as a stranger to help them, and all of a sudden I was one of them.

I was way in the back in the cool section of one of these undercuts, sitting cross-legged, always covered up. I had a big blanket over my shoulders, and I hurt. Then I felt a weight on my chest. I was lying down on the ground, and there were two or three other lepers around me. I was in pain. There was an oppressive weight over my entire body, and it was difficult to breathe. I just wanted to curl up in a ball. Everything hurt. I knew I was dying. Then I felt this tremendous weight taken off of me, and I floated up. It was total release. This terrible unpleasantness lifted away, and I felt like I was floating up in the sky toward a light. It was wonderful. I didn't even attempt to look back.

Then Marsha started calling to me to feel my feet: 'You have to feel your feet. You're here. Feel your body.' She touched my foot. I just laid there. I wanted to continue this floating sensation. The last thing I wanted was to feel my feet. She said, 'Are you all right?' I said, 'Yeah.' She said, 'I'm going to go downstairs. You lay here as long as you want.' I laid there and went over and over and over everything for a long time.

At first, I didn't feel comfortable talking to anybody about it. I told Sue a little tiny bit that day, but no details. For a long time, every time I thought about that little girl, I started to cry. It took weeks before I could tell my close friends that I'd done this [the regression]. Even then, when I talked to Sue or my parents about it, I still cried. The experience was extremely personal, and I didn't want to share it, because I didn't think anyone could understand how intensely personal it was. People have a tendency to talk about it like a joke. I can *joke about it now, but in truth, I take it very seriously. It's still incredibly personal and emotional.*

Asked what seeing this past life has meant for him in terms of his present life, Hobart responded:

It reinforced my belief that this life isn't all there is, and that death is just a transition. My attitude toward my life now is much different. I'm able to put the good—and the bad—that happens into a larger perspective. I don't feel devastated by setbacks. I've been through them before and I'm sure I'll go through them again.

Sex change

Individuals who go through past-life regression often are surprised to find themselves as the opposite sex. Not all, but some, men have a much more difficult time accepting female lives than women do male lives—a reflection of a pervasive male view of women as inferior. In fact, in some cultures which believe in reincarnation, such as the Druse of Lebanon, men refuse to believe it is possible to reincarnate as women; it is simply unacceptable. In other cultures, such as Burma, it is considered punishment for a man to be reborn as a woman.

Ian Stevenson considered the incidence of sex change as the most important variation in features of reincarnation cases in different cultures. His research showed that the incidence of reported sex change does seem to be influenced by cultural attitudes. Stevenson found no reported case of a male being reborn as a female in Lebanon or Turkey, or among the Tlingit Indians of southeastern Alaska, and the Haida, Tsimsyan and Gitskan Indians of British Columbia. Among cultures that do have reported sex change cases, females who remember past lives as males occur three times as often as males who remember female lives.

The incidence of sex change ranges from a low of 3 percent of all reported cases in India to a high of 50 percent among the Kutchin (Athabaskan) Indians of the Canadian Northwest Territories. Sex change accounts for 15 percent of all reported nontribal cases in the United States,

9 percent in Sri Lanka, 13 percent in Thailand and 28 percent in Burma.

If a man believes that it is either highly undesirable, or impossible, to be reborn as a woman, does this mean that he doesn't reincarnate as a woman, or does he merely suppress the memory of female lives? Stevenson said that both answers may be correct. It is certainly likely for undesirable memories to be repressed in order to conform to culture. In addition, Stevenson said, reincarnation beliefs governing sex change might be strong enough to act like posthypnotic suggestions after death, thus avoiding reincarnation as the opposite sex.

Cayce's soul groups
According to Edgar Cayce, souls have reincarnated throughout history more in less in groups in accordance with their alignments to religions, races, cultures, nations, etc. The largest group comprises the planet itself, for earth is not the only place in the cosmos to live. Soul groups are fluid, their ranks constantly shifting as individual souls change course. Generally, however, the groups come and go in earth history in cycles.

In the thousands of Cayce readings, two major soul groups were identified: Group 1 includes souls who lived in early Atlantis, early ancient Egypt, Persia during the time of Croesus I and Croesus II, Palestine, the Crusades, and colonial America. Group 2 includes souls who lived in late Atlantis, late ancient Egypt, early Greece, Rome during the time of Christ, France during the time of Louis XIV, XV and XVI, and the American Civil War.

The souls who lived during the times in these two groups also most likely had other lives; these periods were ones of great importance in the course of human events and evolution. In their reincarnations, soul groups are subject to karma and planetary influences. A particular group may not desire to collectively reincarnate, for example, but be required to do so for the purposes of balancing karma. Some members of soul groups may be present in a particular cycle in spirit form, as guides, rather than in the flesh, and still have an influence upon earthly affairs.

Emerging soul groups

Cayce died on January 3, 1945, shortly before the end of World War II, another great period of world trauma and change. As linear time continues, other watershed periods will undoubtedly mark new soul groups or cycles of groups. Three such groups have emerged: World War II; Vietnam War; and Native American Indians.

World War II. Cases of the reincarnation of souls who died during World War II have been reported; Cayce expressed concern for children killed in the war who reincarnated too quickly and made poor choices for families. The soul group of World War II is complex, for it is interwoven with the ethnic karma of the Jews, which has extended over 3,800 years of history.

Rabbi Yonassan Gershom has collected data in an information study that has yielded interesting information about Jews who died in World War II. According to Gershom, the majority of Holocaust victims in his survey were born between 1946 and 1953. Most of them are not Jewish; those who are typically are marginal in their faith, perhaps, he said, because World War II marked their first experience as a Jew. About two-thirds have light hair and blue or hazel eyes. Experiences reported to him include feelings of familiarity and affinity with the Jewish faith, and religious rituals and traditions not generally known outside the Jewish community; familiarity with the Hebrew language, and *deja vu* or strange experiences upon visiting the sites of concentration camps. One woman who visited a camp felt as though she were walking through mud, even though the paths had since the war been covered with gravel. She recognized the building where she knew she had died, and saw her death. At the end of the tour, her feet and socks were muddy, though her shoes were dry.

Others have reported terrifying nightmares of being killed, and phobias of policemen, barbed wire, doctors and uniforms. Two persons reported asthma attacks brought on by Jewish rituals, reminiscent, Gershom said, of choking to death in a gas chamber.

Some Hassidim believe that Hitler was a reincarnation of Amalek, grandson of the evil Esau, who in the Bible came to represent those who prey on the weak. Exodus 17:16 says that "YH'VH [Yahweh] will be at war with Amalek throughout the ages." This may be taken as a literal reference to the reincarnation of Amalek, or, as Gershom prefers, the indication that God will always fight the oppressor.

Gershom said the Holocaust served as a warning that human rights were in danger, and that it has entered the collective unconscious as an archetype as "an eternal warning about the misuse of our technology."

The Vietnam War. The Vietnam War divided America into bitter factions, and left shattered families and veterans to contemplate the horrors of killing. Unlike World War II and Word War I, there were no black-and-white issues to grasp as to which side was right and why. A popular Age of New Consciousness theory holds the protestors of the Vietnam War were the reincarnated dead of World War II, some even from World War I, who came back angry about the senselessness of war. As the dead of Vietnam return, they, too, are likely to be regretful, angry or outraged over war. The next chapter presents the story of Bill, who in his previous life died as a soldier in Vietnam in 1965.

Native Americans. The Native Americans were made strangers in their own land by the founders and pioneers of this nation. Their way of life was termed savage and held in contempt by the more "civilized" folk who proceeded to pollute and destroy the environment. The New Age has rediscovered that the Native Americans' worthy ideas about life, spirit, healing and living in harmony with nature.

If cultural attitudes have the power to suppress certain past-life memories, as with sex change, they also have the power to release them. Therefore, it is not surprising, in light of the shift in attitudes toward the Indian, that Indian past lives should be on the increase. In addition, I believe that some Indian souls have reincarnated in the race of their oppressors as a teaching tool, to help bring individuals back into touch with Indian culture and stimulate interests that are then pursued long after the regression. Chapters Fifteen, Sixteen and Seventeen present stories in which North and Central Native American past lives figure prominently.

Sutphen's 25,000

Teotihuacan, in central Mexico, is the site of ruins of an ancient city of once grand splendor. A religious, cultural, economic and political center, its population may have reached a peak of 200,000. It was twelve square miles in size, larger than the area contained within the walls of Imperial Rome under the Caesars, a contemporary civilization. By the time the Aztecs arrived in 1325, it was long deserted and in ruins. The Aztecs named the place "Teotihuacan," which means "the place where men become gods."

In 1974, Dick Sutphen and his wife, Tara, visited Teotihuacan and walked among the ruins, including the "Street of the Dead," mounds in which the Aztecs believed were buried the gods. Sutphen felt a sense of *deja vu*. He experienced a dream in which he was in ancient Teotihuacan. Thousands of persons filled the street and night. Elegantly robed men lined the steps of the Pyramid of the Moon, atop which was lit a huge fire. In the dream, he was instructed to "get the books together." He didn't have the foggiest idea what that meant.

Through a channeler friend, he found out that he was part of a group of persons who had lived at the same time in Teotihuacan, and who had made a pact to reincarnate every 700 years to present the spiritual knowledge that they has possessed at that time. Sutphen was fulfilling that past-life pledge by writing books.

Later in 1974, Sutphen had a psychic vision that repeated itself over the years. He was a man dressed in a white tunic with gold braid ribbing, holding a crystal rod and standing on top of the Pyramid of the Sun with fifteen to twenty others. Thousands filled the Street of the Dead. He was projecting his will through the rod, which glowed blue-white, to control masses of people trying to climb the pyramid.

In 1987, Sutphen was awakened in the middle of the might by an inner voice which instructed him it was time for important communications. The voice told him he was one of 25,000 persons who had lived 1,400 years ago in Teotihuacan, and he was to assist others of this group who had reincarnated to awaken to this awareness.

According to information revealed in regressions and psychic consultations, the pact was made in 581 during a time of political upheaval. Sutphen and Tara were part of a secret religious group of sixteen, who in turn were publicly part of a larger religious council. In a change of political power, the new rulers, a hierarchy of priests, misused their powers and blamed the results on the inner circle, which then disguised its teachings by painting over murals on the walls of the Pyramid of the Sun. The inner circle finally was forced into hiding.

In an effort to make a last, public stand, they summoned the population to the Pyramid of the Sun to hear an announcement. One of every eight persons—25,000 people—appeared, and took the pledge to return every 700 years together. The meeting was scuttled when soldiers arrived and arrested the inner circle and other protesters. The scapegoats were buried alive in pits.

Historically, Teotihuacan declined after the late sixth century, and was eventually sacked and partially destroyed.

Sutphen proceeded to search for the 25,000 in his regression seminars. According to their mission, the 25,000 are to once again spread enlightened ideas around the world, so that the fate which befell Teotihuacan will not happen again.

Proving past lives

Most people who see their past lives, especially during a light hypnotic trance, wonder if they are "real" or their imagination, even if they "feel true." There is little way of proving it. As seen in Wambach's findings, most past lives are those of the ordinary masses, for whom few, if any records exist. Through research one can substantiate historical details of the period, but seldom can one find proof that a certain individual lived. Few regressions provide full names, let alone sufficient biographical information to track down an identity.

In the area of research of spontaneous recall among children, numerous solved cases in which a child names his previous personality, identifies his former family members, and discloses personal information known only to the dead or his immediate family and friends, would appear to be proof of reincarnation. Scientists take a more cautious view: such cases are evidence in support of reincarnation.

For a hypnotic regression, one must largely rely upon intuition in judging reincarnation memories. Most persons feel that if they were to fabricate a past life about themselves, they would have conjured up lives of glamour, not the usual mundane ones they encountered. It is common for individuals to receive additional past-life information intuitively, long after a regression session.

Alice T., who uncovered more than thirty of her own past lives, observed, "I believe that we have nonphysical beings around us who care about our spiritual development. In a session, I try to strengthen the communication between the client and his or her guides. Sometimes these beings appear in the regression in human or spirit form, or as lights or colors. They help provide answers. Past-life information is surprisingly accessible."

Sandee Mac believes people do tap into real memories, but she leaves the ultimate decision up to her clients. "I suggest that they trust what comes into their mind, but not get caught up in whether or not they are seeing a 'real' past life. The important thing is that they are being given information they need in order to work through something in their present life."

Psychics also are asked by clients how to judge the information given them. "Why can't you just trust your feelings?" said Laurie McQuary. "With imagination, you have thousands of scenarios to choose from. When one strong feeling comes through, if you really explore it, you're going to see it exactly as the way it was and not how you wish it were. Before you start rationalizing whether it's imagination or not, you've got to decide whether you believe in reincarnation. If you do, you don't think about it being imagination. You trust that it's the truth."

5

Slain in the Viet Nam and Civil Wars

BILL (A PSEUDONYM) is a college student in New England. A native of California born in 1968, he has since early childhood been fascinated by war and the military, and also has felt an affinity with the name "John." It was neither his real first nor middle name, yet as a child he adopted it as a second middle name and called himself by it.

His family moved around the country while he was growing up, and in Texas, where he finished high school, Bill met a friend who introduced him to reincarnation, metaphysics and other topics of the New Age. Just before he entered college, Bill decided to undergo hypnotic regression as an exploration of himself. The night before, he and his friend meditated together as a way of preparing for it.

Three key, related lives appeared in the regression the next day, two of which involved deaths in wars: the American Civil War and the Vietnam War, one soul group and one emerging soul group. The entire experience was intense and emotional, with Bill reliving what he encountered rather than merely observing it.

At the start of the regression, Bill told the hypnotist that he wanted to discover information relating to his back problems, which he had suffered for quite some time. Bill's first scene was a Civil War battle:

> *I found myself wearing an officer's uniform and leading troops in a hill entrenchment alongside what appeared to be a river. The regressionist asked me to look at the aftermath of the battle from a detached point of view. I saw the hill littered with bodies, and found myself still alive and struggling on my back—evidently I had been wounded in the fighting, which had left most, if not all, of my men dead.*
>
> *The regressionist asked me to remove the officer from the battle scene to a place where he would be warm and comfortable, and to tell him that I was from the future. She told me to thank the officer for that life and all that he had learned and done in it. In addition, I should tell him that the injury was in the past and he could let it go so that I could be freed from it in the future. The two of us had something to discuss, she said, and would come to an understanding.*
>
> *I said I sensed there was a bayonet in the officer's stomach. She told me to remove it and take the officer away from the battle scene. 'There is something else that Bill in the future needs to know,' she said. 'What is it?'*
>
> *After a few moments, I shouted out, 'What a waste!... My men...!' and I broke into tears. The regressionist reminded me to take the officer away from the scene and tell him that the incident was in the past and that I was going to set him free. I had come back to earth in a different life with different options, and so had all the officer's soldiers. 'Thank him for what he went through,' she said. I still felt very anxious. She said, 'There is something else, isn't there?'*
>
> *I screamed, 'I was abandoned! They left me!' I went on to say that I had never forgiven myself. The regressionist asked me to forgive myself now, but I cried out that I could not. She then took me to a deeper level to find out why this was so.*
>
> *I saw I was in the Arctic Northwest and was a logger or hunter.*

I got caught out in the cold when my dogsled overturned. I seem to have broken some ribs and injured myself internally, because I was spitting up blood and couldn't go anywhere. It was very cold. Once I had eaten up all my food, I ended up eating my dogs. It was a very cruel and painful thing, and all kinds of emotions popped out that I never realized I had. I was responsible for and loved those dogs, and yet they had allowed me to eat them. I was raging about how faithful they were, because they'd had a chance to get away. They didn't have to stay with me but they did, and they gave themselves to me freely. I was overwhelmed. The connection to the war scene made me feel very cruel, and I could not see how I could ever forgive myself.

The regressionist said I did not need to go through that experience with the dogs anymore, but that I could rescue the man and his dogs. She said the man no longer needed to be angry or blame himself. I still wanted to know why he had done what he did. I felt very confused. She asked me if I now understood about the Civil War experience and being abandoned, and about forgiving. I said that I did, that I knew I had to forgive myself. I let out one final, biting emotion, crying out, 'They were all so young!'

'Forgive yourself for setting yourself up and forgive the men for doing what they had to do,' the regressionist said. I did that. Then she told me, 'See him [the officer] fill with light, strong and whole and healthy, and tell him that you are going to release him and watch him go up into the light.' I did, and I felt that I experienced a very definite healing.

As an interesting footnote, after the regression, I asked my friend if he had sensed anything when we'd meditated the night before. He said, 'You know, I could hear the sounds of dogs and I could taste raw flesh in my mouth.' That was quite a shock. I then told him about the man in the woods.

The experience was so powerful that Bill decided to undergo more regressions to learn what lay in his past. In a subsequent session, his regressionist asked if there was another life related to the Civil War life. Bill, who was but a small child when the United States finally pulled out of Vietnam, suddenly found himself in Vietnamese jungles, an officer or a noncom leading a small group of about ten soldiers:

> *We were dropped off by a boat onto a bank. We wanted to go to some village to set up a school or orphanage for children. I don't think there were any orders for it; it was something I thought was important. We got nailed. We didn't get very far into the jungle before we were attacked. My adrenalin shot up. The next thing I knew, I think all my men were killed, and I was lying on my back in pools of blood. It was shocking. I experienced gut-wrenching emotion from fear to hatred to regret. At one point, I blurted out, 'I goofed. We didn't need to do this!' It was the same feeling of uncommon duty toward my men that I experienced in the Civil War life.*
>
> *In the end I just drifted off. Later I had an eerie feeling that I may have survived for some time, maybe I was rescued and they got me onto a helicopter and tried to stitch me up, and I didn't make it.*

While he was hypnotized, Bill was able to read his dog tag number. He thought his name was either "John" or "Tom."

Intrigued, he delved into that life in additional regressions in order to recover more details. He decided to try to verify whether or not the man he saw in Vietnam had actually lived. The dog tag number led him to a name and a Social Security number of a soldier who was killed in Vietnam in 1965. The man's name was John _____ and his name appears on the Wall, the Vietnam War Memorial in Washington, D.C. Bill was uncertain whether or not he would contact the man's family; such a situation could go off like an emotional bomb.

Bill also discovered that about five members of his Vietnam detail had reincarnated and were among his friends in high school in Texas.

I think in many respects, the purpose of my being here [in the present life] was to come back and check up on them and make sure they were all right. Again, there's that sense of uncommon obligation...

I had a dream one night that I was back in our old house. I was very young and was being chased by a spirit. It wasn't evil. The gist was that I had done what I had come to do: check up on these guys, and having fulfilled my end of the bargain, it was time for me to 'go home.' In the dream I said, 'No, I want to stay.' I was having a tantrum. I did not want to leave. I said, 'There are things to be done here, I'm excited by the challenge.'

That's the way I feel. Life is exciting. I want to put my two cents in and leave this place better than when I came. So I stayed.

Bill did not discuss reincarnation with his friends, feeling that he should not push the matter with others who might not be ready for it. Months after his first regression, he came across information which shed light on his Civil War recall. It seemed like coincidence, but Bill knew it was synchronicity:

I was flipping through a Yankee *magazine and found a story about a colonel in the U.S. Army during the Civil War who was in charge of a Negro regiment from Massachusetts. They led an attack on an entrenched beach facility in North or South Carolina in about 1862 or '63. Most of the men in the regiment were killed, including the colonel. This made sense with what I had seen. The colonel was buried in a mass grave with his Negro troops. Evidently his body was desecrated by the Southern soldiers because he had led blacks. In the official Southern account, the colonel was found lying dead next to his color sergeant. Evidently these two had managed to hold out for a while before they were overwhelmed.*

The colonel was the son of a very wealthy Northern man. At the end of the war, the Army approached the father and said they had located the mass grave where his son was believed to be buried and offered to try to find his body and bury him properly. The father said no, because he felt that his son would be honored to be buried with the men he led. Abraham Lincoln said at the end of the war that the one thing that gave the ultimate edge to the North was the Negro soldier, because of his numbers, his courage and his fighting spirit. I think there is a lot of credibility to that.

I have always had a tremendous respect for blacks and have felt an affinity with them. I think it comes from the respect that I earned for them then.

Bill said that although he could see that in the past, he had enjoyed making war—and still had a fascination with war—he was dismayed by the growth of the war machine in the modern world.

We have pushed our war-making capacity to the limit. There is no need for armies that are so big, missiles that are so powerful. There is no need to turn to genocide and wholesale slaughter to solve political differences. It is wrong. There are always alternatives to killing each other...

The regressions made me look at the 'third' side of every story that is so rarely observed, which is the side of the people who get swept up in the events of history: the soldiers, the civilians, the maimed. As the saying goes, there are those who make things happen and those who watch things happen, and then there are those who wonder what happened. As things unfold in this next century, it's important that we all have an understanding of the significance of the New Age.

If I got anything out of this, it was a unique exposure to the human spirit. So long as it remains strong, so will we.

6

The New Atlanteans

MANY PERSONS WHO HAVE SOUGHT past-life regressions during the 1970s and 1980s have turned up lives in Atlantis. As we saw in the previous chapter, Edgar Cayce identified early Atlantis and late Atlantis as part of two soul groups. He further said that a great influx of Atlanteans reincarnated between the years of 1909-1913. Such individuals, especially those born in 1910-1911, promised to wield unusual powers for influencing world affairs for either good or bad. The Atlanteans supposedly turned their great powers of their advance society to serve evil and thus brought about their own destruction.

Most of the individuals seeking regressions from the 1970s to the present are much younger, however, having been born predominantly in the 1940s through 1960s. This suggests a new cycle of Atlantean incarnations. Why are so many seeing past lives in Atlantis?

There are several reasons why. First, there has been a new surge of interest in ancient cultures and the legendary Atlantis during the New Age. Second, and more significant, is that many Atlantean recalls deal with healing. The Atlanteans are believed to have possessed unusual and remarkably effective healing techniques employing crystals, vibration, sound and music, color and energy transfer. The New Age has witnessed great renewed interest in alternative and holistic healing techniques using the very same tools. Accessing these Atlantean healing lives has in many cases awakened individuals to their own potential healing abilities, as we saw in Chapter One with Pamela Glasser. Another Atlantean healing story appears later in this book. Third, Atlantis is a mirror of our own culture: a high-tech, materialistic and increasingly corrupt and violent society headed down the path of self-destruction. It is possible that Atlanteans have reincarnated in the present in order to help prevent the same fate that befell their land.

But many people do not believe in Atlantis and say the legend is pure fantasy, highly romanticized by film and fiction. What do we *really* know about Atlantis?

The Atlantean legend
According to legend, Atlantis was a island continent with a highly advanced civilization interested in science and technology; their advances were made possible with help from space beings. Their greed, materialism and corruption eventually led to their downfall, and to the destruction of their entire continent by massive tidal waves, floods and earthquakes which sank the land beneath the sea. Some survived, and dispersed to other lands around the world, taking their culture and knowledge with them.

No one has ever found any proof that Atlantis existed, yet the legend has remained a powerful one over the centuries. More than 45 locations around the world on both sides of the Atlantic have been suggested as the site of the great continent.

Plato was the first person known to record the legend of Atlantis in 350 B.C.E. in his *Timaeus* and *Critias* of the *Dialogues*. According to Plato, Solon heard the story of Atlantis from an Egyptian priest. Solon told it to Critias, an old Athenian man, who told it to Socrates. The story, as told in *Timaeus* from the viewpoint of the Egyptian priest, takes place in 9600 B.C.E.:

> *Many great and wonderful deeds are recorded of your State [Athens] in our [Egypt's] histories; but one of them exceeds all the rest in greatness and valor; for these histories tell of a mighty power which was aggressing wantonly against the whole of Europe and Asia, and to which your city put an end. The power came forth out of the Atlantic Ocean, for in those days the Atlantic was navigable; and there was an island situated in front of the straits which you call the Columns [Pillars] of Heracles: the island was larger than Libya and Asia put together, and was the way to other islands, and from the islands you might pass through the whole of the opposite continent which surrounded the true ocean; for this sea which is within the Straits of Heracles is only a harbor, having a narrow entrance, but that other is a real sea, and the surrounding land may be most truly called a continent. Now, in the island of Atlantis there was a great and wonderful empire, which had rule over the whole island and several others, as well as over parts of the continent: and, besides these, they subjected the parts of Libya within the Columns of Heracles as far as Egypt, and of Europe as far as Tyrhhenia. The vast power thus gathered into one, endeavored to subdue at one blow our country and yours, and the whole of the land which was within the straits; and then, Solon, your country shone forth, in the excellence of her virtue and strength, among all mankind; for she was the first in courage and military skill, and was the leader of the Hellenes. And when the rest fell off from her, being compelled to stand alone, after having undergone the extremity of danger, she defeated and triumphed over the invaders, and preserved from slavery those who were not yet subjected, and freely liberated all the others who dealt within the limits of Heracles. But afterward there occurred violent earthquakes and floods, and in a single day and night of rain all your warlike men in*

a body sank into the earth, and the island of Atlantis in like manner disappeared, and was sunk beneath the sea. And that is the reason why the sea in those parts is impassable and impenetrable, because there was such a quantity of shallow mud in the water; and this was caused by the subsidence of the island.

Plato's own student, Aristotle, didn't believe the story of Atlantis and tried to debunk it as fiction. So did Pliny and Strabo several centuries later. The story survived, however, and in the Middle Ages, Atlantis was believed to have existed.

Some modern scholars agree with Aristotle and other ancient critics, that Atlantis was entirely a figment of Plato's imagination. Nonetheless, the story bears striking similarities to legends in other cultures, including a legend from the Middle Kingdom of Egypt (c. 2000-1786 B.C.E.) and one in the Mahabharata of India (composed c. 300 B.C.E.). In addition, legends of the Indians of the Americas speak of space gods and races of highly evolved beings. Finally, the flood of Atlantis perhaps is related to the legends of a Great Flood which exist in cultures all over the world, with the exception of most of Africa and much of Asia.

In the late nineteenth century, "Atlantology," the study of Atlantis lore, flowered with the publication of *Atlantis: The Antediluvian World*, by Ignatius Donnelly, an American Congressman. Donnelly said the existence of Atlantis could explain unusual similarities between widely separated cultures, such as the ancient Egyptians and the Indians of Central and South America. From his research, Donnelly concluded that:

— Atlanteans comprised at least two races, a small and dark-brown, reddish race similar to Egyptians, Berbers and Central Americans, and a large, white race similar to the Greeks, Goths, Celts and Scandinavians. There were many battles for supremacy.

— Atlanteans believed in reincarnation and embalmed their dead.

— There was an established order of priests who oversaw a simple religion.

— The continent itself had 1,500-foot high volcanic mountains, the tops of which were perpetually covered with snow; elevated table-lands where the royalty lived; a lower "great plain"; four rivers flowing from a central point to the four points of the compass; tropical and temperate zones; and fertile soil.

Theosophists, led by Helena P. Blavatsky, also disseminated views about the long-lost land in the late nineteenth century and early twentieth century. Blavatsky believed the continent perished out of natural old age, not the corruption of its inhabitants. She said it was formed by parts of Lemuria, which had been destroyed before it. The Atlanteans, who were descended from Lemurians, were giants twenty-seven feet in height who possessed great psychic powers, she said. They formed the Fourth Root Race of all humans. The priests of the Druids were the descendants of the last Atlanteans.

A different picture was provided by one of Blavatsky's followers, Rudolph Steiner, who said he accessed the Akashic Records to learn about Atlantis. They were weak in logic, he said, but could control life forces and extract energy from plants. Their vehicles hovered a few feet off the ground. They did not possess telepathy, but communicated verbally.

Author Ruth Montgomery, receiving her information from spirit guides through automatic writing, said Atlanteans used a Great Crystal for power, and destroyed themselves by misusing the Crystal.

Yet another theory suggests that powerful ley lines converged at Atlantis, which provided its great energy source. Ley lines are lines of natural earth energy said to crisscross the world; where they intersect, they create powerful force fields. Many sacred sites are believed to be constructed at ley line junctions. Scientists contest the existence of ley lines, but dowsers say they may be detected and mapped.

Taylor Caldwell's Atlantis. In 1913, at the age of twelve, Janet Taylor Caldwell, who later became famous as novelist Taylor Caldwell, wrote a novel about Atlantis. It flowed seemingly from memory, profound in maturity and sophistication for an adolescent. Later in adulthood, Caldwell said she seemed to "know" about Atlantis from infancy, and was "haunted" for years about it before she sat down to write it at the tender age of twelve.

The manuscript remained unpublished for about sixty years; by then, Caldwell had undergone hypnotic regression and had discovered Atlantis among her past lives. Caldwell's Atlantis was a high-tech land of urban overcrowding, rising pollution, power shortages, loss of faith in religion among the masses, social and political upheaval, and a haven for immigrants from more oppressed lands. It was ruled by a monarch, who was among the small elite privileged to prolong life, to about 200 years, by exposure to rejuvenating chambers. They wore crystals to rejuvenate their energy. The continent was divided into twelve provinces, each of which had a certain amount of state autonomy. There were snow-capped volcanoes, great agricultural plains, and a shimmering sea mined for its minerals. The capital city of Lamora was filled with great pillars, domes and walls of gleaming stone.

In the novel, Salustra, the empress of Atlantis, faces the aggression of the neighboring nation, Althrustri. She falls in love with Althrustri's emperor, Signar. Both lands are destroyed by earthquakes and tidal waves, save for a handful of inhabitants and the two leaders, who manage to escape to a new land.

After the novel was published in 1975 as *The Romance of Atlantis* (with co-author Jess Stearn), Caldwell experienced three vivid, exceptionally intense "big" dreams about Atlantis, in which she was Salustra. The dreams left her weeping for Atlantis and yearning for Signar, who she knew in her present life, but whose identity she never disclosed.

Atlantis according to Cayce. Of the 1,600 persons who received life readings by Edgar Cayce, 700 were told they had one or more lives in Atlantis, or "Poseidia," as he also called it. The figure possibly could be higher, as Cayce may not have mentioned Atlantis in a life reading if it were not relevant to issues at hand. Life readings were given to Cayce's family and friends, and concerned previous incarnations that were influencing the present life. The readings were overviews of characteristics, problems and assets; they are distinguished from the more than 25,000 "physical readings" Cayce gave to others.

Cayce said Atlantis was one of the first places on earth where man appeared in material form, as long as 10.5 million years ago. Humans took form and "hardened" by gratifying their material desires. The "red race" developed Atlantis rapidly, especially in science and technology, and particularly in transportation.

The Atlanteans, Cayce said, learned how to amplify sun rays with crystals to generate energy for light, heat, transportation and communication. They wielded "death rays," which perhaps were lasers, and enslaved others. Musicians in temples produced "sounds of all nature" on instruments. The continent suffered three cataclysms, the third of which destroyed it all. The readings give no date for the first cataclysm; the second was said to have occurred around 28,000 B.C.E. After the first two disasters, many Atlanteans left the continent and migrated to other lands. Others remained behind to rebuild, though a great deal of dissent and discord spread throughout the land. The final destruction apparently is the one cited by Plato, occurring around 9600 B.C.E. Of Cayce's Atlantean readings, most dealt with the continent's final phase, when the civilization was in decline and suffering great turmoil. The people faced a choice between following God or indulging themselves; too many chose the latter and the culture became spiritually dead.

Cayce said the ruins of Atlantis lie near Bimini in the Bahamas, "under the slime of ages of seawater." In 1940 he predicted that "Poseidia will be among the first portions of Atlantis to rise again. Expect it in '68 and '69; not so far away." No remains heaved up from the seabed, but in 1968 stone formations suggesting pyramids, roads, walls and circles were found on the ocean floor near Bimini. Some believe they are ruins of Atlantis.

Cayce believed that many Atlanteans have been reincarnating in America, a nation that wields great power in the atom bomb and enjoys advanced technology. It is also a society gone haywire from greed, materialism, violence and the desire for instant gratification of the senses at the expense of our neighbors and our home, the earth. We are now facing the same choices between spirit and matter, the good and the profane. Atlantean past-life regressions call attention to these choices: to the potential of power used for good, the terrible results of power abused, and the need to grow spiritually.

Atlantean regressions
Descriptions of the Atlantis seen in past-life regressions bear striking similarities from widely disparate sources. In general, they support the Cayce readings. At its best, Atlantis emerges as a land of light and crystal, with great, glistening temples and crystal pathways. The air is moist and silky, the gardens lush and the environment unpolluted. The people make use of telepathy to communicate with each other and with the denizens of nature. At its worst, it suffers from a population explosion that has caused overcrowded cities and a polluted environment, and from social and political turmoil.

Some persons, when they first see such scenes in their regressions, think they are in a classical setting, in Greece or Rome, perhaps, though they recognize that there is something strange and different about their surroundings. One man said:

> There was a predominance of white, especially in clothing, which was soft and flowing. A lot of people wore white headbands. The whole area was extremely clean, and was contemporary but not like we know it.

Another description, given by a woman, was this:

There were pyramids which were centers of great energy, like power plants. Only certain people were allowed inside—engineers and technicians, I suppose, and officials. I also saw temples with huge columns. I thought I was in ancient Greece, but the thought came into my head that no, this was Atlantis. I didn't want to believe it at first... The air was very moist, a marine climate. There weren't any cars that travelled on land. Instead, people drove around through the sky in little vehicles not much bigger than a motorcycle sidecar with no wheels.

Many Atlantean recalls also concern the highly developed technology, for example, air ships that traveled on crystal power or magnetic force. One young woman gave this description of her life in Atlantis just before and during its final destruction:

I saw myself in a temple at the age of fourteen, being tutored in spiritual matters. At first I thought I was in ancient Egypt or Greece because of the temples and statues, although they were unlike anything I'd ever seen before. Then it came to me that I was in Atlantis. After my tutoring I went out with a group of friends. We were picked up by others in a strange vehicle that didn't have wheels but floated along. The funny thing about regressions is you can't change them. Now, I'm a pretty rational person, and in my mind, I kept trying to put wheels on the car, to make the picture something I could cope with. But I couldn't change the picture.

We all got into this car and went to a mountain and sat on top of it. There were six of us and we sat in a circle, practicing mental telepathy. We looked at each other, thinking things in our heads and trying to communicate telepathically. [The regressionist] asked, 'What are you thinking about?' and I said, 'What's for dinner!' We were typical fourteen-year-olds just being silly...

I progressed a few years into the future and saw that I and my friends were learning how to rule. Then I progressed and saw the

> destruction of Atlantis. I was about fifty years old when everything fell down and exploded. At the time, I was a member of a governing body with these other people. I knew that somebody was abusing their power and that something awful was about to happen, and it did. Everything blew up and collapsed. I was in an office. Huge stones were falling and I knew I was going to be crushed. I left my body seconds before it was hit by a falling structure. I felt I had chosen the time to leave. I saw myself leave my body.

Shirley MacLaine recalled a life in Atlantis, in which she learned to control the weather but abused her power. Atlantis appeared as a beautiful land of lush gardens, moist air, pink and turquoise water fountains, populated by lean, graceful people who made great use of crystals. There were crystal pyramids, crystal walkways and crystal headdresses, which amplified the higher consciousness. The people communed with each other and with nature by telepathy, and flew about in the air in petal-shaped vehicles propelled along electromagnetic lines.

Dick Sutphen, who has done regressions in seminars all over the country, found that when he asks others to return to a life in Atlantis, if they had one, most are able to do so. That would support Cayce's belief that reincarnating Atlanteans were gravitating to America. Those persons who have little or no conscious knowledge of Atlantis often see great detail which corroborates other accounts. In his book *Past Lives, Future Lives*, Sutphen said, "I believe most of us now living in the United States are ex-Atlantians [sic] who have returned at this time because we function well in the accelerated vibrations of an advanced age."

In the same book, Sutphen tells of an Atlantean regression of his former wife, Trenna, in which she observed herself and Sutphen as young graduates of the School of Philosophy, an ancient school well entrenched in society but resented by the ruling elite. Knowledge of past lives was general among the population, and "proper" incarnations were required for the college. Trenna and Sutphen trained for spiritual work and married. Trenna described their odd wedding, in which the two met in a chamber where there were large pieces of round silver metal. With their minds, they caused the discs to vibrate and create a harmony that would join the two spirits together. They thus were empowered to communicate mentally over great distances and create a healing color for use in their spiritual work.

Out in the field, they promoted education among a downtrodden lower population and were accused of inciting the masses to revolt. They returned to their school, located in a temple high on a hill, overlooking a city, to discuss their activities with their professor. They considered taking their vehicle over the mountains to work with primitive people. The vehicle was disc-shaped and could accommodate two persons. It hovered about four feet off the ground by reversing gravity, but had no great power.

Before they left, a seer warned of impending disaster to the city. A tidal wave struck and hordes of panic-stricken people tried to flee inland as the water destroyed the city. The people's fear could be felt as vibrations through the skin. Those in the temple knew the water would reach it and destroy it as well. Knowing they were doomed, Trenna and Sutphen left their bodies and went to the spiritual plane.

Another story involving the technology and corruption in the waning days of Atlantis was given to me by a woman in her late thirties who suffered from a common phobia:

> *I've always had a horrible fear of flying. My panic attacks were so bad that they affected my life. I never would have remotely considered a job that required frequent flying, and the small amount of flying I've had to do for business has been extremely difficult for me to undertake. Days before I would be scheduled to fly, I would begin to have anxiety attacks and nightmares of the plane crashing. The day of the flight, I had diarrhea and couldn't eat. I prayed desperately for protection. When I got on board, I was your worst case of white knuckle flyer, clutching the arm rests the whole way. I suffered heart palpitations. The slightest change in engine noise would send my pulse rate soaring. I would flag down the stewardess and ask her if we were 'safe.' I tried to deaden myself with alcohol, but it didn't help. I tried to knock myself out with tranquilizers and*

sleeping pills, but they didn't work, either. A flight across the country seemed like eternity, and it was agony all the way. More than once, I would chicken out and come up with an excuse not to go. Or, I would fly out and then be too paralyzed to fly back, and end up taking the bus or train back.

I know a lot of people are afraid of flying, but the extreme nature of my fear seemed irrational to me. Only once in my life was I ever on a real bumpy flight, and I've never been on a plane that had serious mechanical problems or difficulties. I began to wonder if my fear was connected to a past life. If I had to imagine one, I would have guessed that I died in a plane crash in either World War I or World War II—that would have made the most sense to me.

I went to see a regressionist. I found I had indeed died in a plane crash, though the vehicle I saw wasn't really a plane, or anything that we would call a plane. It was a soft oval shape with no wings, rather like a blimp in shape but with no compartment underneath like a blimp. It was a light grey in color and had windows, and was smaller than a jetliner. It seemed to move along on some sort of energy patterns.

I was a man in my forties. I was lean and dark-haired and had very intense eyes. I was a politician or government official of some sort. I was very controversial, but had a wide following among the people. It seemed that there was a lot of upheaval in politics, and I had a lot of enemies in high places. My job required me to spend a lot of time traveling around the land. There were death threats against me. I traveled anyway, because I was very concerned about the evil and corruption I saw around me, and I felt I had to fight against it.

My airship was sabotaged by enemies. There was an explosion and then it went down. At the moment I died, I knew it was sabotage and not an accident, and I was filled with anger and resentment, both at dying while I still had important work to do, and at leaving behind my wife and children.

The regression explained a curious thing to me about my present fear of flying. Part of the fear was that the plane would be sabotaged somehow. This goes back to the days before terrorist attacks on *planes, and there was no reason to think that somebody would blow up an airplane.*

Afterward, my fear of flying lessened. It has not gone completely away, but at least I can get on a plane now without great anxiety and without pills. I'm no longer an emotional basket case about it.

We may never know for certain if Atlantis existed, and if so, when, and how it perished. However, Atlantis can still have a meaningful application in past-life recall. The lost continent most often comes up in regressions in which individuals are searching for information to improve their present lives. In that respect, the question that needs to be asked is not "What proof do we have that Atlantis truly existed?" but "What does Atlantis represent to me?" In other words, Atlantis should be regarded as an archetype.

Archetypes are primordial images, memories and mental patterns that lie deep within the human psyche in a reservoir called the "collective unconscious" by Carl G. Jung. The collective unconscious is shared by cultures, races, ethnic groups and even all of mankind since mankind's beginning. Archetypes are predispositions towards certain behaviors. According to Jung, there is no limit to them, for they are created out of the fabric of human experience, and the endless repetition of countless situations. In myths and fairy tales, archetypal traits are represented by such figures as the wise old man, the nurturing mother, the hero, the ruler, the trickster and others. The archetypes and the collective unconscious exist below the conscious mind, yet permeate and communicate with the conscious mind through symbols, dreams and intuitive and inspired thought. It is possible that they surface in past-life regressions as well.

Perhaps Atlantis exists in the collective unconscious as a group of archetypes. To some individuals, Atlantis represents healing powers and psychic development, while to others it represents the danger of apathy and spiritual death, or the abuse of power, or the misuse of power and technology.

7

Karmic Ties to Others

As we go around the wheel of rebirth, we make our journeys with souls we have known before. More than likely, we have spent multiple lifetimes, but not necessarily *every* lifetime, with the persons who are closest to us in the present: spouse, lover, family, friends, even close business or associates. We have changed our sexes and changed our roles, and some of our present relationship problems—and our present happiness—are the products of what happened before. We also meet our enemies and those we do no like over and over again. In all relationships, the ideal is to work out problems and achieve harmony.

We decide our reunions and roles before we come back in the flesh. The choices are dictated by karma: the unfinished business of the past and the lessons we are attempting to master on the physical plane. Perhaps we are part of a soul group that has agreed to return in certain time periods.

Some of our incarnations bring us together with soul mates. Definitions of soul mates vary. According to one definition, each soul has only one soul mate, who is a true love and other half for all of eternity.

Such a soul mate requires a marital or lover relationship. More likely, a soul mate is any soul to whom we have grown especially close, and with whom we can be a spouse, lover, friend or family member. We may choose to live at a time when we can encounter one or more soul mates in different relationships in the same life.

Too much emphasis has been placed upon finding soul mates as an end unto itself. We should not be running around worrying that we are incomplete or missing out because we have not found our "soul mate." Reincarnation is the evolution of Self. In the course of that evolution, we are aided—and hindered—by other souls, some of whom join us in many lifetimes. The ultimate goal is to shed our imperfections and conquer desire and ego to become self-realized, a state in which we are complete unto ourselves and rejoin the Godhead.

There is evidence that demonstrates how intense desire influences our life choices. Two of Ian Stevenson's cases among the Tlingit Indians of southeastern Alaska involve reincarnation choices made before death, which were announced to others. One case involved William George, a fisherman who wanted to be reborn in his own family. In 1949, he gave his favorite son his gold watch and said he would be reborn with him. They would recognize him by the same birthmarks he had, on the left forearm and shoulder. Shortly thereafter, the man disappeared on his boat, and his body was not found.

Slightly more than nine months later, his daughter-in-law gave birth to a boy, her ninth child. The birth was preceded by a dream in which William George appeared to her and said he was waiting to see his son. The boy was born with birthmarks in the same spots as William George. Little George Jr., as he was named, bore a striking resemblance to his dead grandfather. As he grew older, he called his aunts and uncles his daughters and sons. At age five, he found the gold watch and said it was his.

The second case also took place in 1946-47. Victor Vincent, a stutterer, told his favorite niece, a Mrs. Chotkin, that he would be reborn as her son, and that he would bear the same scars he had now, one on his nose and one on his backside which was a surgical scar. Vincent said he hoped he would not stutter so badly. He died in the spring of 1946.

About eighteen months later, Mrs. Chotkin had a baby boy, Corliss Jr. The baby bore scars in the same spots as Vincent; the one on his backside resembled a surgical scar. At age thirteen months, he told his mother he was "Kahkody," Vincent's tribal name. By age three, Corliss recognized persons know to Vincent. He stuttered until age nine, and demonstrated the same skill with engines that had been possessed by his uncle.

This chapter and the next look at different ways karma ties us to others throughout lifetimes:

She returned as her granddaughter-in-law

Barbara Hand Clow is well known in New Age and publishing circles. With her husband, Gerry Clow, she established the Bear & Co. publishing house in Santa Fe in 1980 with a wide range of titles in religion, ecology, philosophy, psychology, healing, mysticism and spiritual development. (In 2000 Bear & Co. joined Inner Traditions publishing in Rochester, Vermont).

Clow also works as an astrological counselor. In 1982, she undertook a remarkable journey into her own past. For two years she worked with hypnotherapist Gregory Paxson, exploring numerous past lives to discover herself and her true purpose, and to research her master's thesis. Her odyssey spanned 12,000 years of human history, and took her from the depths of intense pain and anguish to soaring heights of ecstasy and enlightenment. She experienced lives of dullness and misery, and wondrous lives in which she served in the priesthood, as both a man and a woman, of the ancient Egyptians, Druids and Greeks.

Clow published her account of her journey in a trilogy, *The Mind Chronicles*. For this book, she talked with me about new insights and revelations concerning her karma with others in some of her past-life experiences.

From childhood, Clow has always had a strong sense of living in other times and places. As a young girl growing up in Saginaw, Michigan, her native home town, and New York City, her other-life memories interfered with her ability to live in the present. She told me:

> *As far as my parents were concerned, I did a lot of inexplicable things, like being able to read Egyptian hieroglyphics and symbology when I was five years old. What explains a five-year-old who wants to study The Egyptian Book of the Dead? I had a very unusual interest in ancient cultures, and I studied them intensely. I didn't feel like I fit in my small Midwestern town. I felt like I got dropped out of a plane and landed someplace. Gradually I oriented myself. I was very close to my grandmother, who acquainted me with the fairies. I was taught very early to see the unseen, and I've retained that ability. I've always had a very strong sense of the other worlds, other dimensions being present with me all the time. I've often experienced* deja vu. *There were inner voices within me clamoring to be recognized...*
>
> *I was raped when I was two years old—I didn't know this until February 1988, when I uncovered it during an all-day 'deep talking' therapy session. During World War II, I was sent away to live with friends in a small town in northern Michigan because my mother couldn't take care of me. The woman wanted to make sure that my mother didn't find out about the rape, so she spent the next six months to a year after it happened, while she was caring for me, to convince me that I did not know what had happened to me. I was subjected to a verbal campaign that what I had experienced was not real. I did 'forget,' but it left an ugly trauma inside...*
>
> *I was a very complex, disturbed child. Dealing with reality was overwhelming, and I tried to commit suicide when I was five and seventeen.*

Clow married at nineteen and had two children. By 1972, at age twenty-nine, she was divorced and supporting her two children alone. She married her second husband and had two more children. She worked as a Jungian-oriented astrological counselor. Her life revolved around taking care of others. By age thirty-eight, her internal ferment reached high pressure and Clow had what she described as "a classic mid-life crisis":

> *I was going crazy. I had never been able to find my purpose and way to express myself. I felt empty inside. These inner voices, these beings were screaming for identification. I needed to finally do something for myself. I began past-life regression therapy with Gregory Paxson, but discovered that was not enough. I went to my husband and I said, 'We've got two choices here: a mental institution or graduate school. I think graduate school is the better choice.' He agreed. I enrolled in Mundelein College in a demanding program then run by Matthew Fox, the controversial Dominican theologian who was silenced by the Vatican in 1988. After I was in school for one month, my husband quit his job and stayed home to take care of everything.*
>
> *I continued to have two regressions each month while I studied at school. I began to see that the regressions were similar to Jungian analysis in terms of the material I was accessing. As a result, my master's thesis was 'A Comparison of Jungian Psychoanalytic Technique and Past-Life Regression Therapy,' which provided the genesis for* Eye of the Centaur *and* Heart of the Christos.
>
> *It didn't matter to me whether I was looking at real past lives or expressions of subconscious need. What was important was the transformation that began to take place deep inside me.*
>
> *The first regression was very traumatic. I was an Assyrian woman, Lydia, who was raped as a teen and had nothing left but to become a prostitute. A group of men grabbed me behind a building in Lastra, where I lived, and raped me. The pain was unbelievable. My little brother, who was with me, tried to stop them, but they hit him and pulled him away. I dragged myself home, only to face my father's fury. My brother and I had been going somewhere we were not supposed to go. My mother was very sad. It was essentially the*

end of life for me. I was soiled, unfit for marriage, and in that culture could only become a prostitute, walking up and down the streets with my head shrouded, a fallen woman, dirty and miserable, nothing but a commodity.

I later discovered that my mother, father and brother in that life are my present mother, father and brother. There's a strong tendency in regression therapy to first pick up lives that concern the primary figures in your life, such as your parents, your spouse, whatever. That regression enabled me to let go of my emotions about the sexual abuse I'd suffered. I also think it helped me later to integrate the discovery of early childhood rape in this lifetime. The memory of Lydia came in 1982, and I recovered the memory of the rape in this lifetime in 1988. The psyche carefully accesses what it can integrate at a given time. I don't see any karmic connection between the two rapes, however. I think most women will encounter rapes when they access past lives.

During the process of regression, I found that after going deep within my emotional body to release trauma, I could then access a lifetime of amazingly high consciousness and development, which has in turn been valuable in this lifetime. This has been a pattern throughout all my regressions: release of pain to achieve higher wisdom. When I am willing to go into the shadow and the deep of myself, then the reward comes. I have re-accessed teaching techniques, healing techniques and sophisticated techniques of emotional bonding with other people, but only after facing the pain and darkness.

The fifth life which Clow experienced was her most recent past incarnation, as a Victorian woman who died of cancer in 1932. She was wealthy and lived in a large corner house in Chicago. In appearance, she was plain: tall and bony in build, with a large nose with a bump on the ridge, brown hair, and soft and loose skin. Her life was one of great emptiness, for despite her wealth, she felt imprisoned and isolated. The care of her children, and all decisions regarding them, were controlled by her husband's mother, who thought her daughter-in-law would be a bad influence on them. The Victorian woman felt useless and resented her husband and mother-in-law, but she did not resist them. Instead, her rage turned inward, and her body became cancerous. She died at the age of forty-six, resigned and apathetic, with her eight-year-old daughter looking on.

As Clow experienced the woman's life, she suddenly realized the woman had been her grandmother-in-law. Now she understood why she bore a striking physical resemblance to her former grandmother-in-law that astonished others, and why her own relationship with her mother-in-law was so unusual:

> When I met my second husband, I was a twenty-nine-year-old single woman with two children, and was not the best choice for a well-educated young man from a very well-to-do family. Yet I received complete acceptance from his mother and her brother, both of whom might have been expected to oppose this match. When we became engaged, my future mother-in-law gave me a diamond and onyx pin that had belonged to her mother. When she handed it to me, it was like somebody was handing me a watch that I had worn for fifteen years —it felt like my pin.
>
> Other unusual things happened in my relationship with her. I always felt like I was older and wiser than her, but I never could understand it. She had a profound, strong and loving emotional connection to me.
>
> Before I began regressions, I had a difficult time not being judgmental with some of my astrology clients. It was a serious flaw and hindered my work as a healer and teacher. Now I could see that the judgment was coming from this Victorian woman. She was inside me like an inner being, creating some kind of intercellular resonant field in my physical body.
>
> I was able to work on it and release the negative energy. The judgmental person inside me left. For about three weeks after the

> *regression, I could feel these gray waves going out of me. They were like spider webs of stickiness. I literally could feel them leaving my body, particularly from my shoulders. It was like a shadow that had been clutching me all those years was gone. From then on I was able to deal with all my clients with an open heart and compassion.*
>
> *I couldn't discuss this with my mother-in-law because her religious beliefs do not include reincarnation. But my relationship with her and my compassion for her deepened tremendously. She was the little girl with blue eyes I saw at the woman's deathbed. Still I wake up at night seeing her blue eyes. A part of her died when her mother did, Her mother's soul was imprisoned to hover near earth until she was reincarnated as me, eleven years later in 1943, to find her daughter again.*

As is often the case, the most recent past life is the most unresolved. While Clow was able to release negative emotions, she sensed that she was still carrying negative physical karma related to the Victorian woman's cancer.

> *She died when she was forty-six and left behind four small children and a husband. There I was, thirty-eight and a mother of four children. I wondered what would happen to me when I turned forty-six. I was watchful about that. In November before my forty-third birthday, which is February 14, I was told by my gynecologist that I needed to have a hysterectomy. My grandmother-in-law had died of uterine cancer. I had a second diagnosis and the need for a hysterectomy was confirmed. I had no signs of cancer, but I worried that I would die in surgery or that cancer would be discovered. I scheduled the surgery for February 27 because I was too busy to do it before then.*
>
> *Around January 1, I thought I better check into the matter. I was seeing Chris Griscom. I said, 'Chris, I think we better go into the Higher Self, go deep inside, and see if there's anything going on that we don't know about.' Chris agreed.*

> Chris's healing work focuses on the emotional body, which is the part of us which holds feelings and experiences. Using acupuncture, she put me in a light state of hypnosis. She started working on my head with her fingers. A voice came through, which is very unusual for me—I don't channel. The voice said, 'You must have this surgery between your birthday and her birthday of your forty-third year. If you do not have the surgery at that time, you will die of uterine cancer.'
>
> I didn't know what her birthday was. I went home and got out her biography and found it was March 19. I had scheduled the surgery exactly between our birthdays.
>
> I elected to have local anesthesia during the surgery so that I could be totally conscious and aware, so that I would not have any astral body invasion. Two days after the surgery, my gynecologist said to me, 'We've gotten the results from your lab test and you have a rare form of endometrial tumors developing. They're not cancerous at this time, but they form first as tumors and become cancerous. They're a very fast developing form of cancer, and detectable only by Pap smear. If you had not come in for a hysterectomy now, you would have had cancer by summer and you wouldn't have known it without a Pap smear, and you could have died.'
>
> I passed a point when she probably first got cancer, when she was forty-three. If I had not had the hysterectomy, I think I would have faced dying from cancer at the same age she did – forty-six. I have now passed her death point at age forty-six, and the imprint from her on my physical body is totally gone. She was with me all the way through my forty-sixth year.

Following her regression sessions, Clow began the task of integrating them all into her consciousness. After completion of her graduate studies, she and her husband went to work at Bear & Co. Clow saw immediate improvements in all facets of her life, in home, work and self. Her therapist, Gregory Paxson observed in the *Eye of the Centaur* that lifetimes are interactive, and, with the collaboration of the Higher Self, contribute to the refinement of energy of the whole being. He said that Clow "is and is not the woman I first met in 1982, or perhaps I should say she is a very different manifestation of that woman. She has worked through many goals, exploring, releasing, expanding and moving deeper into the energies and nature of her being."

Clow was uncertain that all or some of the past lives she saw were "real," but said the benefits were very real:

> *I am happier and feel more balanced. I am content in my own body, my own being. I don't think very many people feel that way. Before, I was 'dead' and didn't know it. If you allow yourself to go to the deepest place of pain and the highest place of ecstasy, what you get is your energy back. I am now capable of an unbelievable amount of work. I write a book every eighteen months, I am an editor, I've got four kids and I have a therapeutic practice. Up until age thirty-seven, I was depressed with a tremendous amount of nervous energy that was not productive.*

The Eye of the Centaur opens with the life of Erastus Hummell, a fourteen-year-old jester who danced in the Renaissance court of a German count in Leipzig. Wearing a gay, green and grey outfit with bell-tipped points, and bells on his moccasin-like shoes, Hummell liked to twirl and whirl in a joyous expression of life. His life was simple and his quarters humble. When he wasn't entertaining at court, he spent long hours in the Count's library, studying the great works kept there. Clow viewed him as a consciousness model, a soul who lived at a time when culture allowed him to expand his mind. Clow felt the same forces at work in her own life: "All magical journeys start with the Jester, the Fool."

Caretaker of the Heart

Sometimes karmic ties arise unexpectedly in regressions. We see people from our present playing different roles with us in our past, and suddenly we see our relationships—and ourselves—from new perspectives.

When a friend convinced Laurel Powers into trying past-life regression, she did so with the greatest skepticism. Powers, who works as a mortgage banker in Houston, was dubious about reincarnation. Even if it were true, she wondered what possible benefit would there be in looking at past lives—they certainly couldn't change the present. She had read a few articles on the subject and knew all about Shirley MacLaine's experiences, but past lives still seemed intangible and very remote from day-to-day living.

In the spring of 1988, Powers' friend took her to one of hypnotherapist Sandee Mac's small group regression sessions. Mac devoted a session to a theme, such as a life in ancient times or a life of importance. The past-life explorers visualized a tunnel, stepped out of it and into a past life. They examined their appearance and view their lives from various perspectives: youth, at moments of significance, old age and death. Then the present self was introduced to the past self so that useful information could be transmitted to help in the resolution of present problems.

Powers didn't expect to get much out of a regression, but thought at the very least the evening would be an entertaining one. She was so surprised by her vivid experience that she explored several other past lives in subsequent sessions. She was even more surprised at the beneficial energy released from getting in touch with her past. What she learned allowed her to see her present relationships in a new light, empowered her with greater self-confidence, and enabled her to achieve a dramatic loss in weight of more than 120 pounds.

> *I had never been hypnotized before. The theme was life in an early culture. I stepped out of the tunnel and knew immediately that I was male, which was something of a shock. I just didn't expect that. I had a completely different physical appearance, that is, I wasn't overweight. I knew it was me standing there even though I looked so different... I began to get images that I was outside in a very, dry sandy almost desert-like environment. There was a little village with little huts.*

It was surprising how clearly things came to me about myself. It was very vivid, like watching a movie. I was totally there. The time period seemed to be the 500s—I'm not sure. I was a shepherd, maybe fifteen or sixteen years old. I could see my sheep. I was average height, had long brown hair, and white skin that had turned real tan. I had an ordinary life. My home was a small hut with shelf or bunk-like bed built into the wall and very bare furnishings. The hut appeared to be made out of stucco, sand or brick—it was built out of the surrounding terrain. I lived alone... There never were other people involved in my life, no spouse or kids. It seemed to be a peaceful, uneventful life. I died of old age in my bed.

When Sandee introduced the me now to the me then, it was a comforting situation. The two images embraced. The message was that everything was going to be okay, that I'll be able to take care of myself and won't be unhappy by doing so; I won't need somebody else to take care of me. It all was real clear to me, undeniable that this really had happened. It was just like my own memories.

After that, I was really hooked on seeing more past lives. You begin to sort of doubt yourself, though, like you've seen too many movies and you're prompting yourself. But because of the integrity of the way the sessions are conducted, and the fact that the experiences of others in the group are so diverse, it gave me a lot of confidence that I wasn't making it up and Sandee wasn't leading us.

I have a real close friend who is English, and he turns up a lot in past lives. I've only known Simon a little over a year, but when I first met him, we developed a close relationship in a hurry; I really clicked with him. In these past-life experiences, sometimes he's male, sometimes he's female, and he takes on different roles: a central character or a minor part of my life, or maybe a presence in a crowd.

I have another real close friend whom I've known almost all my life, Leslie, and she turns up a lot as well. She's always a child of mine and I'm charged with taking care of her. I find that interesting, because that's our relationship to some extent in the present.

The topic one night was to experience a life in which someone in our present was involved. My intention was to find out about Simon. I found myself in London at around the turn of the [twentieth] century. I was a fairly young man in an ordinary sort of life. I worked in some kind of trade and made a modest living. The most vivid thing that happened in this life was my marriage. It was a big festivity. I saw myself standing there getting married. A man who is not known to me now was giving away the bride, who I recognized as Simon. She was small and attractive and had blonde hair. I was average looking, brown hair, nothing real noticeable.

I was propelled forward beyond the wedding and went into the future a few years. We'd had a child, a girl—it was Leslie. She was my responsibility. I moved forward in time again and became aware that my wife had died and I still had this child to raise. I went on into the future and observed that the child had died as well; I observed her in the coffin at the funeral. She was maybe eight or nine years old. The feeling I had was a sense of release from the responsibility. I didn't feel a lot of emotion, but I seem to be emotionally detached in all the regressions... I died of old age.

The message I got after meeting myself in this life was one of having a sense of duty and responsibility that I have to take care of things. Again, that's the way I feel now, to some extent. In another session, we were to pick a time period of interest to us. This was very interesting to me, because I was a history major in college. I picked the Middle Ages. We were also supposed to view an influential life, one in which we were powerful.

I turned up in England again. In all the regressions I've done so far, I've only been female once and that was this medieval English life. I was a sorceress and I seemed to be involved in alchemy. I was a small person with long, brown hair. I was wearing a long, blue dress. I seemed to be fairly affluent, and lived in what looked like a castle. It had banners flying off the top and flags. It was dark inside. I spent most of my time in a laboratory, working on this alchemy. It wasn't witchcraft, it was more of a scientific nature. For some reason, I had to work in secret and keep it real quiet.

Evidently the secrecy didn't work out. As I moved forward in time, I suddenly got a strong smell that was dank, musty and kind of nasty. I thought it actually came over the room I was in [for the regression]. I didn't know what it was. Then I realized that it was part of the past life—that I was now in a dungeon, imprisoned for my activities. I was held for many years and died there alone.

Simon was in that life—he was somebody who was working with me. We didn't have a close relationship, and he wasn't in prison.

The message from that life was a sense of power and ability. I had power that other people didn't know about; it was my secret. Even though I was discovered and imprisoned, no one ever found out my secrets—they died with me.

In analyzing several regressions, Powers observed:

I've had plain lives. I'm often solitary and alone, though I'm aware of people in the distance, a population that I know exists. In the lives I've seen, I've just died of old age—I haven't had any accident or trauma or sickness. Very often I appear the same in old age from life to life, though I don't appear the same during the rest of my lives. I'm usually a man, and have long gray hair and a long gray beard. I'm dressed in a robe-like garment rather than clothes that were appropriate to the time... Some sessions I didn't get much out of, and I think it was because I didn't have a life that was relevant to the topic.

After viewing several lives, Powers attended a session devoted to "most powerful life." The setting that emerged for her was modern, which was confusing. Yet themes from her past and present were crystallized in powerful and moving imagery:

In the other regressions, I was always outdoors when I came out of the tunnel. This time, I saw a lot of light, but it was artificial. I kept trying to say, 'No, you're not seeing that correctly.' A few seconds went by and the image came to me—I realized it was the light of a surgical room, those bright lights that shine over the operating table. I was male and a surgeon. I looked down and observed my feet—I had on those little slippers that look like green shower caps. As the image became clearer, I saw I was operating on someone, a woman. I knew it was Leslie.

I was in a surgical amphitheater, and up above were students looking down, watching me. Simon was one of them. I was doing heart surgery. I was actually removing the heart from the patient. I took it out, and as I held her heart, it became a piece of rose quartz. That was the last image I had.

It seemed liked the United States and very current. That's what puzzled me, it didn't seem like a past life at all. There was nothing gruesome or violent about it. It wasn't frightening to me, but again, the message was one of my responsibilities for protecting Leslie and taking care of her heart.

Asked what she has learned overall from these experiences, Powers summed up:

The recurrent theme is that I can take care of myself—that I have to take care of myself. I may very well be called on to take care of other people, but I'll be okay on my own. There's a sense of being alone—not lonely but alone. And, things are within my power to control. There's also a recurrent sense that if I take charge and do things, they will turn out well, that I can better my situation and be free of problems.

I feel stronger and have a better sense of overall well-being. I feel more secure with myself now. That's something I was never very good about. I try to take responsibility for things and make sure they go well, but previously I didn't necessarily think that I could do it on my *own. I used to feel pretty dependent on other people, and now I don't feel that way as much.*

[The regressions] definitely enhanced my relationships with others. I see and understand things more clearly... I have better intuition. I don't have to spend a lot of time on the getting-to-know-you part. Things that are more important come out more quickly. I don't waste time with situations or people that aren't going to mean a lot to me.

My weight loss was in a way a result of this. I have always been overweight and I always thought I would be that way, I didn't have the willpower or whatever it took to do anything about it. But realizing that I can take control of things in my life made me think I could lose weight, too. I knew if I could do that, I could do anything...

I came to past-life regression with a lot of skepticism, but now reincarnation is undeniable.

8

Keeper of the Jim Morrison Flame

A T THE AGE OF TWELVE, Danny Sugerman was a restless Los Angeles youth sitting on a powder keg of pent-up energy, looking for a hero and direction. He found both in Jim Morrison, the brilliant but tormented leader of The Doors, whose mystical union of poetry and music pushed out the frontiers of rock. The year was 1967, and The Doors had just burst into international fame with their first hit, *Light My Fire*. Sugerman (pronounced like sugar-man) was quickly drawn into The Doors' inner circle as employee, friend and confidante. It seemed like a lucky break then, but Sugerman would find out years later that meeting up with Morrison and The Doors was no accident, but the continuation of a karmic dance that had begun centuries earlier.

By 1967, Morrison was plunging headlong into a psychedelic quest for higher consciousness and the Universal Mind. An intellectual man, he introduced others around him, including Sugerman, to philosophy and poetry, drugs and the pursuit of enlightenment, and, as he quoted from Norman O. Brown, unendurable pleasure infinitely prolonged. The Quest for Consciousness became not only the driving creative force of The Doors' music but a way of life. By July 1971, Morrison was dead in Paris, burned out at the age of twenty-seven. Officially, his death was attributed to natural causes, but his legendary drinking and drug use were whispered to have been contributing factors.

Sugerman played a key role in keeping the spirit of Morrison and The Doors alive, assuming management of their catalog of albums and the career of keyboard player Ray Manzarek, his close friend. With rock writer Jerry Hopkins, he co-authored a best-selling biography of Morrison, *No One Here Gets Out Alive*. Sugerman died at age fifty in 2005 of lung cancer.

Sugerman's own quest for higher consciousness had led him into drug addiction, however, and he struggled against the problem for years. In his effort to find answers and solutions, he undertook a journey into past lives, in which he discovered karmic connections to both Morrison and Manzarek. While I was researching this book, I met Sugerman through Michael Talbot. Sugerman gave me an exclusive interview about his past life discoveries:

> *Back in the good old days before bad habits became addictions, I was taking drugs on a fairly regular basis from the time I met Jim Morrison in 1967. I met him through a Little League baseball game. This umpire was 'umping' for a little extra money, but what he really did was road manage his neighbor's rock band, The Doors. I'd seen their equipment that he carried around in the back of his VW microbus. I had been nagging him to take me to see the band. Then one day he said, 'If you hit a home run, I'll take you to see The Doors.'*
>
> *The concert changed my life. I have no doubt it was a religious experience for me. Jim believed in the spiritual power of music, the shaman's dance, the power of theater and electricity, the drums-and-rhythm healing ceremony. Or, to use another apt description, he was Dionysus personified. Jim identified with these forces and knew how*

to use them. It was a real liberating experience for me, and I'm pretty sure it was for others there that night.

Through the roadie, Sugerman got closer to The Doors, in particular Morrison and Manzarek. It wasn't long before he went to work for The Doors.

> *I knew Jim would not reject me. I was twelve to his twenty-two; he already famous and me still a nobody, but none of that mattered. I started out answering fan letters, doing some press for them—I was an office assistant. He was my hero, like a big brother. I never did get to college. Jim was a college graduate. He once said, 'Just because teachers can't teach and school's a drag doesn't mean you shouldn't read books.' He was a real avid reader. He gave me Aldous Huxley's* The Doors of Perception, *after which the Doors were named, and* Beyond Good and Evil. *I didn't understand all of it, but I understood enough. He gave me [poet Arthur] Rimbaud's life story to read. I identified with Rimbaud because he was nineteen by the time all of his poetry was written and he ran off to Africa. But Jim's knowledge went beyond books. He just had that look. You knew he knew. If I saw that look in your eyes—I'd follow you.*
>
> *I was an obsessive-compulsive hyperactive personality, and when I found something that interested me, I went after it with a single-mindedness that overwhelmed the people around me. Morrison intuitively knew how to direct that energy onto the path of excess, which has no limits. 'The road of excess leads to the palace of wisdom,' Blake wrote and Jim truly believed. By way of Jim's example, my energy became focused, channeled. Everybody up 'til then had always told me, 'Sit down!' and 'Shut up!' Not Morrison. He said, 'Go! Go! Go for it! Get it while you can!'*
>
> *During my experimentation with drugs, I discovered opium. I began smoking it and developed a tolerance to it. I became addicted and started snorting heroin. Before I knew it, I was shooting heroin*

and it was a year since I had taken any psychedelics.

Jim started off on acid and he ended up on alcohol, which is a pain killer. I think a lot of persons with addictive personalities who began with psychedelics and went on to others drugs found their drugs of choice were alcohol, cocaine or heroin, which constrict the consciousness. Huxley talks about the 'reducing valve' that psychedelics enlarge and give us entrance into the Universal Mind. At first I thought I wanted that reducing valve enlarged, with grass and psychedelics. But that wasn't what I really wanted at all. I wanted the reducing valve constricted—I wanted to think less. I wanted that 'falseness of well-being' I'd heard so much about. True or false, who cared? I'd take it. Life was pain and suffering. I wanted to feel good.

Ultimately, I think Jim got to that place, too, where he depended more on alcohol and less on the hallucinogenics he had been taking. At first, alcohol stimulates thought and conversation, but ultimately, booze creates the same thing heroin does: oblivion. There's a saying that ignorance is bliss. The opium flower provides that blissful ignorance, but it's not really bliss at all. It's really indifference, but anyway, I was strung out by the time I was twenty.

Jim had been dead for four or five years and I was managing The Doors' catalog, which continued to be successful. And I also was taking care of two of my heroes, Ray Manzarek and Iggy Pop. I had a house in the hills and a sports car and a beautiful girlfriend, and I was going to all the parties that I wanted and had free drugs all the time. At first I thought, 'This is the life, this is great!' But the truth was, I was scared and very overwhelmed. I didn't know what I was doing. I expected somebody to rap me on the shoulder at any moment and say, 'Excuse me, son, we thought you knew what you were doing, you can't have all this.'

I got higher and higher and went out less and less until finally I was locked in the house and the only people who were allowed over were drug dealers, and even them I didn't want around because I didn't want to share any of my drugs, and I didn't want any of them to learn what was in my house. I hated and resented them, and they knew it. They also knew I needed them. It was not a fun period, but I couldn't stop.

I tried to kick it a couple of times and I couldn't. I thought I could control it. I thought, 'I can kick it whenever I want, but I just don't want to yet.' Then the craving would get unbearable and I'd try to quit again but be back at it within a couple of days. The hell of being clean would become worse than the hell of being strung out, and off I'd go. Eventually I ended up on methadone maintenance.

But one of the things that really did help me for awhile was acupuncture. Jerry Hopkins was in my house when I stopped [heroin] once, and it was obvious to him something was up. He demanded I level with him. I did. I told him, 'I'm going through drug withdrawals and I'm sick.' He asked me if I wanted help, and of course I did, I said. He called a friend of his who's an acupuncturist. He turned out to be The Doors' first photographer, and he had been in jail... While he'd been in jail, he meditated—that was all there was to do, apparently, lots of dead time. He came out remembering a past life as a Chinese acupuncturist. All of his brown hair and his beard had turned white overnight. He took the exam to qualify for an acupuncture license and passed it with no studying. Weird story, huh? The thing was, I'd known him before he went in—we'd met once or twice—and he was totally changed. He resonated serenity. I don't know what happened except that something powerful went down.

So Jerry called him over. He gave me a treatment and I immediately got better. The withdrawals withdrew! Acupuncture takes care of the craving and sickness by activating the endorphins produced by the pituitary gland. The same ingredient that kills pain cures withdrawals. More of it creates pleasure—the body's own morphine, but a thousand times stronger.

But the next morning I woke up sick again and was about to call my dealer when he [the acupuncturist] showed up at the door. I said,

'How did you know I'd need you?' He said, 'I figured you'd be ready for either a fix or another treatment.' He gave me another treatment and it worked fine.

I had to go on tour, and as soon as it [heroin] was around, I got strung out again. About six months later, I contacted the acupuncturist and asked him for help. He came to see me and said, 'Listen you have some real dark energy with you. It feels like Morrison. I knew Morrison and I'm telling you, Danny, before I treat you again, for your own good, you'd better go see a psychic and find out what sort of karma of Morrison's you're carrying around with you and why you can't break this chain.' I said, 'That's a real interesting question.' Mainly, I was just interested in getting some more treatment from this guy. There weren't a lot of acupuncturists at that time [1974-75], and I didn't want to go to another one and say, 'I'm coming off heroin, treat me.'

He took care of me just once to get me well enough to go see this psychic that he referred me to. She didn't interpret any past lives for me, but told me to go see a regression hypnotist. She told me she couldn't help me, that there was stuff I had to see for myself. So I said, 'All right, fine, I'll try it.' So she sent me to see this guy up in Topanga Canyon.

I've always been a good hypnotic patient because I'm susceptible to altered states of consciousness. I'm willing to let go so I can go right into a trance state. That first doors concert was an example. I was entranced by that hypnotic music and the spell Morrison cast.

The theme of the session was my relationship with Jim Morrison. In one life he was an older brother, in Amsterdam. Our family owned a general store and I worked in it, but he refused to. In another life, we were pirates. There was a lot of looting, pillaging and raping going on, very intense feelings of shame and remorse. I didn't dig it at all. I mean at that time—I had too much of a conscience to get into it. I tried to stop them and they tortured me. They put some sort of wood down my throat that expanded as they poured water on it, so eventually I choked to death. Jim was really into the pirate's life, and if I remember right, he was my protector, ya know, 'the kid doesn't have to do what he doesn't want to do. But Jim got stabbed and died and then I was fair game. I don't know what the time period was, because I don't have anything to compare it to. I'm not real versed in history.

Then the regressionist told me to go back, back, further back in time. Eventually I saw this floor take shape, a path of stones and pebbles and earth that I couldn't have imagined. The details, the carved craftsmanship was amazing, beautiful. I saw plumbing and water and an irrigation system, very intricate yet different as well as beautiful. I know nothing about irrigation. I saw meditation gardens with waterfalls. All the water was used very constructively: this going to the washing, this going to the well, that going to the waterfall, that to the garden and so on. I could hear the water... I could hear the sound of sandals on these rocks that made up the path, the echoing into the hallway... Something inside me said, 'This is real, this is not a dream, this isn't your imagination, this is real.'

It was somewhere in China on the border near India, up in the hills, totally isolated, way before the Communist invasion, before Christ. I was a young monk, if a monk is what you call it. My head wasn't shaved but my hair was very short. We had on these dhotis covered by robes, and these sandals. The robes seemed light in color, beige or a grayish beige. I didn't get the sense I was on any religious quest. I had more of a sense that I had been put there by my family. It was something that was expected me.

Ray was there—he was an elder. Jim was like the abbot, and his body was dying. Several of us were called in. I was Ray's charge now that Jim was dying. Jim said to me, 'I want you to take these notebooks, and I want you to make sure that people know what I'm saying. Don't let people interpret me. If you wait and it is passed down by word of mouth, it's going to be misinterpreted. I spent my life writing this, and it's important. If you care about me, which I know you do, you'll pass this on. You'll continue the work and make it yours, *and Behari'*—that was Ray's name—*'will be with you.'*

I said, 'No I can't do this, I don't want to deal with it.' *I was a novice and I was too upset by the body dying.* 'How can you talk about lessons when you're leaving me?' *I didn't take the books. I didn't stay. The books said one thing, I don't know what, and the ashram believed another. I split. It was too much for me. I went back to my family.*

Afterward, the regressionist wanted me to come back for another session, but I didn't go back. I wasn't ready to own what I knew, what I'd learned. I wasn't done with using drugs, and using wasn't done with me. Ultimately, I just burned out on it. It's not the sort of lesson that you can learn. You either live to get sick of it or you don't. I was lucky I got sick and tired of being sick and tired.

The regression did explain a lot to me about a lot of things, including this recurring dream I'd been having. I could never remember what it was about, except the sensation that I was filled over brimming, beyond pleasure and pain. It was real disturbing and powerful. I'd wake up and feel my jaw shoved open and my head back, like I was drinking something that was incredibly powerful, with some incredible force behind it, that something solid was just pouring down my throat and an incredible rate, overflowing, filling me up. But it was hard [not liquid]. My lower jaw was snapped open and I couldn't use my mouth. When I came to [from the hypnosis], I knew the dream was related to the pirate life: at the moment of release from the body, there was a sense of relief and gratification and pleasure, but at the same time there was this physical pain.

There was another life in which I worked on the Mississippi and was your standard real drunk. So what I had to deal with were the residual effects of the life of drinking and the need to satisfy this oral compulsion—I think those two lives concerned basically the same theme—and the fact that I had not taken responsibility. I didn't take responsibility in the monk life with Jim, and I didn't take responsibility in the Amsterdam life. In this life I have to take responsibility, *and I'm doing my job. It's nice to know. If I don't [take responsibility], I'm bothered by the possibility, however remote, that I'll have to go through all this again.*

I don't disbelieve in reincarnation, but I also think the mind can't help but filter and color these images in a way that it can relate to them. I don't think all the experiences I had were true reincarnation experiences. I think the gist of them was true, but the mind interprets in a way that it needs to color. It might make one person a boy instead of a girl because it can't relate to a spirit being feminine, for example. However, the feeling I'm left with even to this day is that something is there that is very real, very mysterious and very powerful. All I'm saying is, this was my experience. I don't find reassurance in the plausibility of reincarnation, I don't derive comfort in the concept of returning again and again to grow and learn, because I'm a slow learner and growing hurts. At the same time, this same knowledge causes me to get on with the work and to stop procrastinating. On the other hand, you can't consciously remember, anyway, so what different does it make?

Some years after his hypnotic regression, Sugerman met Manhattan author Michael Talbot, and the two worked together on a project for a while. Talbot had powerful memories of having lived long ago as a Tibetan monk. When Sugerman related his own past life regression and the images of the remote mountain monastery, Talbot felt certain he had been there at the same time as a fellow monk. With the help of Jim Gordon, a past-life psychic, Talbot pieced together details, which he described below:

Without explaining anything that Danny had told me, I asked Gordon one simple question: Have I had any past-life experiences with a friend of mine named Danny Sugerman? To my surprise, Gordon immediately started telling me more about the past life Danny had described. He didn't mention Morrison by name and only referred to him as the abbot of the monastery. He said the abbot was very old and was dying, and wanted Danny to take charge of this set of sacred books. Gordon then added some information that had not surfaced in Danny's regression.

As Gordon explained, there was a controversy over the books because the monks had discovered plants and roots with hallucinogenic properties. One school of thought in the monastery held that drugs should be used for spiritual advancement and another school of thought held that was not the proper path. The abbot wanted Danny to take over the books, but Danny was reluctant because he didn't know how he felt about the issue of whether or not to use drugs to open spiritual doorways. He didn't take the books, and that is why the drug issue bubbled up with him again in this life, because he was still wrestling with the question.

I asked if there was anything I could do for Danny. Gordon alleges he communicates with the constellation of souls that have contracted to be your guides. It's like having a three-party call. Most often they communicate to him via images; occasionally they give him sentences. He said, 'They're telling me that no one can do anything for Danny, he has to do it for himself. You made the right choice in that life by not using drugs. You came together in this life so that he could continue to see you making a lot of right choices, and that might possibly help him.'

Sugerman did at last "do it" for himself; he kicked his drug habit in 1984, and wrote about his battle with drugs in his second book, *Wonderland Avenue*. He felt he had chosen to be with Morrison in this life, and that he balanced the karma over those ancient notebooks by carrying on the Morrison flame.

I feel I'm about done with it, finally. I've done just about everything I can for Jim. The book I wrote on him introduced him to millions of souls. That feels good to me. I've been involved with bringing out a new poetry album of his—he always wanted to be taken seriously as a poet. He kept a lot of notebooks and journals. In 1986, some previously unknown notebooks of his were discovered. I thought that was interesting, in light of the regression.

The things that Jim knew and what he was able to write about, and the beliefs he had, are not those of a twenty-seven-year-old man. This guy had wisdom at twenty-seven that few of us will have, if we're lucky, at eighty-seven. He was a real old soul. And, he was not only a good man but a very brave man. He went out on a very precarious limb—he was out there all alone, with no religion to comfort him, no God to have faith in. He tested the bounds of reality in every way I have known him. We have the findings. We got Jim's life even as he lost it. The conclusions are all ours to wrestle with. Jim is free. I hope.

9

The Karma and Grace of Love and Hate

Edgar Cayce once observed that the scars of wounds created in one lifetime stretch on down the centuries. So, too, do decisions made by the soul, to love another, hate another, or seek revenge against another. Love has its own sweet rewards, as we have seen in the previous chapter. Love redeems and furthers spiritual growth. The repercussions of hate, guilt and revenge reverberate in chain reactions through lifetime after lifetime, creating more tragedies and disasters, until a lesson is learned and the karma is discharged by love and forgiveness.

The fidelity dilemma of Mrs. X
On the surface, Mrs. X appeared to live an enviable life. She possessed the kind of beauty that made others look twice. She had been married for eighteen years to a successful businessman, and led a life of material comfort among wealthy friends.

For years, she hid the dark stain that blotted her life, until at age forty-one, she consulted Cayce and confessed her troubles. Her husband was impotent, totally incapable of providing the kind of physical pleasure she desired from him. She loved him deeply, however, and did not want to hurt him by annulling the marriage or divorcing him. At first, she had found outlets for her needs in relationships with other men, before learning how to sublimate desire through meditation and spiritual study.

The crisis which motivated her to seek out Cayce was the reappearance in her life of an old flame, a man who had loved her from childhood but had lost her to her husband. They were still deeply attracted to one another, and Mrs. X was tempted to have an affair. She resisted because her old love was married, too, and she knew his wife and did not want to hurt her, either.

Cayce gave Mrs. X a reading. The cause of her husband's sexual impotence went back 600 years and two lifetimes earlier, to the days of the Crusades. Mrs. X was a woman named Suzanne Mercelieu, married to her present husband. Monsieur Mercelieu was a religious zealot who joined the Crusades. He mistrusted his wife and forced her to be locked into a chastity belt during his absence to guarantee her fidelity. Suzanne was so resentful of this cruel and uncomfortable prison that she vowed she would get even someday with her husband. She took that resentment and vow to her grave. Two lifetimes later, it came back like an ugly boomerang. She was, said Cayce, coming face to face with herself.

Essentially, Mrs. X had already overcome much of her negative karma from the past life. She could have indulged in her revenge by leaving her husband or ridiculing his impotency. Instead, she had stayed married to him out of deep love, and had overcome her urges to have relationships with other men. She had resisted entering a potentially destructive affair with her old flame. It was not her place to punish with revenge, for the law of karma had punished her husband with impotency. By forgiving him through unselfish love, Mrs. X was presented an opportunity to allow both of them to grow spiritually.

Anthony H. learns the law of grace
The law of karma operates hand in hand with the law of grace, an innate guiding force which prompts a soul to keep improving itself to perfection. To right one's wrongs, one must first forgive oneself. At that moment, said Cayce, one begins to move under the law of grace.

Anthony H. was a college student in Connecticut, prior to World War II, when he fell in love with a young woman who dropped him for his best friend. He discovered through readings with Cayce that he had been married twice to this woman in past lives. One of those lives was in ancient Egypt, where she had jilted him for the same man. Their relationship, it seemed, had always been troubled.

Anthony got over his lost love and got on with the rest of his life. He married, and in 1944 was drafted into the armed services to fight in World War II. One of his chief faults was a short temper, which he strove mightily to control. During his military service, he suffered a bizarre problem with choking on small objects that lodged in his throat: a plum pit, gristle and bits of bone. Each time, he was rushed to the hospital.

After the war, while dining with a friend one evening in Manhattan, a bit of chicken bone stuck in his throat and sent him once again to the hospital. He hovered on the edge of consciousness as he was rushed into the operating room and administered an anesthetic. As he went under, an angry face with dirty, unkempt yellow hair hovered in front of him. Anthony realized, to his astonishment, that it was himself! Suddenly, he was no longer in the hospital, but in surroundings that appeared medieval and Nordic. What was more, he was in the middle of a homicidal rage against a young woman—his wife. He had just discovered her infidelity, and was so consumed with hatred that he was on the verge of killing her with his bare hands. The vision ended abruptly.

A few nights later, Anthony dreamed of the medieval woman, who took on the features of the woman who'd jilted him in college. In the dream, he strangled her to death. He woke up in a cold sweat. He knew enough about reincarnation and the laws of karma and grace to realize the implications of the vision and the dream. Mortified, he began praying fervently for forgiveness for himself and the unknown Nordic woman. The prayer seemed to work, for after a while he felt an enormous burden lift from him.

Several days later, Anthony was surprised to get a telephone call from the long-lost college girlfriend. She was in Manhattan and had thought wistfully of him, and how shabbily she had treated him in college. She hoped he could forgive her. Of course, he told her, to his great relief.

The choking emergencies were retribution for Anthony's strangling of his wife; perhaps one might have eventually claimed his life. His victim had exacted revenge by loving and leaving him, with the added insult of marrying his best friend. For her, it was a hollow victory, for the marriage had ended in divorce. So had a second marriage. She was lonely and unhappy. Now both forgiven by themselves and each other, they were free of the need to hurt each other again.

The lives and murders of Gail Bartley
Gail Bartley's life took a strange and downward turn following her divorce in 1981. Despite the trauma of ending a six-year marriage, the signs were positive for new beginnings. Bartley was still very young, only twenty-eight, and quite attractive with shoulder length, curly dark brown hair, expressive brown eyes, and a slender five-foot-five build. She had a stimulating and challenging job as an art director in a Los Angeles advertising agency, which brought her into professional and social contact with scores of interesting people and potential dates. She was her own woman.

Why did she fling herself headlong into an abusive and destructive relationship with a man named Roger (a pseudonym)? For years, Bartley was unable to answer the question, and unable to unhook herself from the relationship. Finally, after exhausting conventional forms of therapy, Bartley got her answers through past-life regression. She discovered that the seeds had been planted centuries earlier in ancient Rome, and had grown, misshapen, through a series of unhappy lives.

For Bartley, meeting Roger was the beginning of a compulsion. She didn't feel she had known him before, but she felt compelled to become involved with him—against her better judgment. Her mother took an icy dislike to him after one brief meeting during a social occasion, which Bartley found odd. Her mother was not one to make snap judgments about others. And a voice inside Bartley's head kept screaming, "Get away, get away...he hates you...he's trying to destroy you...!"

The relationship that developed between Bartley and Roger was one of intense love and hate. Bartley found herself riding an emotional seesaw of emotional highs and lows. She suffered from emotional and verbal abuse, and, occasionally, physical abuse. One of those times, during a rage-filled argument, Roger wrestled her to the floor and started choking her.

Bartley wondered what was wrong with her. Her self-esteem diminished. Why was she putting up with this? Who needed this pain? She'd never let anyone treat her so badly before! Where was her pride?

In 1984, Bartley moved to Manhattan to take a job as art director for a New York ad agency. Roger followed her and wouldn't let go. She was able at last to end the relationship, but couldn't heal the scars. She tried counseling and psychotherapy. Nothing worked. She felt low and depressed.

In 1985, the solutions to her dilemma materialized. At the time, they seemed to be mysterious coincidences, though Bartley now understands that there are no "coincidences" in life, but synchronistic events which occur at the right time and place.

Her search for meaning led her to books, and several volumes on reincarnation and past-life therapy found their way into her hands. Bartley was intrigued. As a child, she had believed in reincarnation, then abandoned the belief under peer pressure from taunting teenaged friends. That left her without a spiritual rudder, for organized religion had never had any appeal to her. Now, Bartley felt ready for spiritual growth.

Bartley decided to try past-life regression. But where to find a regressionist? The answer that popped into her said seemed incongruous: *Go to the Pineapple Dance Center.*

The Pineapple Dance Center in Manhattan offered ballet classes, and Bartley had been interested in taking one. During her lunch hour, she followed her hunch and went to the center. There, on the reception desk, she found a brochure about a Manhattan regressionist, Alice T. Thrilled, Bartley called her and scheduled an appointment.

Upon arriving for her regression, Bartley felt nervous, despite the comfortable surroundings. Nervous anticipation is common, and Alice put Bartley at ease by explaining the procedure. First, she would help Bartley relax in a comfortable reclining chair, by using a guided meditation and background music especially designed to synchronize the right and left hemispheres of the brain. The music, Alice explained, would enhance the vividness of the regression. Then Alice would guide Bartley through an imaginary tunnel with a light at the other end. Upon emerging into the light, Bartley would find herself in a past life.

Before Bartley's arrival, Alice had meditated for spiritual guidance, and to surround their working area with a protective white light. Of the many lives that Bartley undoubtedly had experienced, Alice would ask for the revealing of the one or ones which would shed light on Bartley's present situation with Roger. She would see scenes, and move backward and forward in time to significant moments.

Bartley followed Alice's instructions. She closed her eyes, settled back into the easy chair and let Alice's soothing voice take her through a progressive relaxation. She had no trouble visualizing the tunnel and the bright, white light at the end. But as she moved through the tunnel toward the light, a cold anxiety crept into her bones. The hairs on the back of her neck prickled. She felt a profound dread of something unknown. At the end of the tunnel, the light gave way to darkness, and Bartley did not want to step out into it. Alice relaxed her again, and Bartley felt secure enough to move forward.

She found herself standing in a bedroom with high ceilings. Her name was Joyce, and she was twenty-three years old. The time frame seemed to be the 1920s. Her long, straight brown hair fell down her white nightgown. She was barefoot. The scene was eerie. Part of Bartley felt she was watching a movie, and part of her felt *in* the movie. As she stood in this darkened bedroom, she was filled with apprehension and fear. The source was the man lying in the bed near her: her husband. She watched him get out of bed and approach her until he was standing in front of her. Bartley's fear escalated, and she hyperventilated. The drama of past love and hate unfolded:

Alice: What do you feel?

Bartley: Really scared. My heart's beating. (She begins to gasp and moan). I don't believe it!

A: What's happening?

B: He's putting his hands on my throat. (She continues to gasp and hyperventilate)... He's strangling me... I'm dropping to my knees... I can't breathe!

(Alice instructs her to be able to look at the scene and breathe very easily. Bartley gasps for a few more moments, then calms down.)

A: Breathing very easily, very effortlessly... Tell me what's going on now.

B: He' still holding on to my throat, and I'm lying on the floor... He lets go and stands up.

A: Are you in the body or out of the body?

B: I'm in the body. He walks away. (She indicates that she can breathe again. She watches Joyce sit up, dazed.) I think I'm okay... He goes to the door and walks out and he shuts it... I'm kneeling now and I'm touching my throat... Now I just hang my head, and I get up... I'm just standing there. I don't know what to do. (Alice moves Bartley forward a little in time. Bartley sighs.) I'm walking around the room, and I don't know what to do. I'm thinking I want to leave but I don't know where to go.

A: Stay in this scene until the next time you see your husband.

B: I see him coming up the stairs... It's the same night. I go out in the hall... He has a cold look on his face... I feel hate. I don't know if I say, "I hate you" or if he says, "I hate you." I just feel it... I don't feel as frightened as I did before. He walks by me, back into the room, and shuts the door.

(Alice asks Bartley to move back in time to a scene that will explain why this hate and confrontation developed. Bartley immediately finds herself at a wedding party—her own. She is wearing a beautiful gown of white and lace. The reception, attended by a large crowd of people, is taking place in the garden of her family's elegant home. Her husband approaches her.)

B: He's pulling me by the hand, and he grabs me around the waist to kiss me. He kisses me... I don't think I like that—he's rough.

A: How long have you known him?

B: Ten years (there is a question in her voice)... A long time.

A: Are you in love with him, is he in love with you?

B: No.

A: Why do you marry? Is it an arranged marriage?

B: I don't know. I'm afraid of him.

A: Are you in front of a lot of people when he's kissing you?

B: We're in the garden still, but he has pulled me away from the crowd. I'm pushing him away. I'm saying I want to get back.

A: What does he say?

B: "*Bitch*." (Alice asks Bartley to go to the moment at which she agreed to get married. Bartley sees herself in the study of her parents' house, with Joyce's father and her fiancé. Her father is a banker and well-to-do. Her fiance also comes from a wealthy family.)... We're all talking. We're telling him [father] we're getting married. He doesn't seem very happy... I don't know [why]... He's listening... We're smiling... [My father] says, "He's not right for you, he's not good enough for you."

A: Why doesn't your father think he's the right man for you?

B: He doesn't like him [because] he's irresponsible and he's violent.

A: How do you feel about your fiance right now?

B: He's exciting... He's passionate. He scares me.

A: Have you made love with him before?

B: No.

A: How does he feel about you?

B: He tells me that he loves me.

A: How much time is it before you get married?

B: A couple of years. (Alice asks Bartley to move to another scene that will shed light on the relationship. Bartley sees the two of them in a shiny, new yellow convertible, driving along some cliffs near the ocean. It is before they become engaged.)... We're driving fast. We're laughing. I kiss him. Our hair is blowing... He puts his arm around me. I love him... We're still driving, he's driving too fast. I ask him to stop, to slow down. He's angry at me for asking him to slow down, and he stops and he gets out of the car and he just stands there and he won't talk to me. I say, "Don't be upset, I only asked you to slow down." He says, "You're trying to dominate me." (Alice asks Bartley to go to the next significant scene.)... We're kissing.

A: How did you make up?

B: He just stopped being angry. (Bartley moves to another scene. She sees Joyce and her fiance back in her parents' home, alone having tea. Bartley begins to tense visibly, and Alice relaxes her. Bartley continues with the regression.)... I'm telling him I don't think we should get married. He says, "Don't be silly."

A: Why don't you think you should get married?

B: Because I don' like him. He says I'm crazy.

A: Let go of this scene and move forward without pain to the very last day of your life in this incarnation... How old are you?

B: I can't see anything.

A: Is it dark?

B: Yes... I'm young.

A: I'd like you to move backward in time a few moments until it's light enough for you to see.

B: I'm back in the bedroom.

A: How old are you?

B: Twenty-three! (Bartley is surprised—this is where the regression started.)

A: What's happening? Are you alone?

(Bartley begins to gasp for breath and cannot answer immediately. Her breath is heavy and labored. "I'm getting scared again," she says. Alice instructs her to stay calm and relaxed.)

A: Is he with you?

B: No, I think I hear him downstairs... [Now] he's at the door.

A: Does he say anything?

B: No... He's holding something behind his back.

A: What is it?

B: I don't know. (She gasps again.)... He's walking towards me... I think he has a knife but I don't believe it! (Bartley pauses while she struggles to get control of her anxiety)... He has a knife. He rips my nightgown with it, in the front... I push him away. He just looks at me and he gets real close. (Again Bartley cannot continue. Her heart is pounding. She breathes heavily for a few moments, and Alice helps her to relax.)... I'm not sure [what's happening]... I'm not sure... He stabs me. I'm standing by the window... I'm holding myself. He's just standing there in shock. I can't talk... I sink to the ground. (Bartley realizes these are her last moments in this life as Joyce. She has been murdered by her husband, the man she now knows as Roger. As she watches herself die, she feels no pain. She feels herself float out of Joyce's dying body, and hover in a corner of the room, looking down on the scene.)

A: Can you see him?

B: He's standing there with a knife looking down at me and then he looks at the knife.

A: What is he feeling?

B: Shock. He throws the knife. He starts to cry. He runs to me and holds me... He's just holding me. (Bartley feels her soul floating away.)

A: Let go of this now and move backwards in time... I want to go back to the scene prior to where he murders you, the scene that precipitated this... I want to know specifically what the argument was—the straw that broke the camel's back. (Bartley finds the two of them at the dinner table.)

B: I'm laughing at him. He's upset about something. I'm being mean... He's saying he doesn't love me, that he has never loved me... He says that I've never loved him.

A: That's when you laugh?

B: Yes.

A: Let go of this scene and let go of this life... I want to go back to the life where we will find the cause of why he murdered you in this life where you were Joyce.

(Bartley releases the memories of Joyce and, guided by Alice, moves through time. She arrives in the life a seventeen-year-old boy named George, who lives with his mother and ill-tempered, domineering father in a cabin, somewhere in the Old West of America, in the late nineteenth century. George is tall and lean, with sandy-colored hair. When Bartley first sees him, he is standing outside the cabin, wearing a long-sleeved red shirt, blue pants and scuffed boots. It is night, and the crickets are singing. George's mother comes out of the cabin. She is a small woman with gray hair, wearing a light-colored dress.)

B: She puts her arm around me. She asks me why I'm out here alone. I say that it's just a nice night and I wanted to listen to the crickets... My dad appears in the doorway. He says, "Get in!" (George reenters the cabin. The interior is bright and cozy with a fire.)... I don't like my father. I don't know [why]... I like my mother. She's afraid of him. (Alice asks Bartley to move forward or backward in time to a significant scene. She finds George and his father camping in the wilderness. A fire blazed at the campsite.)... We're drinking coffee. My father is talking. He's angry at me for doing something wrong... something with the horses—I didn't tie them up right... I'm in my sleeping bag. I think I hear noises. It's real quiet, but every so often I hear a noise that's not an animal... I think he's digging.

A: What is he digging?

B (incredulously): A grave... a hole! I think it's for me!
(Bartley becomes agitated. Alice pauses to relax her, and asks her to go on.) He hits me in the head with a shovel! I'm already down, I'm in my sleeping bag. It's funny, I'm observing it like I'm out of the body... I'm leaving the body. He throws down the shovel and he drags me to the grave and he puts me in and he covers me up!... He's thinking, making up a story about how I died.

A: Does he feel any remorse?

B: No! (Alice asks Bartley to move to a scene which will shed light on the hatred between George and his father. Bartley observes George, still seventeen, at a community dance, dancing with a beautiful girl named Sally. He is in love with her and hopes to marry her someday. The fiddling is lively and the crowd is having a good time. George's happiness radiates from Bartley's face.)

A: You look like you're very happy. I'd like you to enjoy this moment of happiness with Sally. (Bartley hums a bit of the tune being played.)

B: People are laughing and spinning around!

A: How long have you known Sally?

B: All my life... She loves me. (Alice moves Bartley to the next significant scene)... We're up in the barn and we're kissing. I'm touching her, and we just love each other very much... He [father] catches us.

A: Are you clothed, the two of you?

B: Halfway. We pull things. He gets real angry. He's yelling at me and I'm yelling at him. I'm saying, how dare he, that I'm old enough to have my own life. Sally is crying... I'm a little bigger [than him] but we're pretty much the same size... He orders me to go home. I leave and walk down. (Bartley becomes distressed.)

A: Are you all right?

B (crying): He rapes Sally. (Bartley sobs and Alice comforts her, then asks her to probe further into the events in George's life. She sees George back at home in the cabin.)... He walks back in. He's smiling, he's smirking. I lunge at him.

A: Do you know what he's done?

B: I don't know how I would know... I know for some reason.

A: There might be some way that you found this out.

B (speaking rapidly): He's laughing. I lunge at him and I hit him with my fist, and then I strangle him. He pushes me away. He's just as strong as I am. We're fighting.

A: Does anybody get hurt?

B: No. My mom comes in and stops it.

(Alice asks Bartley to let go of George's life, and search her Higher Self for the lifetime in which the hatred first took root. Alice surmises that the incarnations as George and Joyce were consecutive, and that their premature deaths by murder had a common cause. Bartley moves once again through time and finds herself a strapping, blond young man of about eighteen in Rome. He has command of a chariot drawn by a single white horse, and he is awaiting the start of a race. The race begins, and the horses thunder down the course. The young man is on an adrenaline high in the competition to win. Then something unexpected—and tragic—happens. His chariot swerves and hits a chariot abreast of him. The driver loses his balance and is knocked from the chariot. He dies instantly when his head is crushed by the wheels of the blond youth's chariot.

The shock to Bartley is overwhelming—especially when she realizes that the dead driver was her brother in that life. She is instantly filled remorse and guilt. She moves to other scenes in which they share drinks and laughter and the company of young women, and one in which Bartley, as the Roman charioteer, lay sick in bed while his brother tended him. The bond between the two brothers is intense, full of admiration and love. After these glimpses, Alice asks Bartley to let go of this life.)

A: I would like to move you up to your own higher mind. You might look at these relationships that you had with Roger in the past and analyze how they relate to the present time... How does [the life as Joyce] relate to the present?

B: It's the same verbal abuse, not as much physical abuse... He has strangled me before, once badly... I thought I was going to die.

A: What about the life in which you were George and he was your father?

B: That was more of a very cold relationship, with more distance, not as much physical violence. We had a lot of hate.

A: What about the relationship in Rome in which he was your brother?

B: We had a good relationship, we loved each other.

A: I'd like you to look at that life in Rome and be able to forgive yourself for that accident... It was not your fault.

B: But it doesn't matter that it wasn't my fault!

A: Why?

B: (Crying) Just the fact that he was gone... I missed him.

A: It's important for you to be able to forgive yourself, let go of that baggage. You don't need to carry it around any longer... If you've carried that guilt with you so long and into so many other lifetimes, it might be that you are feeling that you deserve the violence... You feel you did this terrible thing to him and you bring this guilt forward into other lives and you allow yourself to be abused... You allowed yourself in two of these lives to be murdered... It's time to let go of that guilt. Do you think you can look back on that life in Rome and truly forgive yourself for what happened?

B: (Crying) I think so... I forgive myself for that (unconvincingly).

A: I'd like you to make me believe you.

B: (Emphatically) I do forgive myself.

A: If that's truly the karmic cause for these two murders in these previous lives, that's a very big price to pay for an accident. You have more than paid for it now.

B: I don't understand why, if my brother forgave me for an accident, why he would come back in every life and murder me.

A: There might be some other lives involved as well... It is time for you to let go of that guilt, and be treated with the love, respect and dignity that you deserve...

(Alice then has Bartley forgive the previous incarnations of Roger, as Joyce's husband and George's father. Bartley lets go of the anger and hate she experienced. She knows the violence must stop.)

A: Great wisdom can come out of this for you. It is up to you to change yourself.

Because the regression has been traumatic for Bartley, Alice believes she could benefit by looking into the future in a progression. She needs to see the positive effects of change, and know that a loving, happy relationship is possible. At first, Bartley is uncertain. The idea of looking into an unknown future is a little frightening. But she has felt safe and guided throughout the regression, so she agrees.

Alice takes her ahead in time. The scenes are misty, not as clearly defined as those from the past. Bartley experiences a dramatic shift in emotion. She sees herself married to a tall, Englishman named Peter, with curly blond hair, who works in the creative arts. She observes herself and Peter enjoy a vacation. She stands overlooking art of the Grand Canyon at sunrise, as he drives up in a car. She experiences a tender moment of intimacy shortly after the birth of their baby daughter. In this progression, Bartley is no longer at her present job, and is living somewhere else than New York. Words float into her head. *Perfect. Fine. Wonderful.* She guesses she is in 1989. She returns to full consciousness.

Later, as Bartley went over and over the regression in her mind, she was awed by the power and intensity of the experience. Everything she had witnessed had been vivid and real. Most incredible of all were the emotions she'd felt. *I've never felt such emotional pain, or been so emotionally high in love,* she thought.

The past-life regression and future-life progression proved to be an enormous catalyst for transformation for Bartley. She felt liberated of oppressive energies weighing down her life. She went through a period of rapid growth and change, during which she gained a feeling of being spiritually centered. She was able to let go of Roger and put the relationship behind her. She felt like a new person.

Bartley embarked on an exploration of other past lives in additional regressions. She discovered her long-time affinity for England stemmed from a series of at least six lives there. Her present work in advertising took her often to England. Now she knew why she always felt at home there.

Several months after her first session with Alice, Bartley entered the elevator in her apartment building one evening. Inside the car was a tall blond man. Bartley knew she had never met him before, yet she recognized him. *Your name is Peter,* she thought, her pulse quickening in anticipation.

The man looked down at her and smiled. "Hello, my name is Peter," he said in an English accent. "What's yours?"

I can't believe it! thought Bartley. She flashed on the warm, wonderful feelings she had enjoyed in the future progression. She had half believed it, half not. Was this the man who would make that vision come true? Bartley grew even more hopeful when, in their short conversation, she discovered Peter was a writer. Everything—his name, height, hair, occupation and heritage—fit the progression exactly.

Peter took Bartley's telephone number but did not give her his. It was unlisted, he explained. He promised to call. By the time Bartley left for a trip to England two days later, he had not made good on the promise. Nor did he call after she returned to New York two weeks later. Bartley would have shrugged it off as another of the vagaries of single life, had it not been for the progression. She manufactured a tale to obtain his unlisted number from the telephone company operator and called him. No, no, he hadn't forgotten her, he assured her. How about lunch?

Bartley's fragile bubble of hope burst on the lunch date. Peter was not at all what she was looking for; in fact, he reminded her of Roger in some ways. He admitted he was living with a woman, whom he was more than willing to deceive by seeing Bartley on the sly. Bartley saw immediately where that would lead: to more pain for herself. She didn't want any part of it.

What is going on here? she wondered. *I thought I was through with men who'll hurt me!* She was devastated by the unexpected turn of events. Doubts lingered in her mind. Was she giving up that marvelous, happy future? She resolved to work through her feelings and discover the reason why meeting Peter had happened. After a great deal of meditation, she got the answer. She had been given a lesson in making choices. She had arrived at a crossroads. Peter represented the old path to yet another unhappy experience. Before her lay a new path. If she took it, she was certain she would find happiness.

Bartley continued her spiritual growth through study and meditation. She had relationships with men, but none of them caught fire. One day in 1986, she consulted a well-known trance channeler in Manhattan. The channeler told Bartley that she had a soul mate on the planet, but whom she wouldn't be with until May 1987. He had blond, curly hair and worked in the creative arts. The elusive mystery man again!

In May 1987, Bartley went to London. For the past three years, she had been working a great deal with an English photographer named William, who aspired to be a film writer and director. They were good friends but not romantically involved. He had wavy blond hair which he wore short. But when Bartley saw him that May, he had let his hair grow, and the waves were now curly.

One evening, Bartley and William went out to dinner. Both had recently broken up romances. All of a sudden, they seemed to see each other in a new way. It was electrifying. Bartley knew immediately that *this was it*.

Events in Bartley's life then moved swiftly, as though directed by unseen forces. Within months, she lost her job at the New York agency. Her apartment went co-op and she had to move. She did: to London. She left the advertising agency world and went to work styling, which is finding props for commercials and still photography. In June 1988, Bartley and William were married. *Perfect. Fine. Wonderful.* The progression will be completely fulfilled when a baby arrives, and Bartley is certain there will be one somewhere in the future.

She surmised that she got the name "Peter" in the progression because her meeting with Peter was approaching on the horizon. Did she really see the future, or was the progression a fantasy which she then materialized through her own desire? Perhaps it was a little of both.

Bartley's journey through past lives led to inner changes that left her feeling like a brand new person. She had learned both the law of karma and the law of grace. Her overwhelming guilt had caused her to allow herself to become a victim of violence again and again. In order to break the cycle, and grow spiritually, she had to first forgive herself for taking a life, then forgive the soul who was her brother in that Roman life, who had allowed resentment over the tragedy to fester into hate and revenge. It wasn't easy, but it literally was a matter of life and death.

10

Phobias and Physical Karma

IN HINDUISM, they're called *samskaras*: subtle impressions, or imprints, carried over from one life to another, manifesting in physical appearance and personality traits. A death, the soul passes into its subtle body or astral body, which retains all of these impressions and carries them into the next physical body. A similar concept in Buddhism is the *skandhas,* remnants of the personality, including form, perceptions, feelings, impulses and personal consciousness, which remain after death and are reincarnated in a new personality.

Phobias and physical traits are among the *samskaras* which are troublesome and debilitating. Many persons have phobias which cannot be attributed to traumatic events in their lives, and which have been present since the earliest memories of childhood. How does one account, for example, of a fear of horses when one has seldom been near horses? The answer lies in past-life traumas.

In his research of spontaneous past-life recall among children, Ian Stevenson found a high incidence of phobias related to the mode of death of the previous personality, especially when the death was violent or involved prolonged or great suffering. Of 252 cases of violent death, 127, or 50 percent of them, involved phobias. One of the most unusual cases is that Ravi Shankar, an Indian boy born in 1951 six months after a boy who lived near his family, six-year-old Munna Ashokumar, was savagely murdered. Little Munna's throat had been slit and his head nearly severed, apparently by a barber and a washerman. The men were arrested and one confessed, but retracted his confession. They were released due to lack of evidence, and the crime went unpunished.

Ravi Shankar was born with a startling birthmark: a long, jagged line slashed across his throat. It varied from about 1/8- to 1/4-inch in width, and was dark and stippled, much like scar tissue from a healed knife wound. When Ravi Shankar reached the age of two or three, he talked spontaneously about "his" murder. He named his murderers and described the murder site, and painted a rich picture of his life as Munna. He also had a strong phobia of razors, barbers and washermen. He said he wanted to avenge his own murder. Munna's father wanted to avenge the murder, too. When he heard about Ravi Shankar and verified to his satisfaction that he was Munna reincarnated, he sought to reopen the case against the accused killers based on evidence provided by Ravi Shankar's past-life memories. Not surprisingly, the courts wouldn't hear of it.

Curiously, the ragged birthmark began moving up Ravi Shankar's throat. By 1964, it was under the ridge of the chin, and had shortened to about two inches in length. At that time, he no longer was afraid of one of the accused murderers and no longer recognized the second. By 1969, it had moved up further under the chin, near the chin's point. Ravi Shankar was eighteen and a student in college. He had lost all memories of Munna's life and death, and no longer harbored feelings of revenge. He had gotten over his fears of razors, barbers and washermen. No satisfactory explanation has ever been given for the movement of the birthmark.

Other death-related phobias are tied to places, such as bridges and cliffs, and foods, in cases related to poisonings.

In many of these child cases, the phobia diminishes or disappears with the passage of time, as do the past-life memories themselves, as happened to Ravi Shankar. Some phobias remain life-long.

Persons who undergo past-life regression often discover that their present phobias have past-life causes, and that most are related to death and severe trauma. Many persons are surprised to find their phobias disappear after the discovery of the root cause. There is no known reason why this happens; apparently the process of examining past lives releases beneficial or healing energy which alleviates the problem. The results are often so swift—sometimes occurring after a single regression session. Thus, some people seek past-life regression solely to try to cure themselves of phobias that are interfering with their lives. Sometimes past-life regression works when other methods have failed.

Alice T. has done a great deal of work with clients who have phobias. Two clients once shared a similar but unusual phobia, in terms of its cause:

> *A woman came to me with a terrible fear of injections, having blood drawn, or having any kind of invasive procedure, whether she was herself experiencing it or merely witnessing it. Her phobia was so profound that it would cause her to faint. In fact, the day before our session, she had passed out while attending a circumcision.*
>
> *The cause of her phobia was based on two lives—her present-life birth experience, which was by Caesarian section, and an earlier incarnation somewhere in Central or South America. In it, she was a woman whose infant was to be sacrificed in a ritual. It was considered an honor to have one's child chosen. But I would imagine that even in such a culture, it's not easy for a mother to sacrifice a child. In her case, the sacrifice was done by fire. The baby was put into a fire, but it didn't die right away and was in a lot of pain. The suffering of her infant horrified her, and she felt compelled to end the suffering. So, she grabbed the first thing she could find, which was a tool or weapon with a blade, and killed her baby so that it would not*

suffer through the burning.

The soul who was the infant in that life is her mother in her present life. During birth, the soul is sometimes in the fetus and sometimes out of it. She was out of the fetus and observed her mother being cut open. She associated her mother's surgery with the sacrifice and believed that she was once again causing this soul, whom she loved dearly, excruciating pain. This caused her tremendous grief and guilt, which caused her phobia. About two weeks after the session, she had to go to the doctor's and have blood drawn. For the first time in at least six years, she didn't pass out.

Another client had a similar phobia with a similar cause. Lynn L. of New York City explained:

I had severe anxiety whenever I was given an injection. Even the prospect of an injection or surgery prompted anxiety. I would hyperventilate, want to cry, break out in a cold sweat, get nauseous and, less frequently, vomit. If I so much as saw a surgical procedure on TV, I would begin to experience the phobic symptoms and have to turn off the program. A couple of times I had minor surgery that usually was performed on an out-patient basis, yet I had to stay overnight in the hospital and have general anesthetic, so that I would be totally unconscious during the experience.

In an earlier lifetime in Africa, I was a woman who was pregnant but not by my husband; I had been unfaithful. To punish me, the villagers tied me to a stake and slashed my stomach open. I died and my baby died. When I was born by Caesarian section in this life, I viewed the birth. I remembered the degradation and humiliation I experienced in the African life, and, as I witnessed my mother being cut open, I perceived her suffering degradation and humiliation and thought I was the cause. Once I discovered the cause of this phobia, I was able to release it. Now I don't think I'm any more squeamish than the average person.

For Laurie McQuary, her own fears of death by fire and drowning have roots in past lives. The information was revealed to her in past-life dreams, which she described:

> *A dream opened with me walking down cobblestone streets which turned into dusty roads. I was walking amidst a group of people. I was dressed in a burlap or rough material that was either creamy colored or white. I had long red hair down to my waist. I had this real sense of calm, that these people were protecting me and taking me someplace and I would be fine. All of a sudden, off to my right was a house. It was more like a cottage, very simple. The group of people was trying to get me to go into the cottage to exchange identities with another person who was going to take my place. They were trying to protect me from wherever I was going. I wouldn't change. I said, 'No, I have to go where I'm going.'*
>
> *They continued with me, and I ended up at a fire pit that was probably a good five or six feet deep. I was thrown into the pit and fire was thrown on top of me. The most amazing thing was, as I lay in the pit, I could see the fire above me. I couldn't have crawled out of it easily at all. As the fire was falling towards me, I had such a sense of calm. I said, 'I'm going to die, and I'm fine.' When I woke from that dream, I knew I had died for being a witch in a past life. I feel it might have been in Ireland or Scotland. It felt like a very long time ago—it might even have been in ancient Druid times.*
>
> *I have a fear of drowning, especially in anything covered like a car. I had a dream that I was on a floating plank-like object in a huge river. I could see across the river and see other people clinging to plank-like pieces. As I passed this one group, I thought, 'That's my mother, though it's not the mother that I have in this lifetime.' In the dream I said to myself, 'This is part of the reason why I'm so afraid of drowning.' I knew I had lost my mother in that lifetime through drowning.*

Physical karma

Edgar Cayce was twenty-one in 1898 when his remarkable ability to give medical diagnoses by clairvoyance was discovered. He suffered laryngitis and lost his voice. No amount of medical treatment helped, and he was forced to give us his job as a salesman. A traveling hypnotist who came to Cayce's town was able to hypnotize Cayce and improve his voice during trance, but post-hypnotic suggestion failed to work. Cayce's condition caught the attention of another man, Al Layne, who hypnotized Cayce and ask him, while in trance, to describe the nature of his affliction and a cure.

The hypnotized Cayce said his condition was partial paralysis of the inferior muscle of the vocal chords, caused by nerve strain, and that increasing the circulation to the vocal chords would relieve the condition. Layne gave that suggestion, and then watched Cayce's neck turn bright red as blood circulation increased for about twenty minutes. When Cayce awoke, his had his voice back. Layne suggested Cayce try to diagnose others while in trance. Cayce was dubious. His success was astounding.

After word of his ability spread, thousands of suffering persons contacted Cayce for help. Over the course of his life, Cayce gave more than 25,000 physical readings. He knew nothing of medicine, yet he was able to describe in medical terms the nature of a person's affliction, and give instructions of alleviation or cure. To give a reading, he simply lay down and relaxed. The client did not have to be present; he could give readings long distance, for someone who was anywhere in the world.

Cayce began giving medical diagnoses in 1901. He didn't allude to reincarnation until 1923, and from then on many of his physical readings involved past lives. He often attributed the cause of physical problems to past-life actions, and told the client he or she was experiencing the effects of karma. Not all conditions were karmic, and of those that were, he was frank in stating whether or no they could be cured. Some could not be cured but could be alleviated. He repeatedly emphasized that the health of the body depends on the health of the mind and spirit, and that ill health could not be cured without first changing attitudes. He stated:

The body, the mind, the soul are one within the physical forces; for the body is indeed the temple of the living God. In each entity there is that portion which is a part of the Universal Force, and is that which lives on. All must coordinate and cooperate. (Reading 1593-1)

But remember, mind is the builder... Don't look to material things—look for the spiritual. Plan what you will do for others, and what you will do with the healing grace that maybe manifested in the body-forces through the power within and the prayer to the Christ within the self. (Reading 3681-1)

The effect of the mind and emotion on health is ancient knowledge and has been at basis of many healing systems, such as the 5,000-year-old Ayurvedic system in India. In the industrialized West, mind and body became separated in medicine, and have only recently been reunited by researchers in the relatively new field of psychoneuroimmunology, the effect of the mind on the body's immune system. From the standpoint of reincarnation, there is an added incentive to purge negative emotions from one's life, for in addition to affecting present health, it may affect future health as well.

According to the Cayce readings, the cause and effect of karma is not necessarily literal, nor does it occur immediately in the next life. Cayce was sometimes asked by clients why karmic debts sometimes skipped lives. His answer was simple: "because it [karma] was unable to do so before."

One of the most important points to be drawn from the Cayce readings is that *attitude* and *intent* can create physical karma; here he echoes the Eastern teachings that karma is created by thought and motivation. The paybacks for mockery, scorn, hate, jealousy and indifference may take the form of physical deformity, debilitating illness, loss of limb or bodily function in accidents and degenerative diseases. A number of Cayce's clients were told their problems stemmed from lives in Rome, when they participated in the persecution of Christians by mocking and scorning them, and taking delight in seeing them torn apart by lions in the Coliseum. Such persons in their present lives suffered from polio, tuberculosis of the hip, lameness and the like. The readings also show that *tacit approval* of cruelty and abuse also incurs negative karma.

Tacit approval also may be experienced collectively, as in a group, race or nation which tolerates violence to others. Given that, we may expect to see many karmic scores settled by not only those who actively helped the Nazi massacres of Jews and other innocents, but the millions who stood by and allowed them to happen.

Some karmic effects seem to manifest in unusual ways. For example, Cayce said that a young boy who was anemic had lived in Persia, where he had caused great bloodshed; hence in the present, his own blood had been robbed of its vitality.

Cayce's cases serve to remind us that it is not just our deeds which speed or inhibit our spiritual growth, but our words, thoughts and emotions. As Cayce said:

> *For, as given of old, each soul shall give an account of every idle word spoken. It shall pay every whit.* (Reading 3124–1)

Past-life regression and physical karma

Many of Cayce's recommended treatments were elaborate, and, depending on the problem, improvement was sometimes slight or gradual. More recently, past-life regressionists have helped others to alleviate or cure some types of physical problems by finding the past life responsible and facilitating a release of negative energy. It is not understood exactly how or why this process works, but, like phobias, it is in some cases very effective.

Obesity, for example, is often found to be related to either starvation or sexual abuse in previous lives. The individual overeats to prevent starvation again, or to make the body undesirable and therefore prevent a repeat of sexual abuse. In addition, Cayce attributed obesity to neglect and abuse of the body in a previous life. Making these past-life connections seems to resolve the matter on some level of consciousness, and the individual often is able to marshal the resolve to shed the unwanted pounds.

Past-life regression has been found to help alleviate some chronic physical complaints, such as headaches and back pain. Here again, it must be understood that past-life regression is no magic bullet and is not a substitute for medical treatment. Nevertheless, relief has been found in cases where traditional medicine has been unable to diagnose the cause of the problem or treat it successfully. Said Laurie McQuary:

> *Medical conditions come through often in a past-life reading. Once someone came to see me who had terrible pain in his side. He'd been to doctor after doctor but could never get a diagnosis on it. Fortunately, he is metaphysically oriented, and he figured it was psychically tied to a past life.*
>
> *We narrowed it down to something that was cyclical in nature and revolved around a friend of his in the present. Whenever he spent a lot of time with this friend, he would get a stabbing pain in his side. They were friends from childhood, but the friend was irresponsible and had a lot of problems in life. This man, on the other hand, was very responsible, and was always trying to counsel his friend and help him out.*
>
> *In a past life, they were two monks, standing out in a garden and arguing. The one who is the friend now was in that lifetime very unhappy as a monk and wanted out. He was always questioning his faith. My client was always trying to counsel him. Suddenly this friend picked up a sharp stick or hoe and struck him in the side in anger, and it killed him.*
>
> *It seemed that in the present, whenever my client argued with his friend, he relived the moment when the friend lost control and killed him in that life. From that time on, the man's pain started to diminish and it was gone within two months.*
>
> *I send a lot of people who have medical conditions that may be*

> tied to past lives to a hypnotherapist [Sam McMains]. One was a woman who suffered chest pain. The doctors could find nothing. She was absolutely opposed to the idea of reincarnation, yet she knew she had to do something. Sam regressed her. She saw herself as a slave in the United States, standing on a slave block. She couldn't understand a word that anyone was saying around her, because she had just come from Africa. She was hauled off the block and put in chains. She tripped and a wagon ran over her and crushed her chest. She came out of that regression remembering everything, and was totally convinced of reincarnation. Her pain went away.

From Sandee Mac, hypnotherapist:

> Sometimes physical problems relate to more than one past life. One woman I worked with had chronic colon problems, a lot of pain and blockage. The condition was tied in with more than one past life, including one in which she was stabbed in the colon area. Another woman came to me because she had suddenly developed a fear of flying. She had flown extensively throughout her life without a problem, until she took her first trip to Europe. The fear was activated when she was coming home and flying over the water. In regression, we found that in World War II, she was a soldier in a military plane that was hit and went down over the water. I asked her unconscious if there was another lifetime involved and got the answer yes, in another life she had drowned in a shipwreck.

The hangman's headaches

Past-life regression helped Pat, a New York woman, to recover from severe and chronic headaches:

> I went back to a life in England where I victimized others. The first thing I saw was a great castle with a moat. My first thought was that I was the queen or princess of the castle. As soon as the thought mate-

rialized, I instantly found myself on the other side of the castle. Then I realized that I was the hangman! I saw a scaffold. I began to see a lot of pictures of people, old people, young people, men, women, and I knew that they were people I had hung. I don't know what century it was. I had the feeling there were political difficulties, a time of great strife, and many people were being hung.

I felt a great deal of emotion, of horror—how could it be me, this mild-mannered, nice person who chases a roach out of her apartment rather than kill it? I was horrified that I had taken part in such violence!

That was all that I saw about that lifetime. I was able to get a sense of who I was as a man. I was between the ages of thirty and fifty, and was not educated or capable of doing much else. I was emotionally frail, but I had no conscious moral conflict about what I was doing. It was my job, I did it and I did it well. I didn't see a picture of myself, but I got a sense of my appearance. I was about five to ten with reddish brown hair and a slight build.

Seeing this life enabled me to get over chronic headaches. When I was about nineteen, I began to suffer from headaches that started with a pain in my neck and worked their way up. They got progressively worse over the years. Sometimes they were debilitating, forcing me to go to bed. I had various medical tests, including a scan, because my doctor thought I might have a brain tumor. I didn't. I tried acupuncture but received only temporary relief. Finally, after regressing to the life in England, I stopped having those headaches. They were a product of guilt. Once I was able to view the life and look at it closely, the guilt was released.

The regression also stimulated a desire in Pat to visit England, a country previously of little interest to her—perhaps for past-life reasons—despite her enjoyment of travel. Within a few months of the regression, she planned her trip. While browsing through travel folders, she was startled to see a picture of the very castle she had seen in her regression: Warwick

Castle on the Avon River near Stratford-on-Avon. Warwick is considered one of the finest medieval fortresses in all of Europe. It housed a dungeon where many people were tortured for various crimes throughout the years. The water that Pat had thought was the castle's moat was the Avon River. She visited the castle during her stay in England.

A few years later, Pat discovered that the hangman's life was connected to her most recent past life. As the hangman, she had given her tacit approval to the executions, which created a karmic debt:

> *I was a Jewish girl who was killed in a Nazi concentration camp, Dachau I believe, in the early 1940s. I was only about five or six.*
>
> *I have gotten information on this life from five different sources. The first was an intuitive flash, a picture of a Nazi officer in a woolen uniform coat as seen from behind. All I could see was the right lower quadrant of his coat, although I knew what the front looked like. The second source was a channel who told me my most recent life was as a concentration camp victim in World War II. The third source was a friend who was regressed to a life where he knew me in that World War II life. The fourth source was my own regression to that life by a colleague. The fifth was my astrologer, who said my chart showed that in my last life I died violently as a child.*
>
> *For me, this seems to be the perfect karmic balance. In the life in England I hanged people I didn't know or have any personal vendetta against. I was simply doing my job, following orders. In the life in World War II, the people who killed me had no personal vendetta against me—they were just doing their job.*

The castrated Roman

Physical karma from a victim's trauma occurs in this account from Barbara Hand Clow:

> *Three or four years before I had my first past-life regression, I began*

to develop a cyst in my neck. It was about the size of a pea or bean and felt like it was in one of the neck glands. I was very fearful that it was cancer, even though I have always felt that I would never get cancer in this life. I did not go to the doctor.

The cause of the cyst was revealed when I began past-life regression with Gregory Paxson in Chicago. I relived part of a past-life in which I was a Roman man, small in stature and about twenty-one or twenty-two years in age. I was taken to a prison, but instead of being put in a cell, the soldiers took me into a room and forced me to lie on a wooden table. A man in a white tunic came in and castrated me with a thin, razor-sharp knife. The pain and terror were incredible, and I saw myself witness my mutilation from outside my body. It was horrible.

As Greg and I went over the incident, I noticed that I had a sharp pain in my neck. Greg said, 'Go to that part of your body and find out what's going on.' I then saw that one of the soldiers was holding a small knife right next to my neck, cutting my neck as they were castrating me. If I struggled to rise off the table and get away, he cut into my neck. Reliving this incident enabled me to release negative energy in my emotional body, which in turn was affecting me physically. Three weeks later, the cyst went away and never returned.

Stabbed by a jilted suitor

Annie B.'s experience with a physical condition was triggered when the man who created her problem in the past reappeared in her present life:

> I woke up one morning with a pain in my chest that wouldn't go away. I went to a doctor but he couldn't find anything wrong. After about three months of having this pain, someone suggested I look into past lives. I was skeptical but gave it a try. I was regressed, and immediately saw a side of a building and some bushes. It seemed to be in Italy in about the 1300s. There were three persons besides myself. Two of the others were a man I refused to marry and my

> mother in that life, who wanted me to marry this man. The man was stabbing me in the chest because I wouldn't marry him. I could feel the knife going in, right in the same place where I was having the pain. He killed me.
>
> I realized that the man who stabbed me was now a man I'd recently started dating. I didn't like him very much, though I was strongly attracted to him physically. I realized that the pain had begun several weeks after meeting him. It must have been triggered by the past-life connection. After I saw the past life, the pain healed by itself. I guess there is such a thing as old psychic wounds.

The experience also helped Annie see that she was dating this man for the wrong reasons. She broke off the relationship.

Raped and hanged

Alexandria (a pseudonym) lives in Connecticut and works as a hair designer. Her co-workers and customers see her as an attractive young woman with an abundance of energy and enthusiasm, who always thinks of others first. Privately, has struggled with physical discomfort, depression and problems in her relationships, the solutions to which seemed to elude her. Past-life regression gave her a new perspective, and insights which surprised her. Here is Alexandria's account of her experience:

> There were three main reasons why I decided to have a past-life regression. About five years ago, I started doing yoga and lot of things got stirred up. I began to feel a lot of tension, a tightness, in my groin. I noticed it a lot when I was driving, like I was holding a ball between my legs. It was a very uncomfortable feeling.
>
> Secondly, I felt unhappy. It was a vague unhappiness, around me all the time. I could be anywhere, like at a party, and be outwardly happy but be unhappy on the inside, like I didn't know where I belonged. It was weird.

Finally, I felt stuck in a pattern of bad relationships that invariably involved alcohol or substance abuse. My father was an alcoholic, and the men who came into my life also had problems with alcohol or drugs. I always questioned the abuse or put it down or tried to stop it. I also did that with my father before he died. It seemed like a chain, a progression of events and I wanted to break it. I tried group therapy for a while but that issue was never resolved. Then I did est, which made me more aware of the pattern I was in. A friend recommended past-life regression, and I thought perhaps it would help me let go of the tightness in my groin, and discover why I was unhappy and stuck in a pattern of bad relationships.

I was raised Catholic and didn't believe in reincarnation until I started the yoga. The first yoga book I read was [Jess Stearn's] Yoga, Youth, and Reincarnation. *I also read Edgar Cayce. I was attracted to the whole Eastern philosophy of eternal oneness and eternal spirit, and the idea of coming back to resolve things until we get everything right.*

Alexandria's past-life regression was done under light hypnosis, in which she asked to see lives that would shed light on her three problems.

The first thing I saw was that I was in a cabin. There was a fire going in the fireplace—I could hear it crackling. I was alone. I was in my early thirties, about the same age I am now. I was wearing a long blue dress.

I heard Indians outside. They attacked the cabin and broke in. There were about a half a dozen of them. They dragged me out and put me on a horse. The next thing I saw was that I was somewhere in a forest and was tied up on the ground. The Indians raped me. I was very frightened—I was afraid they were going to kill me. They eventually did, but I don't know how. I didn't go through the death. I don't recall that I tried to defend myself.

Then I moved on to another experience. I got a real clear picture of it. I was sitting at a dark and heavy table in my house with my younger sister. I had been reading. I had glasses and gray hair that I wore tied back. I had a long dress on. I got the feeling that it was sometime around the seventeenth century, but I don't know where. There was a village.

My sister had come over to warn me that the town men were after us. They were after us because we were supposedly witches. We were healers and they didn't understand about healers. We ran away with other women who were also healers. My sister had her child, a girl, with her. I don't remember any other children. We ran into a cave and huddled together. My sister's child fell and needed some kind of root or leaf, a medicinal plant. I said I would get it. I went outside and *the townspeople caught me. They took me out somewhere and raped me and broke my back—I've always had back pain—and they hanged me from a gallows.*

I felt very sad because I couldn't get back to my sister and help her child. She is my sister in the present life, a year older than me.

Afterward, I understood why I had the tightness, and I was able to let go if it. I also felt on a different plane with my sister the next time I spoke to her. I saw her relationship with her daughter differently. Before I was judgmental about how she was raising her child; now I give her credit for being the loving mother that she is. I felt moved by that... She's always loved and adored me and I never felt worth it... Seeing this relationship in a new light was unexpected.

I didn't get to work on why I'm in a pattern of bad relationships, but I did get something else out of the witch life. The men hunted witches and had no understanding of me. That's like the same thing now. The men I get involved with have no understanding of who I am. It also has to do with me not communicating, and I am going to have to work on that.

The sadness lifted and now I feel great. I'm much more confident in my work. I still have back pain, but not as often, and it occurs only when I'm under very great stress. I can release it on my own... I'm happy and I truly believe that the universe will support me if I go with the flow.

Sometimes the physical karma left by a past life is a birth defect or birthmark. Ravi Shankar, as you recall, had a birthmark around his neck where his previous personality had suffered his death wound. Another unusual birth defect case in Stevenson's research is H.A. Wijeratne, who was born in 1947 in Uggalkaltota, Ceylon, with a pronounced deformity of his right breast and arm. His parents attributed it to an unknown past-life karma. As the boy grew older, he reminded the father of his younger brother. The child was dark-complected and distinctly different from the other, fairer children in the family. At age two-and-a-half, the boy talked about murdering his wife in his previous life, and that was why he had been born deformed. The father's younger brother had been executed in 1928 for murdering his wife.

Stevenson collected more than 250 cases of birthmarks in reincarnation cases in cultures around the world, and found many of them to bear a correspondence to violent deaths in the previous lives. Ma Tin Aung Myo, a Burmese girl who was afraid of airplanes, said in her previous life she had been a Japanese soldier in World War II, and had been killed in a strafing. She was born with a thumb-sized, itchy, brown sore on her groin that remained open and runny until she was about three. She also had a phobia of airplanes flying overhead.

Off with his head!
Andorian, a young man who lives in the Southwest, has a birthmark similar to the one Ravi Shankar had at birth:

> *I have a very large birthmark around my neck. It's a reddish, jagged line that circles my neck at about the collar line. I believe it comes from a past life in which I got my head chopped off. It was life I spent with my ex-wife in the present life in a Middle Eastern country, about 600 A.D. I worked as a palace architect. I was well-educated and lived very comfortably. I designed our home for my wife and*

three children, two boys and a girl. It was pretty elaborate, with a swimming pool, big rooms and long silk curtains. We had servants.

A man framed me for stealing one of the palace objects—it was a vase with a lot of gold decoration. This other man was very deceptive and manipulative, while I was straightforward and believed the truth would take care of itself. I think he was the one who really stole the vase. He convinced the king no one else but me could have done it, because I had a lot of power and access throughout the palace. I was sent off to jail and sentenced to be executed. The king felt that he had treated me like a son and I had stabbed him in the back. The execution took place in the throne room, because it was for his pleasure to see me being executed. I knelt over a stone block and the executioner cut of my head with a mammoth, crescent shaped sword. I wasn't so much afraid of dying as I was of my family being scarred by shame.

I'd hidden all our money and told my wife where it was before I was killed. Afterward, she grabbed the money and took herself and the children far away to start a new life under a new name. It was hard for her; I don't think I was supposed to die like that in that life. She was a lot younger than me, and she had to learn how to adapt and cope without me. The oldest child was seven and the youngest was three when I was killed.

The birthmark hasn't caused me any problems. I think I was able to accept what happened to me at the time, and not go out angry.

11

Skills and Talents

OTHER FORMS OF *samskaras* are skills, talents and inclinations toward certain professions and occupations. Those who are at the top of their chosen fields perhaps have honed their skills and paid their dues many, many times over.

In Eastern doctrine, reincarnation and the law of attraction, or soul connections which are not apparent on the surface, are responsible for genius and child prodigies—not heredity or environment, or a combination of the two. Mozart, then, was not a miracle, but one who had served a musical apprenticeship over a series of lives, building his talent and skills until he achieved a genius of creativity and knowledge.

Ralph Waldo Emerson alluded to genius as a product of reincarnation in *Representative Men*, his essay on Emmanuel Swedenborg, the Swedish mystic of the eighteenth century. The reason for the "intuition of genius," Emerson said, "would lead us into that property which Plato denoted as reminiscence and which is implied by the Brahmins in the tenet of Transmigration."

According to Ian Stevenson, no empirical studies of investigated reincarnation cases provide sufficient evidence to justify reincarnation as an explanation for child prodigies. No known child prodigies of the West have claimed to derive their skills from previous lives, though a few in Asia have done so. Stevenson believed the musical gifts of Mozart, Beethoven, Brahms and Bach, for example, most likely were influence by hereditary and early environment, for they all had musician fathers and were reared in a musical environment.

Stevenson did not dismiss reincarnation as a possibility, pointing out that numerous examples exist of exceptional talent and unusual abilities that cannot be attributed to heredity and environment. George Frederick Handel, for example, developed his musical talent despite both lack of interest and opposition on the part of his family. Likewise, Florence Nightingale (1820–1910), the English nurse who founded modern nursing, and Elizabeth Fry (1780–1845), the English Quaker who achieved major reforms in the English prison system, also received no support from their families.

Still other highly talented individuals do receive family encouragement for their ambitions, but exhibit them in such a remarkable way at such a young age that reincarnation seems to be the only plausible explanation. Take the case of Jean Francois Champollion (1790–1832), who announced his intention to decipher Egyptian hieroglyphics before he was twelve years old. He was trained in archaeology by his older brother, Jean Jacques Champollion-Figeac, and succeeded in deciphering the Rosetta Stone in 1821. Similarly, Heinrich Schliemann (1822–90) displayed an unusual passion for the writings of Homer as a child, and was less than eight when he said he would discover the ruins of Troy. He went on to earn a fortune in business, and retired at age forty-one to search for Homeric sites. He not only unearthed Troy but made significant archaeological finds at Mycenae, Ithaca and Tiryns.

Unlearned languages

One of the most exceptional skills linked to past lives is that of xenoglossy, or the ability to speak in an unlearned tongue. To past-life researchers, xenoglossy provides some of the strongest evidence for reincarnation, for language cannot be transferred by telepathy; it must be learned. Cases of authentic xenoglossy are rare. "Recitative xenoglossy" is the recitation of unlearned languages with neither comprehension nor ability to converse. "Responsive xenoglossy" is the ability to converse in an unknown language. When xenoglossy occurs, it usually does so in hypnotic regression in a fragmented, recitative fashion. In most cases, there is a high degree of inaccuracy; or, it is difficult to disprove that the individual did not pick up the phrases at some point in his or her reading or learning.

There are, however, some cases of responsive xenoglossy which seem to have no natural explanation. In 1862, a mesmerist named Prince Galitzin hypnotized an uneducated German woman who began speaking fluent French, a language she did not know. She said she had lived in 18th century France as a woman who had murdered her husband, and now was being punished with a life of poverty.

Three modern cases of responsive xenoglossy have been studied extensively:

"*Gretchen.*" Carroll Jay was a Methodist minister in Elkton, Virginia, who began using hypnosis on his wife, Dolores, in an effort to relieve her back pain. During such a session in 1970, he asked her, while she was entranced, if her back still hurt. She answered in German, "*Nein.*" In a subsequent session, she began speaking German again, identifying herself as "Gretchen." Dolores Jay had never studied German.

Gretchen continued to appear in more hypnosis sessions. She understood questions put to her in very simple English, but answered only in an imperfect German. She said she was Gretchen Gottlieb, daughter of the mayor of Eberswalde, Germany, who had died at about age sixteen after a severe beating. She did not know when, but based on her descriptions of her life, it appeared she had lived in the second half of the nineteenth century.

Dolores Jay was afraid she was being possessed by the spirit of the dead girl; she did not believe she herself had lived before as Gretchen. Others theorized that "Gretchen" was a fictitious personality brought forth from Jay's subconscious as a way of expressing deeply buried memories.

"Jensen." Another American woman hypnotized by her husband, a physician, who began speaking an unlearned language was "T.E." (a pseudonym) of Philadelphia. In sessions from 1955–56, T.E. began speaking an archaic and colloquial Swedish in a deep voice. She identified herself as "Jensen," a male peasant farmer. Jensen was not fluent in his conversation; however, his diction was like that of one who speaks in his native tongue. T.E. had never studied any Scandinavian language.

Jensen provided sparse details about himself, except that he had died after suffering a blow to the head. Interestingly, T.E. suffered from headaches. It was estimated that Jensen had lived in the seventeenth century.

"Sharada." Uttara H., an Indian woman born in 1941, was thirty-three years old when a Bengali-speaking personality named "Sharada" manifested in her life. Uttara spoke Marathi, but had made an effort to learn some Bengali when she was a child; she had felt a great affinity for it. The appearance of Sharada came after a long period of physical illness and psychological stress. For about eight years, Sharada would completely take over Uttara's life for periods lasting from a few hours to forty-one days at the longest. The spells were preceded by premonitions on the part of Uttara.

Sharada spoke fluent Bengali and sang Bengali songs. She said she was of the brahmin caste (Uttara's family was not) and refused to believe she was dead. She had lived in the first half of the nineteenth century, was married and had been seven months' pregnant. The last thing she remembered of her life was falling unconscious after a snake bite. She woke up in the body of Uttara. She was greatly distressed to learn her family was long dead.

Sharada favored nineteenth-century dress and mannerisms, and was much more extroverted than Uttara. Existing records (few) indicated that a man who may have been her father died by 1827.

Prof. A.A. Akolkar, a parapsychologist of Pune, India, who investigated the case, theorized that Uttara's regression, of which Sharada was a part, was brought on by several factors: her "extreme psychophysical exhaustion"; unfulfilled aspirations for marriage and motherhood; and a practice of meditating, which speeded her spiritual progress (Akolkar pointed out that the Bhagavad-Gita says that persons who cannot attain the higher states of yoga are born into spiritually-inclined families). The Sharada spells diminished when Uttara reached her forties. Akolkar said this perhaps coincided with diminished prospects for motherhood.

The blind virtuoso

A remarkable case of unexplained musical talent is that of "Blind Tom," a black slave of the nineteenth century. He was born blind in 1849 to a slave woman owned by Perry H. Oliver, a farmer of Muscogee County, Georgia. As a slave, the infant had no value; rather, he was a liability, a useless mouth to feed. Oliver determined to rid himself of his liability as quickly as possible, and when the boy was a year old, he put the mother on the auction block. A General James Bethune of Columbus, Georgia, bought her. When the sale was made, Oliver gleefully announced that the woman had a child who would be thrown in for free, and he produced the blind boy from a hiding spot.

Perhaps Oliver congratulated himself all the way home for his cleverness. He had no idea, however, that what he had done was a blessing for the boy. Many slave owners might have been as indifferent as Oliver or worse, but Bethune graciously took the infant into his care. He named the child Thomas Greene Bethune.

The Bethunes were quick to observe that Blind Tom, as the boy became known, had a keen ear for music, and for all sounds in general. At age three, he astonished the household by spontaneously joining the Bethune girls in song, singing perfect harmony. The Bethune girls, like all young ladies of culture at the time, studied the piano. One evening when Blind Tom was four, the girls spent several hours playing the piano in the parlor. After they departed, the boy sat down at the keyboard and played back everything he had heard. He demonstrated complete familiarity with both major and minor scales, though no one could recall him ever touching a piano. His fingers rippled up and down the keyboard with the confidence of a seasoned artist.

General Bethune attempted to get formal instruction for Blind Tom, but Carlo Patti, one of the leading piano teachers in Columbus and who taught the Bethune girls, declined, saying the boy knew more about music than he. "All that can be done for him will be to let him hear fine playing; he will work it out by himself," Patti said.

Blind Tom began giving public concerts at age eight. During the Civil War, he entertained troops on both sides with the music of the great classical composers. He gave concerts in Britain, Europe, and the White House. In addition to his talent for playing whatever he heard, Blind Tom demonstrated a considerable talent for improvisation. Critics and reviewers were amazed at his mastery of music, which seemed to come from the very essence of his soul.

No explanation was ever advanced that satisfactorily explained how a blind, uneducated slave boy could possess such brilliant musical gifts. Perhaps reincarnation is the only plausible one.

Stevenson found indications of skill carry-over in many of the childhood cases of spontaneous reincarnation memories that he has investigated. Such children display at a very early age interests or skills that they could not readily have learned from older persons, either through instruction or imitation; they say that they remember using the skills in a previous life. In Chapter Seven, we saw the case of Corliss Chotkin, Jr., who claimed to be his deceased uncle born again, and who, as a child, displayed remarkable skill in handling and repairing marine engines without having been taught. Corliss' father had no such interest or skill, but his deceased uncle had been very fond of boats and engines.

It is possible that children tap into past-life memories without being aware of it when they play at some imaginary occupation. The child who sets up a restaurant or pretends to be a horse trainer with persistent and amazing passion is perhaps acting out a drama from the past. Consider the following story:

Forever a fighter
George Smith Patton, Jr., the tough American general whose brilliant command of the 3rd Army in World War II helped liberate France in 1944 and defeat Germany in 1945, knew from childhood that he would be a soldier. He was certain of that not only because the Patton lineage included many illustrious military men, but because he possessed a mysterious sense of having lived as a soldier many times before. As he grew older, he came to believe that his military skills had been honed over a series of lifetimes dating back to classical times.

Patton believed in a God of Battles, and felt it was his destiny to be a soldier in lifetime after lifetime, cheered on by a spirit host of ancestors. He once told his nephew, Fred Ayer, Jr., who wrote a biography of his uncle, *Before the Colors Fade*, that there was no question that he believed in reincarnation. "I don't just think it, I damn well know there are places I've been before, and not in this life," Patton said. To illustrate, Patton told of his first command in France in Langres, a town with Roman roots, which Patton had never before visited—in his then-present life. A French liaison officer offered to show him around. Patton stunned the young man by telling him he knew the place well.

As the two drove around, Patton gave directions, feeling as though someone were whispering them in his ear. He knew the way to the sites of the town's Roman amphitheatre, Forum and Temples of Mars and Apollo, even though some of the structures no longer existed. He also found the military drill ground and the spot where Caesar once had pitched his tent. He knew the town so well, he said, because he had been there himself as a soldier in Caesar's Tenth Legion, and he could still smell the sweat of the men and feel himself mingling with the Roman crowds.

Patton often surprised others with his past-life beliefs. Once in Africa during World War II Harold Alexander of England remarked to him, "You know, George, you would have made a great marshal for Napoleon if you lived in the eighteenth century." Replied Patton, "I did."

Patton believed he had fought with the Greeks against the Trojans in the Trojan War, had served under Alexander the Great at Tyre, had fought against the Huns as they invaded Europe, had fought on the side of the Crusaders in the Holy Land, had served Henry V at Agincourt, and had served with the Scottish Highlanders of the House of Stuart. He had battled on the side of Napoleon at Jena and fought for the Confederates in the American Civil War at Winchester and Gettysburg. Patton's sense of having fought in battles throughout the centuries gave him an exceptional gift for planning strategies. The spirits of all these warriors were impressed into his blood and soul, preparing him in his most recent life for one of his greatest and most important roles, to help ensure the defeat of Hitler's Nazi machine.

Patton succinctly summarized his views about his many lives and his destiny in his poem, *Through A Glass Darkly*, which he wrote in 1944, a year before he died. He wrote that he had fought in many guises and under many names, but always in God's will. His destiny forever was to be reborn again and again a fighter.

Many modern reincarnationists believe that times of great crisis are foreseen and planned for on the other side of the veil, and that reincarnations are prepared so that the appropriately developed souls descend into the flesh in order to provide the needed leadership.

Edgar Cayce said that each entity must have spiritual ideals, or purposes, for entering into each life experience. The ideals help the soul, through its mental and material associations and activities, to grow in grace, knowledge and understanding. The abilities of the soul which are manifested on earth must be used in service to others for the glorification of the Creative Force and not for self. The channels of expression in a given life depend in part upon the channels used by the soul in previous lives. Patton's example certainly supports Cayce's views.

The Cayce readings contain many examples of skills and talents built up over lifetimes. That is not to say that every soul returns to the same task in each lifetime; the primary occupation may be separated by lives in unrelated jobs, if such are needed for the soul's overall karmic balancing. In many cases, a soul develops skills by serving in a variety of related occupations. For example, one Cayce client was a successful osteopathic physician, whose skills could be attributed to at least three past lives: one as a doctor who worked closely with American Indians and learned their natural and herbal lore; one as a supervisor of baths and massages in early Christian times; and one in ancient as an embalmer.

Similarly, a New York composer and arranger had past lives as a music teacher, a wood carver of musical instruments, a buffoon in the court of King Nebuchadnezzar, and an Atlantean who worked in sacred music.

In her book *Many Mansions*, Gina Cerminara observes that vocations are both "the matrix through which some aspect of man's spiritual growth takes place" and a crucial part of the realm of matter which must be mastered by spirit. Perhaps the mastery of vocation is necessary for man to become a co-creator with God, "a poised, pure, and potent spirit, a harmless, radiant, loving and creative center of expression, capable himself of generating forms and lives and worlds."

The question naturally arises as to when and how a soul decides to pursue certain vocations. Unfortunately, Cayce provided no definite answers, although his readings do show that souls do change their vocations and interests. In analyzing Cayce's readings, Cerminara found that changes seem to come about through two forces of equal strength, desire and karmic law. A person may have experiences in one lifetime that inspire new directions, or, a change may be necessary to balance karma. It may take several lifetimes to make the transition to a new vocation. This, perhaps, may explain why some are more successful in their fields than others, but should never be used as an excuse for lack of initiative or poor performance. Whatever conditions and obstacles are present in a given life, the soul always must strive to fulfill its destiny and highest potential.

Persons who are experiencing difficulties or failures in their vocations sometimes find reasons in past lives. Invariably, the present problems are karmic repayment for past abuses of a spiritual nature. Cerminara tells of one Cayce client, a man who was suffering from an increasing dislike of the social requirements of his job as a real estate agent. Cayce told him that in a past life, he had been a rigid, harsh and dictatorial teacher, and now was learning a lesson in relating to others. Cayce advised him to stay in his vocation and absorb the lesson.

Professional problems are one of the main reasons why people seek out past-life counseling, according to Alice T., a regressionist. "They feel very talented, capable and qualified for the work they're doing, yet they're having little success. Everything is a struggle; nothing is easy. The cause often turns out to be a past life in which they were successful and powerful and abused it in some way. Sometimes it is guilt—they think they abused their power or failed others by not helping them, and therefore, they do not deserve to be successful in this life." Discovering the roots of such problems in past lives can help a person cope or find a solution.

The Faberge jeweler
Past-life vocations which are not vocations in the present life often manifest as hobbies, strong interests and leisure pursuits. Michael Talbot had a

resonance for Russia, but hadn't pinned it down to a time period. He pieced together fragments, "almost like a detective story," as he described the process. One key piece fell into place one day while he was out walking on Central Park West, and had a spontaneous memory concerning St. Petersburg during czarist Russia. The memory was touched off by his recollection of a Smirnoff vodka advertisement he had seen in a magazine, which showed a gilt-framed portrait of the czar. Talbot recounted:

> *What hit me was that picture frame had cost a lot of money, and who had stolen it? I was instantly outraged. I was on my way back to my apartment to search for it when I thought, 'What on earth am I thinking?' I have not owned a beautifully framed portrait of the czar in this lifetime. I then experienced visual images of a large and beautiful house in St. Petersburg. I knew that in this past life, I was a man. I carried a cane. I can almost feel it in my hands. I didn't need it for walking—it was more for style. I had a strong sense of riding around in carriages, and that my father in this life was there.*
>
> *I knew that I had been a jeweler before, but I hadn't pieced it together with the Russian life. I have this fascination for building miniatures, and I've always tinkered with watches and other small objects. When friends' eyeglasses and things like that break, they bring them to me for repairs. When I was fourteen, I was in a bookstore and saw a book on Faberge [Peter Carl Faberge, 1846-1920, Russian goldsmith famed for his elegant jewelry and exotic Easter eggs he designed for the royal family]. I was riveted to it, but nothing bubbled up enough in my subconscious for me to question why I was so interested—at that age I wasn't looking for past life information. Yet I knew that name.*

Psychic Jim Gordon gave Talbot additional information. He had lived in just before the Russian Revolution of 1917, and was trained as a jeweler in the house of Faberge. However, he never worked as a jeweler, because his family income was sufficient. His father had been his uncle in that life, and the uncle's two sons, both of whom fought in the war, were now Talbot's nephews in the present. Without knowing about his son's past-life recollections, Talbot's father revealed that he had a feeling he had once lived in Russia.

> *My father had a dream that he was shot during the Russian Revolution. He didn't know which side he was on, but someone was after him and was going to shoot him. He ran in front of this beautiful marble building, and he thought they wouldn't shoot him there because they wouldn't want to injure the building. They shot him anyway. Later, he was watching a television special on Russia and saw this beautiful marble building. There were bullet holes in the building because during the revolution, people had been shot in front of the marble.*

If yesterday's occupations form today's hobbies, then it is just as likely that today's hobbies may become one's vocation in future lives.

12

The Traveling Interplanetary Musician

WHILE SOME PERSONS TURN to past lives in hopes of solving career problems, many more do so to find new careers. "An amazing number of people seek past-life therapy because they know they want to make a career change but they don't know what they should do," said regressionist Alice T., "They aren't sure where their talents lie. What we do is look at a past life that reveals their strengths in practical areas. If you live a city, it's not going to be useful to find out you once were a terrific blacksmith. When we investigate careers in past lives, we are somehow able to call upon latent talent more clearly. Talent is yours forever. It's just a matter of finding a way to awaken it." One career changer who came to see was Ornyece Prince.

Prince has a composure and style that most persons would envy. A striking woman, she has the ability to carry off distinctive clothing and jewelry. It comes as no surprise, then, to learn that Prince has worked in fashion virtually all of her professional life, as a designer of costumes for the theatre. In 1986, she launched her own line of jewelry, which she manages from her home in New York City.

To the casual observer, it might seem that Prince had carved out a nice niche of independence. Deep down inside, however, she felt something is not right about her life, that she was not in the right place doing the right thing. Meeting with me over coffee in Manhattan, she confided she has felt this way for a long time, and it has left her quite frustrated. Despite her work as an artist, she has always had the odd feeling of being in service to others. "While it's good to serve people," she acknowledged, "I have always felt that I was here to pay some sort of a humbling debt. I've wanted to find out why."

Prince had glimpsed previous lives and had encountered dark mysteries at an early age. She came into the world feet first, her large, thirteen-pound, eleven-ounce body covered from head to toe with weeping eczema from a dry birth. The eczema gave her skin the appearance of having been burned. From the earliest that she could remember, she was aware of the presence of a spirit woman.

> *I used to see this woman all the time. She had a German shepherd dog. She was very pale and had dark hair, and she was very still and peaceful. Her hair was cut in a pageboy and she wore a shirtwaist dress. She would just stand there with this dog. Sometimes I would walk around a corridor and see her. She wouldn't be looking at me, but I knew she was there for me, there was a connection. I never tried to think it out, I tried to think it away. I was never afraid of her, I thought it was normal. She never spoke to me or did anything. If I mentioned her to my family, it caused such an uproar that I thought there was something wrong, something bad about it.*

By the time Prince reached her teens, the woman ceased to appear, but the German shepherd remained. "Even after I was a grown woman and had my son, I would walk down a corridor and swear I saw a dog, and then suddenly it wasn't there anymore," she remembered.

Years later, Prince thought the spirit woman might have been an aspect of herself or former self, from another life. Her son said he was afraid that one day he would walk into a room and see she had been replaced by a woman who resembled the Walt Disney character, Cruella, a pale woman with dark hair and long nails. The Cruella woman would then try to convince him that she was now his mother. "When my son told me about this woman, I asked him to describe her. He said she entered his dreams occasionally when he had been very young. It's the same woman I used to see growing up as a child," Prince said. Prince encountered her again in her past life regressions.

Also during childhood, Prince spoke of believing in reincarnation and the possibility of human life on other planets, which left her father, a conservative minister, aghast. "To shut me up, he would say, that can't be God speaking, it must be the Devil," Prince said. Like many children who learn it's not appropriate to speak of past lives, Prince kept quiet about her private thoughts.

For most of her life, Prince had lived with a vivid memory of once being a wise woman who lived in the forest with a little boy. Both of them were burned alive because others believed she was a witch. The little boy was her father in the present life. Here is her story:

> *I stayed away from people—they came to me. They knew about me through word of mouth. I was a healer. I lived in a covered wagon with a lot of shelves and pouches and glass jars with herbs and things. I had clairvoyance, but it seemed natural. I was a peaceful, young person, I would say between the ages of seventeen to twenty-eight. One day this little boy found me where I lived in a campsite site. I don't know if he ran away or was lost, but he tried to give me the impression that he was just a loner. He didn't want to be returned to wherever he came from.*
>
> *I wound up being a mentor to him... I would tell him about spiritual things, and how things could not happen to you unless you*

allow them to happen. Somehow the wrong people found out I was living there, and they looked on me as a witch. They were going to burn me at the stake... I was tied to a stake or a tree, with dried grass or bushes around me, and the boy was tied to the left of me. He was looking at me, starting to panic and cry. I tried to tell him telepathically that everything was all right, and he was going to be okay and not to worry. He looked at me and trusted me. We both still burned. In his passing on, I think he was confused, that he was registering my teaching about spirituality on a mundane level. He really thought that something was going to happen to rescue him and he would not burn, and that was not what I was trying to get across.

In this life, my father and I from day one battled. I could never understand how a man could look at a little child and say such negative things... In this life, he was not going to listen to me. He, a minister, sure of everything he said. In effect, he was telling me, 'Now it's your turn to listen to me.'

Prince also recognized a connection between her death by burning in that life and her arrival in this life looking as though her skin had been burned.

Questions about her relationships and her true purpose in life led Prince to Alice. Prince didn't know what to expect from viewing past lives. She asked to see a life in which she possessed a skill or talent that enabled her to lead a satisfying life in all ways—professionally, spiritually, financially and emotionally. It was her hope that she would unlock creative energies deep within her that would help her redirect her present professional activities. She also had another question: Why am I such a procrastinator? The life that was revealed in answer caught her so completely by surprise she at first did not know how to respond.

Alice, using guided meditation, relaxed Prince and let her drift back in time through a dark tunnel. When she stepped out of the tunnel, Prince was astonished to find herself on what seemed to be another planet. And she was not human, but an odd, large human-like being. "I feel I'm a creature!" she said, bemused, when asked if she was male or female. "I think it may be male."

She took in the scene before her bit by bit. She saw it from both the viewpoint of herself, and the viewpoint of this creature. The creature—Prince dubbed him "Og"—had his huge, wide feet planted on a flat, vast plain that shimmered in metallic hues of blue, gray and silver. The sky was colored the same metallic hues, and so were objects which appeared to be clouds. There appeared to be no sun, no moon, no trees or large rocks. The only land formations were small mounds which rose up from the plain, which seemed to stretch on forever.

It dawned on Prince that the metallic hues represented Og's vision, like a person who is colorblind sees only certain colors. Looking down at Og's feet, she saw he wore brown sandals, yet Og saw them in the same metallic colors that clothed everything else, including his skin. His clothing consisted of a tattered toga, which registered also as a metallic silvery blue.

His human-like feet were wide, about nine inches across. Prince gazed in fascination at his toes. Og seemed fascinated, too, and very proud of an ornament on the nail of one outer toe which appeared to be a gold nugget. It seemed to be a symbol of achievement.

Og's entire body was thick and wide, like his feet. He was at least nine feet tall. His face was large with bold features. His hair was coarse and silvery gray, almost like steel wool in consistency, and piled on his head in a mound.

Prince sense a great deal of gentleness and pride within Og, despite his warrior-like physique. He felt secure, yet he was of limited intellect—so limited that Prince felt embarrassed for him. He seemed to be very old, even thousands of years old, yet was young at the same time, as though many, many Earth years represented a short time to beings of his race.

As Og stared out over the shimmering plain, Prince realized he had 360-degree vision, and she could see everything behind her as well as in front of her. *What was he doing in this place?* she wondered. With one hand, he was leaning upon a cylindrical object. She guessed it was her tunnel to the past. His other hand held a strange tool or instrument. It was taller than he and was unlike anything Orneyce had ever seen. It was shaped like a half-U. The straight portion had separations or perhaps strings, and was pierced by pegs or frets. The bottom, curved portion seemed to be computerized and bore buttons and bars.

Prince tried to get Og to move, but he wouldn't budge. Gold stairs appeared in front of him, leading up to a building with pillars. Og registered the golden color as the same narrow band of metallic hues. Prince knew there were other beings in the building, though she neither saw nor heard them. When Og still refused to move, Prince and her regressionist decided to leave that life and go on to another.

Afterwards, Prince felt a bit disappointed that the regression hadn't given her the answers she had sought to her professional situation. Og was intriguing, but what did it all mean? He had simply stood there, grasping his weird object, refusing to budge.

Sometimes the energies and information unlocked by past life regressions do not manifest immediately, but bubble up slowly to the conscious mind. Prince went home, listened to her tape, and put it out of her thoughts.

Later, she attended an opening night party for a film. She met a famous singer who was making his acting debut in the film. Impulsively, she asked him if he would be interested in setting to music some poems she had written. He agreed to take a look at them.

Back home, Prince examined her poems and found them too personal. She decided to try her hand at writing fresh lyrics. The words came effortlessly. To her surprise, so did the melodies. She had never written a song before. Though most of her immediate family studied classical music, and one of her aunts was an opera singer, Prince had never had the slightest interest in learning about music. She had never taken a single lesson, and knew nothing about composing.

But now the melodies were pouring into head, compelling her to set them down. She fetched her son's electronic keyboard, took a soft pencil, and wrote the scale letters on the keys. As she composed the music, she jotted down the letters on a piece of paper. In this crude fashion, she quickly finished three songs.

The singer declined further involvement, but for Prince, it was only the beginning. Song writing was fast becoming an obsession. She made inquiries through friends and contacts, and found a musician who agreed to teach her how to compose sheet music in a sound studio. She told him she knew nothing, but he hardly believed her. Not only did she have perfect pitch, he said, but she knew enough to appear formally educated in music. Prince shrugged it off. "Maybe it's because I grew up in a musical home," she said. "I just never thought I was paying attention."

One night, Prince played her regression tape again and fell asleep while listening to it. Through her dreams, the pieces of the puzzle of Og began falling into place.

> *I began to understand him and recognize things. Og was an interplanetary, travelling musician, and this thing he held in his hand was his instrument. The cylindrical object next to him was his ship. When he travelled to different places and landed, he didn't move until he was sure it was okay, especially if the place was new to him. That answered my question about why I procrastinate...*
>
> *This particular place in my regression was known for war, so he didn't feel that secure. It was the demilitarized zone where nothing would happen but he had to be sure and he had to know who was sending for him, and were their intentions honorable. The instrument was complex but not to him. It had special tones that most people couldn't handle, but they loved the music and felt it was worth sending for someone like Og to entertain them. He was known as the best.*
>
> *I put two and two together that perhaps I was supposed to be in*

the music field, and that my success will eventually come in music. I went to a producer with a demo tape. I didn't tell him it was mine, but belonged to a friend of mine who was a musician. He listened to the tape and was impressed. The first thing he said was, 'This is different, very different. As a matter of fact, I don't know where to place this music. Maybe it's the kind of music that has to go to Europe first and then come back here because people won't be ready to understand it, it's too different. Yet it has a good beat and it's danceable.'

The producer told Prince he wanted to hear more samples, and she set to work. At the close of 1988, she had copyrighted nine songs, and was exhilarated with the new creative energy she had found. Though she was still earning her living from her jewelry, she foresaw a time in the future when she would be earning her living from her music.

Prince's exploration of past life regression answered one other key question: Why did she feel part of her purpose in this life was to repay a debt of humbleness? The answer came in the form of a woman Prince had been over and over again: tall, slender, regal in bearing, cool and aloof, distant—and very much alone.

Prince regressed to a life in which she was a wealthy, assertive business woman. She owned a shop that sold imported and handmade, fashionable clothing, and traveled extensively in her business dealings. She lived alone, with a bevy of servants, in a luxurious mansion, where she hosted elegant balls. In her pillared ballroom of ivory and gold, she danced in her pink satin and tulle dress and white satin pumps. It was a busy life, well-planned and controlled, her calendar jammed with commitments—but she was bereft of emotional ties.

The woman surfaced in another life, in a primitive setting that appeared to be in the Middle East. She was tall and thin with caramel skin, and acted as ruler and judge over her people. She lived in an ivory and gold palace with marble stairs, and an upper window that looked out over the marketplace of the city. Here, accused criminals and violators of the law were brought to her for sentencing for punishment. She was in her thirties and wise beyond her years.

As this life unfolded, a man was kneeling before her, trying to explain his transgression and begging for mercy in a most pitiful voice. The scene shifted, and Prince saw another man brought before her. He had been on a rampage through the marketplace, knocking over carts and damaging merchandise. Prince recognized him in that life as a known thief, a con man and a liar, who had created the disturbance in order to gain access to the palace. She also recognized him from the present life: he was yet again a con man, who had tried to convince her to enter into business deal with him.

As the judge, Prince sentenced the man to have his head cut off. The punishment was not solely for his destruction of the marketplace. Prince was made aware that the man had intended to cause her harm, and that he had planned the marketplace incident as a way to gain access to the palace. She never watched executions, but for some reason, she decided to witness this one. It was carried out immediately.

After the execution, she went upstairs to an ornate room with a cot or bed, window seats, and a table with a bowl of fruit on it. She lay down on the cot and contemplated suicide. Her life as a judge of others overwhelmed her and seemed pointless. She had no regrets about the punishments she'd meted out, but had no more desire to continue doing so. She felt cold-hearted and depressed. She got up and went to the table. The bowl contained red berries which were poisonous, and which she kept on hand in anticipation of this very moment. She had thought about suicide for a long time. She took the berries and sat on the window seat, where she could watch the bustle of the city as she ate the poisonous berries. People walked about with huge loaves of bread on their shoulders, and pushed carts laden with fruit and hay. The noise wafted up to her window.

She felt dreamy. She knew it was wrong to take her own life, but she was bored and tired of it, tired of answering the demands of her people, who, she felt, forced her to execute them for their wrongdoing and never seemed to learn anything from it. She was so self-assured that she felt she could control what happened to her as she passed on—that she would not go to a hell, but would go to the light. She would shed this life and move into another existence. As the poison took effect, Prince was shocked to find she had no control over her transition.

> *Everything became dark and got as dark as navy blue. I never saw a light. That did throw me. I still felt I could still change things and go to the light, but it wasn't happening. I remained in this state in the dark. It was pulsating like electricity. It was a void. I was thrown because for the first time I was not in a position to control things the way I wanted them to be. I stayed in this limbo for an indefinite time and then was released into another life.*
>
> *There always was a person inside of me who felt she was in control, and had this power that put her above the spiritual laws. I have never had a relationship that was fulfilling. I found out through this woman that just being judgmental can distance me from others. I've always felt I'm not judgmental, but I guess I am, to a certain extent.*
>
> *I noticed that in every life, I didn't see a lot of people around me. I was alone. I had position, I didn't love intimately, and I didn't have domestic responsibilities—I always had someone to do that for me. There were a lot of people around who were servants, rather than friends or relatives. Even Og was a loner. It seems as if he didn't need much in life. He didn't have an entourage—he travelled alone. His space capsule seemed to seat one or two persons.*

In analyzing what she had learned from her past lives, Prince still felt a need to be in control of all situations, but realized that control in itself would not necessarily bring her everything she wanted. She appreciated the strength and assertiveness of the "power woman," but not her judging of others. She felt she could integrate the best characteristics of the woman and Og into her present life. "I haven't the right the judge anyone," she concluded. "It only causes disharmony with others as well as with oneself. From Og I have learned that livelihood and contentment should be synonymous."

13

The Past-Life Muse

THOSE WHO WORK IN the creative arts have various theories as to the source of their inspiration and ideas. A majority believe they are somehow influenced by supernormal forces. Some believe their inspiration is divine, while others believe they are aided by spirit guides or spirits of the dead. Some feel their inspiration comes from their own imagination triggered or enhanced by guiding forces. Some believe they tap into some sort of cosmic currents, while still others believe that they tap into their own past lives. Perhaps all of those possibilities, and more, come into a complex play.

In his book *An Encyclopedia of Psychic Science*, the respected psychoanalyst and psychical researcher, Nandor Fodor, defines *inspiration* as "a psychic state in which one becomes susceptible to creative spiritual influence, or, to a varying degree, unwittingly lends oneself as an instrument for thought-flowing ideas." Mozart and Beethoven were among stellar composers who felt blessed by a mysterious inspiration. Mozart described how thoughts streamed in on him at certain times, when he was in a relaxed state or when he could not sleep at night. Beethoven felt his inspiration came from an exalted state of awareness in which he felt the intertwined harmony of all things.

Henry David Thoreau, the Transcendentalist whose famous works include *Walden* and the essay, "Civil Disobedience," studied Hindu philosophy and the concepts of karma and reincarnation, which he reflected in his philosophical writings. He wrote in *Walden and Miscellaneous Writings* that the hawk had earned his power of flight "by faithfully creeping on the ground in a former state of existence." Of his own past lives, Thoreau stated in a letter to Harrison Blake, that the sky at night looked the same to him as it had when he was a shepherd in Assyria. In other letters, to Blake and to Ralph Waldo Emerson, published in Thoreau's *Letters and Journals*, he said:

> *I lived in Judea eighteen hundred years ago, but I never knew there was such a one as Christ among my contemporaries...*
>
> *And [Nathaniel] Hawthorne too, I remember as one with whom I sauntered in old heroic times among the banks of the Scamander amid the ruins of chariots and heroes... As far back as I can remember I have unconsciously referred to the experiences of a previous state of existence.*

Novelist Louisa May Alcott also believed she had lived before. In a letter she wrote:

> *I think immortality is the passing of a soul through many lives or experiences; and such as are truly lived, used, and learned, help on to the next, each growing richer, happier and higher, carrying with it only the real memories of what has gone before... I seem to remember former states and feel that in them I have learned some of the lessons that have never since been mine here and in my next step I hope to leave behind many of the trials I have struggled to bear here and begin to find lightened as I go on. This accounts for the genius and*

great virtue some show here...

Inspiration is of particular interest to writers, especially novelists, who create characters and worlds and make them real. From where do these fantasy people and worlds come? William Makepeace Thackeray once admitted surprise at some of the things his characters had to say. "It seems as if an occult power was moving the pen," he wrote in 1862. "The personage does or says something and I ask: 'How did he come to think of that?'" Thackeray did not speculate upon past lives; however, because novelists create imaginary worlds, perhaps they are attuned more than others to past lives. This attunement may be conscious or unconscious.

Joan Grant's past-life biographies

London-born Joan Grant did not turn to writing until she discovered her past lives. In 1937, at age thirty, she published the first of seven novels that she said essentially were her own biographies of her past lives. The wealth of information she presented in these novels was obtained in an enhanced recall technique she called "far memory," which she described as the displacement of a major portion of her consciousness from her present life to a past life. In this altered state and reality, she became her past self, and dictated what happened to her as she relived bits and pieces of her previous life. Her far memory sessions sometimes lasted for hours. She never knew what she was going to see, and had to fit her pieces together later in order to relate a chronological tale.

Grant's incredible ability to tune into her past was a product of her innate psychic gifts. As a small child, she was aware of having other selves: she possessed fragments of memories of seven previous lives, four male and three female, including a young Greek boy who was a runner. By the age of eleven, she was having strange dreams, some precognitive, and others in which she was another and much older person who helped the newly dead cross over to the other side. During World War I, she dreamed of being a nurse on a battlefield, telling soldiers they were dead and helping them on their way. In her waking hours, she could perceive ghosts and received piano lessons from a dead woman's spirit. Her contact with the spirit world increased through use of the planchette and automatic writing.

After her marriage to Leslie Grant, a barrister, in 1937, she vowed to get a better understanding of her interface with the unseen, and began recording her dreams. She learned psychometry, a psychic skill in which visions and other sensory information is perceived by handling objects. For example, a psychometrized ring yields information about its owner.

In 1935, the Grants went on an archaeological dig in Iran, where Grant put her psychometry skill to use in handling Sumerian artifacts. She touched the objects to the middle of her forehead, the spot of the third eye, and immediately saw moving images from the past. In 1936, when a close woman friend named Daisy gave her some Egyptian scarabs to psychometrize, Grant discovered Sekeeta, daughter of a pharaoh.

At first, Grant did not realize she had tuned in to one of her own past lives. Her sense of identification with Sekeeta intensified, until she realized she had found one of her past selves. Daisy had been Sekeeta's mother. Initially, Grant continued to use the scarab as the stimulus for reaching Sekeeta. She eventually was able to teach herself the far memory technique, in which her "I" expanded and became the subject of the past life. She learned how to distinguish imagination from recall: the details of a recall, she said, could not be changed, no matter how hard she tried.

In the story that unfolded, Grant learned that Sekeeta had spent ten years in a temple, training to be a Winged Pharaoh, a ruler and healer. Sekeeta herself learned far memory as one of her necessary skills of leadership. She was required to remember at least ten of her own deaths, so that she would be able to comfort the dying. Her initiation test for learning far memory was to spend four days and four nights in a tomb-like chamber, during which she left her body to see other levels of reality. Sekeeta also had to undergo seven initiatory ordeals to test her courage. In the Seventh Ordeal, she had to overcome a huge cobra. It was a terrifying experience, made all the more traumatic for Grant because of her fear of snakes. The recall left her so physically shaken and exhausted that she suffered headaches, cramps and fever for two days.

Grant collected 200 episodes from the life of Sekeetka and wove them into her first novel, *Winged Pharaoh*, published in 1937. Sekeetka's world sprang to life in minute and colorful detail. Interestingly, Grant had visited prior to discovering Sekeetka, and had felt no *deja vu*. As her past life explorations continued over the years, she recalled numerous lives in ancient Egypt.

Material for her second novel, *Life As Carola*, spilled out unexpectedly when a friend asked Grant if she could simultaneously hear Egyptian music while she listened to harpsichord music by Hayden. Grant "shifted level," as she called her entrance into far memory. When she returned to full consciousness, she was told she had given details of a past life as Carola di Ludovici, a sixteenth-century Italian girl who played the lute and died at the age of twenty-seven. The harpsichord music apparently triggered the connection.

Grant's new-found literary success contributed to the breakup of her marriage, for her husband was ill at ease with the subjects. It was one thing to entertain friends in the parlor with psychometry, quite another to go public with a book. Leslie Grant was a man concerned with appearances, and what the members of his club would say.

Grant returned to Egypt for the subject of her next two far memory novels, *Eyes of Horus* and *Lords of the Horizon*. She had lived 1000 years after Sekeetka in the last reign of the Eleventh Dynasty as Ra-ab Hotep, the Nomarch (the equivalent of a lord lieutenant in England) of the Oryx. Ra-ab Hotep belonged to the Eyes of Horus, a resistance movement against the corrupt priesthood. According to Grant, his family's tombs do exist and are located at Beni Hasan in Egypt.

Scarlet Feather, Grant's fifth far memory novel, recounts a female life in North America in the second millennium B.C.E., in which she underwent the ordeals for male warriors and earned the right to wear the sacred scarlet feather. *Return to Elysium* tells the story of Lucina, a Greek girl of the second century B.C.E. who was the ward of a philosopher who preached against immortality. Lucina, who, like Grant's other incarnations, also retained far memory, knew this was not true. After convincing the philosopher that he was wrong, she left him to establish her own practice on an island in the Tiber.

Grant's last novel, *So Moses was Born*, is set in Egypt, and concerns a male contemporary of Ramesses II. Published in 1958, it marked her last past-life biography. All seven novels remain popular to this day.

In 1958, Grant's life shifted her away from her novels and into psychotherapy. She met Denys Kelsey, a psychiatrist and hypnotherapist who became her second husband. The two established a practice in which Grant used her far memory to validate the past-life recalls of patients under hypnosis. Regression was employed when Kelsey believed the cause of a neurosis, phobia or guilt might lie in the past. Grant's ability to tune into the patients' recalls enabled her to sort out true recall from fantasies, the latter of which she said appeared to her as static, while recalls were active.

According to Grant, man has four phases of evolution, spending many lifetimes in each phase as his consciousness expands. He begins as a molecule of energy, graduates to the mineral kingdom, then the plant kingdom, then the animal kingdom, and finally the human realm. As a human, his consciousness eventually expands so that it becomes too large for a single personality, and an incarnation includes both a personality and a component of his total self.

A vampire drawn from past lives

Michael Talbot, who wrote both nonfiction and fiction, felt pieces of his own past lives become material for his novels, as he discussed in an interview:

Frequently when I write, I think past-life material channels through. I don't go into a trance, but somehow I tap into the past. I think this is true of writers in general. We draw upon what we know although we think it's imagination.

I wrote a book called The Delicate Dependency, *a vampire horror novel which takes place in the 1890s. I wrote a lot of stuff I thought was purely out of my imagination. It turned out to be taken from past life memories.*

One character is a monk who is a wandering troubadour. I discovered later that this comes from a past life I had in the 1500s in which I was a troubadour, a mountebank like Cagliostro who knew mystical things. I courted a beautiful woman, whom I also know in this life. She saw through me, that I was a bit of a charlatan. Through gossip she destroyed me and I was imprisoned and died of a lung infection. All of those things have resonance for me: being a troubadour, being in prison, dying of a lung infection.

In the novel, I made the troubadour monk a vampire. The reason I wanted to write a vampire novel is because I wanted to write about immortality and how being immortal would change consciousness... When I assess anything in this life, I find I'm always looking at other lives. I think it gives me a real odd take on life in general. I don't feel either young or old, but in a way I've always felt really old. My family has always commented on it. My parents have always said I was never a little boy, I was always a little man. So, I thought that if you really had lived for centuries it would change you; a nine-hundred-year-old is not the same intellectually or emotionally as a thirty-year-old person.

[In the book] the vampires are very respectful of life. They have a coterie of humans that they feed on, but they loathe killing because a brutal and violent act is the only thing that can bring an end to their own lives... The thing they're most intrigued by is knowledge. Because they live for so long, they have the opportunity to study

things in the way few humans can.

I seem to have drawn on my past life as the troubadour to make the monk vampire like the Illuminati or an alchemist... In one place he says there is a secret language written into the doors of Notre Dame. I thought I was making it up. Later I read that it was believed that alchemists had put a secret language on the original doors of Notre Dame... These vampires knew to meet under the rose window of Notre Dame. I thought I was making that up, too. One day I was looking through the dictionary and saw the term subrosa, *which in Latin means 'under the rose,' and which means a meeting held in secret.*

The main character is a British virologist who forms a hypothesis after he encounters a vampire that they may be a victim of some sort of virus. In the course of his searching, he is incarcerated in a hall on the Isle St. Louis by this nine-hundred-year-old vampire. The vampire says that he can't let the neurologist go now that he has broken into the vampire's home, because the vampire's life depends on people not knowing about him. He guards the neurologist with a trained falcon. The doctor knows that if he gets ripped by the talons he will die. Later in going through some of my old stories and poems, I found I had written about a falcon ripping someone several times before... My hypothesis is that in some past life this had a meaning. One past life which has left a powerful resonance on me is a life in ancient Persia, where falconry was important.

Taylor Caldwell's past lives

Janet Taylor Caldwell (1900-1985), who wrote as Taylor Caldwell, penned a number of best-selling historical novels that brimmed with information she did not consciously possess. At age six, she exhibited the first inkling of reincarnation when she was handed *The Mill on the Floss*, one of the novels of the Victorian writer, George Eliot (the pseudonym of Mary Ann Evans). She had never read the book, and without opening it, discussed the plot in detail and said the book was "my favorite book over all the other I have written."

A prolific and imaginative writer from an early age, Caldwell at age twelve began work on a novel of the life of St. Luke, who healed in the tradition of Hippocrates, which later was published as *Dear and Glorious Physician*. Throughout childhood and into her adult years, she was plagued by an intense, recurring nightmare of being imprisoned by Dominican monks in a Mediterranean city. Just before three men entered her cell to torture her, she flung herself out the window and rolled down a steep tiled roof. At this point, she invariably woke up screaming and crying.

As Caldwell met with literary success in adulthood, book after book was filled with explicit details of life in earlier times, and the personalities and actions of great people, including Christ and those around him. In particular, her knowledge of medicine and healing astounded doctors. sensed an unseen Presence who gave her inspiration, and she also believed she may have tapped into genetic memory. She very deliberately rejected the idea of reincarnation, calling it a "curse" of whatever gods there might exist. She said the "very thought of it horrifies me."

Nevertheless, she was persuaded by writer Jess Stearn to undergo hypnotic regression after the death of her beloved husband, Marcus Reback, in 1970. In a series of deep trance sessions, journeyed back through the past, reliving previous incarnations. She assumed the personalities, mannerisms, speech and voice of her previous selves. Stearn's account, *The Search for A Soul: Taylor Caldwell's Psychic Lives*, was published in 1972.

Caldwell's knowledge of Christ apparently derived from a life she described as Hannah bat Joseph, mother of Mary Magdalen. She called Jesus "Yeshua ben Joseph," and recounted how he rescued her daughter from stoning by the Pharisees, who called her a "harlot." Hannah died before Christ was crucified, but at the moment of her death, her heart burst into fire and she had a wonderful vision of him as the Messiah. He was clothed in lightning, larger than life, with rays of light streaming from his hands. His eyes were more brilliant than the brightest star, and his hair and beard were like golden fire.

Her ancient medical expertise was learned in Greece, where she lived as Helena, an attendant of Aphrodite, goddess of love, a type of courtesan who worked in the house of Aspasia, the mistress of Pericles in the fifth century B.C.E. As leader of Athens, Pericles brought Greek civilization to its zenith. Many learned and famous men visited Aspasia, including a physician, Heracleus, who took an interest in fifteen-year-old Helena when he treated her for a broken arm. He taught her the healing arts and sent her to school disguised as a man, for women were not allowed into the medical schools. The students learned the teachings of Hippocrates, which included astrology. Helena excelled and eventually surpassed Heracleus in skill. While in trance, Caldwell, completely absorbed in Helena, delivered lengthy lectures to her long ago medical students.

The regressions also solved the mysteries of the nightmare and the familiarity with the works of George Eliot. The nightmare seemed to be a fragment of a life as Sister Maria Theresa, a follower of Fra Girolamo Savonarola, a fifteenth-century Italian Dominican who led an effort to reform the corrupt court of Pope Alexander VI. Savonarola was excommunicated in 1497 and was burned at the stake a year later as a false prophet. According to Caldwell, Maria Theresa was denounced as a witch and heretic and imprisoned in a bell tower in Florence. To escape torture, she threw herself out the tower window to her death.

Although Caldwell had exhibited startling familiarity with the works of Eliot, she had not lived before as the famous writer. According to her recall, delivered in an Irish brogue, she was Jeannie McGill, Eliot's Irish chamber maid. McGill had been put out to work at age ten, eventually being taken by Eliot. She worked for the writer for three years, until a woman in the household accused her of stealing a ring, and McGill was turned over to the police. She was sent to a workhouse, where she hanged herself.

Caldwell recalled other lives in Atlantis, Lemuria, Egypt, Peru, China, France and Mexico—she had thirty-seven lives in all, according to a psychic reader. In most of them, she was poor and abused, and forever cold and miserable. In her last life before that of Caldwell, she had been Wilma Sims, a blue-eyed, flaxen-hair girl born in a Battersea workhouse. Sims had died in 1898, two years before was born. Throughout Caldwell's life, she had a great fear of poverty, and felt wretched, depressed and abused.

Weaving through her many lives was an ongoing love triangle of cosmic proportions. The unseen Presence who aided in her work was identified as the Lord Darios, archangel of the planet Melina, which was ruled by his brother, Lucifer. Darios had taken Caldwell as his bride when she was fifteen and lived by the seashore on the lost continent of the legendary Lemuria. She described Lemuria as almost a Garden of Eden, a land in which there was no disease, and people lived to six years or more before they died of old age. One night as she was alone in her garden, watching the moon rise, he appeared to her, a brilliant being with rays of light streaming from him. She thought he was God and worshipped him. He told her he had seen her many times and wanted her for his bride. He transported her to another plane of reality to Melina, where they were married.

Though she loved Darios, she was lonely most of the time, isolated in a huge white palace protected on one side by a bottomless black chasm. She fell in love with another man, Estanbul, one of her tutors. Jealous, Darios exiled Estanbul from Melina. There followed these many lives on Earth, in which searched for Estabul, hoping to redeem him with love so that he could return to Melina. She found him over and over again (he had been Savonarola, for example) but never gained his love; she was constantly thwarted by the invisible presence of Darios. At last she met Estabul in the form of Marcus Reback. The two enjoyed a soul-mate marriage for more than forty years. Between lives, said her spirit always returned to Melina.

In her book *Dialogues with the Devil*, an exchange between Lucifer and the archangel Michael, Caldwell wrote about the planet Melina, which was destroyed by God out of displeasure. Under hypnosis, said Earth was in danger of being destroyed because of the corruption and greed of its inhabitants, and that Darios had laughed at the puny efforts of Christ to sacrifice himself to try to save the planet.

When shown the transcripts of her regressions, Caldwell could scarcely believe them. They failed to convince her of reincarnation. Her own life, she said, had been filled with despair, and she could imagine nothing worse than having to come back and live again. Caldwell died on August 30, 1985. Perhaps she has gone home once again to Melina.

14

Marion Zimmer Bradley's Mirror to the Past

MARION ZIMMER BRADLEY (1930–1999), best-selling author of science fiction, fantasy and historical fiction, believed in the possibility of reincarnation and made use of some of her own past-life memories in her works. Her recalled lives include that of a Spanish soldier and a male cowherd in Scandinavia in the thirteenth or fourteenth century, as well as others which she discusses below. The past lives which have been particularly meaningful to her work as a writer deal with Pagan religions and mysteries, Goddess worship and magic.

One of her most popular works, *The Mists of Avalon*, retells the story of King Arthur from the viewpoints of the women around him, including the central character, Morgaine (Morgan Le Fay), priestess of the Goddess and the Mysteries, who spent seven years learning the magical arts from Viviane, the Lady of the Lake. *The Firebrand* concerns the fall of Atlantis, as seen through the eyes of Kassandra (Cassandra), prophetess and priestess. Kassandra herself is vaguely aware of having a previous life as a serpent-handling priestess of the Sun Lord.

Bradley described herself an occultist, having had since childhood a strong interest in classical ceremonial magic, the mystery religions and the Arthurian legends. She was for a time a member of the Rosicrucians and various occult groups, including her own. She had numerous friends in the Wiccan community. She was an ordained priest of the Neo-Catholic Church, a vaguely Theosophical group. Perhaps it was her own past lives as a priestess that helped to make her characters so compellingly real.

Bradley's past lives involved her two husbands, Robert Bradley, from whom she separated in 1959 and divorced in 1964 (he died in 1966), and Walter Breen, from whom she was separated in 1979. They remained close friends. Her awareness of her past lives began surfacing as spontaneous recall when she was in her teens. Bradley, whom I met in person at one of her lectures in Rye, New York, granted me an exclusive interview for this book. She said:

> *I started experiencing them [past lives] more or less on my own. I was about fourteen. You could say it was a form of dissociative reverie. They would go away for awhile and then I'd find myself remembering something else [from the past]. For a long time I thought I was going nuts and then I realized that this is something that just happens... When I was sixteen, I almost got killed in an automobile accident. I was crossing the street in front of the school bus and a car came straight at me from the other side. I was hit in the leg. I found myself facing death and I felt a weird resignation. I thought, 'Well, that's it, I'm dead. Isn't that strange?' I felt myself flying through the air. Then I woke up and I picked myself up, rather surprised and disappointed to find that I wasn't dead.*
>
> *I think around that time in my life I realized, as I said in one of my books, that death is the least final thing in the world. From that time on I have never had any fear of it. When my daughter, Moira, was born in 1966 my heart stopped and I did die, and I had one of these classic near-death experiences, a meeting with a sort of person*

who said I wasn't supposed to come yet. Actually, they said in effect that I could come if I wanted to, but I had the girl I'd always wanted and I didn't think Walter could raise a girl alone. So I went back.

Bradley said she was not shocked by the near-death experience:

When these things happen, you sort of say, 'Well, yes, of course.' It's hard to put these things into words. They're more impressions. The main things that surprised me were the lights and the music. I got the impression of a tremendous city, you could say a city of light. The one thing I wanted in the world was to join the music and be part of it. The music was, well, the nearest I've ever heard to it is a famous piece by Ralph Vaughn Williams called Fantasia on a Theme by Thomas Tallis [a medieval churchman], which sounds more like heavenly music than anything I can think of. I always thought I would be cheated if I didn't get to be part of the heavenly choir, because I've always cared so much about singing. I'll be perfectly happy if they give me a harp and tell me to play it.

She used her near-death experience in two of her books, *In the Steps of the Master* and *The Firebrand*; the latter includes a description faithful to what Bradley encountered herself. In *The Firebrand*, it is Kassandra, priestess in Troy's temple of Apollo the Sun Lord, who comes to the threshold of death. In the fall of Troy, she is raped and nearly killed by an enemy soldier. She feels herself leave her pain-racked body, rise and move over a flat, featureless and gray plain that is and is not the city of Troy. It is the plain of the dead, and she sees others who are dead, some of them confused soldiers. The dead include Priam, her father, Penthesilea, the Amazon Queen who raised Kassandra and taught her many skills and who was slain by Akhilles (Achilles), and the handsome Khryse, a priest in Kassandra's temple. When Kassandra sees Penthesilea, smiling and unwounded, she runs into the Amazon's arms and is surprised to find them solid:

Beyond Penthesilea the plain of the dead faded away, and Kassandra could see what looked like blinding light—twice the brilliance of the Sun Lord as she has seen Him in her first overpowering vision; and through the light, she made out the form of a great Temple, larger than the one where she had served in Colchis, and even more beautiful.

She whispered in awe, "Is that where I am to go?"

Beyond the light she began to hear music: harps and other instruments, swelling and filling the air with harmony like a dozen—no, a hundred voices, all joined together in song, clear and high and coming closer. This was what she had thought the Sun Lord's house would be. Khryse was standing in the doorway, beckoning to her; his face was free of the dissatisfaction and greed she had seen in it, so that he was at last what she had always believed him. He held out his arms, and she was ready to run into them...

But Penthesilea was standing in her way—or was it the Warrior Maiden Herself, wearing the armor of the Amazon?...

"No," Penthesilea said; "no, Kassandra. Not yet."

Kassandra struggled to form words. It was the place she had seen in her dreams, the place where she had always known she belonged. And not only Khryse, but everyone she had loved was there, awaiting her, waiting for her voice to fill the place open in that great blended choir.

"No." Penthesilea's voice was sorrowful, but inflexible, and she held Kassandra back as one restrains a small child. "You cannot go yet; there is still something you must do among the living. You could not leave with Aeneas; you cannot come with me. You must go back, Kassandra; it is not time for you."

The beautifully molded face under the shining helmet was beginning to break up into a sunburst of brilliant sparkles. Kassandra fought to keep it in focus. "But I want to go... the light... the music..." she said.

The light was fading, and around her was darkness; she was

> *aware of a ghastly smell, like death, like vomit; she was lying on the dirt floor of some kind of rough shelter. Then I'm not dead after all. Her only emotion was bitter disappointment. She fought to hold on to the memory of the light, but already it was disappearing. She was conscious of pain in her body. She was bleeding, and part of what she smelled was her own blood on her face and covering her shift...*

Bradley explored her past lives by using a self-induced trance, sometimes with others:

> *I'm quite certain I have known Walter many times before... I think he's been a musician in many lives. I think he was one of the minor Bachs. There were about forty of them in at least five generations that we know of, most of them somewhere in the sixteenth century. Walter once sat down and played the harpsichord without ever having had piano lessons, as though he'd belonged to it for all of his life. He picked up a harp one day and just played it...*
>
> *I remember being a sort of official in the Roman Empire under Tiberius. Walter was my adopted son. He was Greek. We're still always arguing about the Romans and the Greeks. We make jokes and say it's a habit we've kept up for nineteen hundred years... I think I met Tiberius once. He seems to have been very much of a tough guy. I was at that time some sort of army official, an inspector of military camps. I died when a house collapsed on top of me. It was a slum someplace. I'd gone there to inspect it and it collapsed.*
>
> *When I went to England in 1978, I went to some of the Roman sites and found them very interesting. Sprague de Camp, who was very much an archaeologist, said that there couldn't have been cavalry in the Roman times because they hadn't invented the stirrup to control the horses. I know [from this past life] that they did, because they had Parthian archers who were cavalry. Sprague said no one has ever found irons for the stirrups. I seem to remember that the stirrups had been made of leather in those days...*

> *I did at one time know my name in that life but I don't remember it now. I remember seeing an inscription with my name on it. It was something like Lucius Valerius. I can't be exact about it. I saw a tombstone of one of my family, I think, in a book Walter had of Roman inscriptions.*

Bradley said her past lives may have included that of Charlotte Bronte (1816-55), the English novelist and poet whose novels include *Jane Eyre*, *Shirley* and *Villette*, and whose lyric poems are considered to be among the best in English poetry:

> *I have a feeling that I might have been Charlotte Bronte because I understand a lot of things about her that other people don't. I seem to understand about how she felt about Branwell, her brother, who was a drunk. She said in one of her letters that she had suffered a great deal with him, seeing a man whom she loved and respected deteriorate into the worst sort of person. I can relate to that because the same thing happened to my father, of whom I was extremely fond.*
>
> *Two or three times, I've had past life flashes about Charlotte. I thought I heard someone calling to me on one occasion. I later discovered what I didn't know then, that "Talli" was one of her nicknames, and I thought I'd heard someone calling me by that name. She'd evidently been called that as a small child...*
>
> *There was a poem that I kept seeing in my mind's eye, and I thought it was Emily Bronte's. I went all through her work. Then it flashed in my mind that it might have been one of those that Charlotte burned after Emily died—she burned everything she found because she knew that Emily did not want them printed. I used the poem in the end of my book,* Darkover Landfall.

Asked if she has felt any influence from Charlotte Bronte upon her writing, Bradley made this observation:

I have been very meticulous about emotions. If emotions are true, that is much more important that anything else. My late friend, Theodore Sturgeon, said that writing is the telling of passionate emotional relationships. I've always felt that way. She [Charlotte] seems to have, too. From reading her letters, one would assume that it was the most important thing in her life...

Although I believe in reincarnation, I also disbelieve it. I am not emotionally committed to the idea. I like believing that it might have been true, because Charlotte is, after all, somebody I admire tremendously. I am definitely not one of these people who gets my teeth into a theory and hangs onto it for dear life.

Bradley said her most recent past life took place around the turn of the twentieth century:

During the First World War, I was a young kid in school in Belgium someplace. I seemed to have known Walter then. And I seem to have from that life a series of very strange memories of between lives, in which I remember that I died in bombings [of my school] in the First World War around 1913–1914. I was a boy [Marty] about seventeen years old. As I was dying, I saw the kid whom I think was Walter—his name was Teddy—standing outside the door waiting for me. I said, 'Is Teddy all right?' And the school people were telling me, 'Oh, yes, he's fine.' But I knew that he'd been killed in the bombing, and that I would probably die very soon, and I did. The stranger thing is, I think I died by accident, that I should have lived and been part of that Edwardian scene. Brad [Robert Bradley] actually fought in World War I—he was in France...

Once or twice, looking in a mirror, I have seen Marty. I'll be looking in a mirror and suddenly my face will dissolve and I will see his face looking out at me. It's very much a masculine face and not at all like mine. I would say it has very sharp features, very slender and very blond.

> *In the between lives period, I seem to have realized what I was meant to do in this life. My purpose is to pick up people who have left the path and who are into a terribly materialistic thing. That's the reason why I write fantastic stuff—but almost all of fantasy is based on Hermetic philosophy. If I can convince [materialistic people] that I believe in these things, and I'm obviously not crazy, then they can believe it too and not be thought crazy.*
>
> *This is why I've been shoved into science fiction. Every time I've tried to get out of it, to write straightforward books, I've been shoved back in... I remember once a teacher asked me why did I waste my mind on something like this. I said, 'Oh, you think it's better to write stories about adultery in the suburbs?' At least in science fiction, you're thinking about the future. Science fiction is a basic sort of affirmation, in a way, that there will be a future, that the human race will survive.*
>
> *I've used [what it's like in the between lives] several times in the Darkover books. There's something I call the Overworld, which I think resembles the astral planes. In that world you present the visual image as you think of yourself. For instance, one man in my books realized that his wife and his wife's sister weren't really identical twins because they looked different in that world. Also, you can be where you want to be with the speed of light.*

In the late 1960s, Bradley's dissociative reveries of past life memories interfered with her waking consciousness, and she made an effort to suppress them:

> *Around 1967 or so I discovered that I was having these [reveries] and they were something like focal seizures. I would get wound into them and it would seem that everything was happening in slow motion very far off. I'd find myself not able to cope with the outside world. I said this wasn't doing me any good. I would stop thinking about it and turn my attention very quickly away so that I wouldn't get*

caught up in these things. I got to where I stopped them. Now they're just flashes...

I have taken LSD a few times [mostly between 1965–69]. I can't anymore because it lowers my blood sugar too much—I am diabetic. I don't think it [had anything to do with past-life recall]. It's true that the central vision of The Mists of Avalon *came from it. The last time I took it was when I started working on* Mists. *It was in 1978. By then I had tapered off to taking it about once a year as a sort of religious experience: the sort of thing where you take two days to prepare, one day to take it and two days to integrate the insights from it. There was never any case of taking it just for fun. I'd read a lot about its use in psychology [when] it was not illegal...*

The flood of ideas that I got coalesced into the central vision [of Mists*]. I focused on the training of the priestesses, which was another of my past lives. I think I have always been a priestess, on several occasions, through most of pre-history and up until about the fourth century. In the early days most women did nothing but sit around and spin. Priestesses were entrusted with almost all the medical knowledge and time keeping... I wrote a lot about that in* Firebrand.

Bradley had past life memories involving her first husband, Robert Bradley. However, Brad, as he was called, didn't take them very seriously. Bradley portrayed him (to his annoyance) in two of her works: as Frobisher in the short story *Hero's Moon* and as Riveda in the novel *The Fall of Atlantis*. None of her past life recollections involving Walter has shed light on why she and he met time and time again:

I have sometimes thought of this Platonics idea... that the real thing is complete in some other basic world and in this world we're just trying to attain it as if it were there in perfect form. Here in this world we get a dim echo if it. This is the true theory of 'archetypes.'

15

Lessons and Missions

LOOKING AT PAST LIVES often fosters growth. As Cayce noted, every soul reincarnates with a specific agenda of karmic lessons to learn and debts to repay. Sometimes, in the course of a life, one loses sight of that agenda, resulting in the need to return yet once again. By examining past lives, a person can see reasons for present situations and relationships. One also may see patterns of behavior and mistakes; in many cases, repeated opportunities may have been presented for a particular balancing of karma, yet were ignored or missed. The knowledge gleaned from past lives can quicken karmic growth by keeping us on the right track.

Past lives also can bring us into a greater understanding of who we are. The memories which surface, no matter by what method, do so for a reason: to teach us about ourselves. We view our tragedies and triumphs, failures and successes, and strengths and weaknesses. It is then up to us to put the information to good use.

To know thyself

Laurie McQuary extensively explored some of her own past lives and learned a great deal about herself. Most of her information surfaced spontaneously through intuition and what she called a "cognizant knowing," which enabled her to tune into the past. She also obtained past-life information from her own dreams, from consultation with other psychics and regressionists, and from her own readings for others.

Earlier in her present life, McQuary felt like she was always on the run, from abusive relationships and financial hardship. Past lives helped her put those circumstances in perspective and break negative patterns so that she could become stronger and whole. In addition, she got closer in touch with her deep feeling of kinship with the American Indian. She talked about some of her past-life recollections:

> *As early as eighteen, I recognized I was on my own trying to figure out where I belonged in life. I investigated up to eight religions, trying to find one where I fit. I never found anything until I discovered the Spiritualist Church, which is quite a believer in reincarnation. This was twenty-six or twenty-seven years ago, and reincarnation was not a big fad then—people didn't talk about it and I had never heard about it. But the moment I heard the theory, it felt right. I knew there had to be some explanation for everything I'd gone through even up to eighteen.*
>
> *I've had a problem with men in my life, being mistreated mentally and physically from the time I was little. I was always trying to understand why. I was sexually abused as a small child by my stepfather, whom I believed was my father. I was only two when my mother married him and he died of cancer when I was seven. The day he died, she told me he wasn't my father.*
>
> *I had other incidents of abuse from strangers, until I was eleven or twelve. Then my mother remarried for the third time and that man beat me until I was eighteen. In his past lifetimes, I always see*

him as an inquisitor and a judge. I'm sure I've met him before. Any time you have strong feelings about someone, either good or bad, you can bet it's from a past life.

As I began to tap into past lives, I realized that I had several lifetimes as a man who abused women. In one life, for example, I was a man in Spain, and worked for a circus or traveling show. I beat women. I was just horrible, and I ended up getting hung.

What better way to understand what it's like to be abused than to come back as an abused woman myself? After suffering childhood abuse, I then had a tendency to be drawn to the same type of man that I was in that Spanish life, sort of the self-made, off-the-wall, risque, irresponsible woman-hater. My second husband shot at me once with a forty-five-caliber. The bullet missed, went through the wall and hit the bed of the people next door.

Once I accepted what reincarnation meant, then it began to make sense to me why I've felt so attracted to certain cultures and so repelled by others. One culture in particular that mystified me for years was the Orient. Aside from not liking Chinese food, I even had an aversion to Chinese people. I didn't know why I didn't like them, I just felt turned off.

I had a dream that led to an explanation for this. In the dream, I was in the Orient and was standing next to an ox cart. There was a little, fat baby boy sitting on straw. He was naked. It was apparently summertime. I was terribly upset, crying and crying. The dream was lucid, so I was able to look at myself and say, 'That was me in a past life.' The reason I was so upset was we—the boy and I—were travelling over two hundred miles over the mountains because we had been forced to flee our homes. When I woke up, I realized the Orient had never appealed to me because of that unhappy experience in that lifetime. I have always hated making a home move, yet I recently made my seventy-fifth move in twenty-eight years. Obviously, it is a lesson for me to learn how to cope with moving.

I got more information about my negative feelings about the

Orient from a friend who did dream reincarnations for others. She was in her eighties. You would ask her for information, and she would come up with reams of paperwork about where you were and what you did. The dreams she dreamed about me in the Orient concerned another life in which I was a well-to-do physician's wife. I'm not sure of the century. My name was something to the equivalent of 'Orange Blossom,' and I had long, long black hair that was braided and coiled on top of my head with shells and ornaments. I went through the streets of China delivering my husband's medicinal herbs. I was dressed in black silk pants and an embroidered jacket done in pinks and oranges. The jacket had an elongated neck and long sleeves. I wore a lot of bracelets that were hidden up inside the sleeves. For some reasons, I carried some jewels sewn into the inside of the coat.

I was kidnapped and held for ransom by bandits from the mountains. From the way I was dressed and the jewelry I wore, and possibly because of the little rickshaw I was travelling in, I'm sure they could ascertain that I had money. They found out who my husband was, but for some reason, it never came about that he was able to rescue me. I was taken to the mountains to live with these people, and I never got to go home.

While I was in the mountains, I became impregnated and had a child. When she was about six, we ran away, but got lost and starved to death in the mountains. She is the daughter I have in this lifetime [Kirsten]. We've been alone a lot together in this life. I lost her father [first husband] when she was five months old, and we experienced the same feeling of survival from that past life. Also in this lifetime, I had a deep seated anxiety that bordered on fear about getting home before dark, especially in the wintertime. I feel it was connected to that kidnapping.

Another past life of hardship and desperation involved McQuary's son, Scott, from her second marriage:

> *It was back in ancient times in the Middle East, and we were very poor. I had several children and the boy who was Scott was my oldest child. To make ends meet, I sent him out to beg. So that he would be more appealing to people, I maimed him on purpose, by scarring his face with a piece of burning wood. When I flashed on this, it nearly killed me. It brought tears to my face. I told Scott about it. He's very psychic and has tremendous past life dreams himself. This struck chords with both of us.*
>
> *In the present life, things were real hard financially for us for years. I was divorced from my second husband for seven years and it was nothing but hard times. The same emotions, and sometimes the circumstances, will be the same as what you've gone through in another lifetime.*

In another of the many lives she recalls, McQuary remembers again running from trouble:

> *I was in Spain around the sixteenth century. My second husband in this life was a priest and I was an important lady and had money. There was some kind of war or upset going on, and I had great fear for my land, my money and my life. The priest sheltered me by taking me into a monastery or abbey. He was a like a mentor and taught me a lot.*

Also during that life, McQuary said she abused horses, a karmic debt that led, ironically, to the flowering of her psychic talent in the present. When she was eighteen, she was bucked off a horse in California, struck her head and lapsed into a coma for three weeks. A few months after she regained consciousness, she began having precognitive dreams and experiencing telepathy. The experiences initially frightened her, but she eventually accepted her new ability and learned how to control and use it.

While she was a lady of position and power in sixteenth century Spain,

McQuary said that in a subsequent life, about two hundred years later, she was a working class woman who ran away from responsibility:

> *I was a curly-haired blonde in eighteenth century England. I wore a white dress with a corset and bodice. I was probably nothing more than a call girl, and I had absolutely no responsibilities in life. All I wanted to do was party. I saw myself playing on this hillside. There was another woman and we were just having a high old time, drinking and running around. I knew that this is why I now have a problem with women who are totally irresponsible and misuse their sexuality.*

While some past lives have explained to McQuary some of her aversions and difficulties, others have explained the reason for her lifelong identification with the American Indian, particularly the Apache of the Southwest, and also the Cherokee and Sioux. When she has participated in shamanic workshops, she immediately has found herself transported back in time about one hundred to two hundred years. Her affinity with Indians is so strong that she contemplated relocating to the Southwest, a move that for her would be "going home":

> *From the time I was about seven, I would tell total strangers that I was an Apache Indian. My parents probably thought I needed a psychiatrist! We lived in Cleveland, Ohio, and we had nothing to do with Indians, but I was absolutely convinced that I was part Indian. In the eighth grade, I once got up in social studies class, furious because my teacher said the Indians were 'savages.' I had never read anything about them, but I gave a discourse in class on the Indians, what their society was like and that they were not savages, but had rules to live by. The whole class laughed at me.*
>
> *All through my growing up years I continued to be fascinated with American Indians. I read all I could about them. When I was*

about fifteen, I decided that one day I would live on an Indian reservation. When I was thirty-four, I went to live on the Warm Springs reservation [in Oregon]. My husband at the time was hired as the drug and alcohol counselor, and I was a nurse. I lived there for a year and a half and I loved it. It certainly didn't happen by design. I think I had to complete that part of myself. While I was there, I often was asked if I was part Indian. I find many times that if you have a particular lifetime that you're still tied to, you will reflect that look no matter what your nationality is in this lifetime.

Through past-life recall, McQuary discovered that she has had numerous lives as an American Indian, including one in which she and Scott were husband and wife. In another Indian life, she was a young woman with an unusual occupation:

I was Cherokee or Sioux, in the North Plains. I was very different for that time in that I didn't want a man in my life. I wanted to be left alone and free. I became a runner for my tribe, carrying messages to and from other tribes. The Indians did allow people their individuality. I probably wasn't totally accepted by everyone, but I was given other accolades and told I could do certain things and be my own person. I saw myself running and getting lost, and having a bad fall in a crevasse, where I died. I was probably in my twenties. There also seems to have been a thwarted love affair, a young man in my tribe who loved me. I cared about him, but I needed to reject him.

McQuary also remembers several past lives in ancient Egypt, another culture with which she feels a strong connection. She believes she may have been the only female pharaoh, Hatshepsut, who ruled in the Eighteenth Dynasty of the New Kingdom, from about 1506 B.C.E. until her death in 1482 B.C.E. When Pharaoh Thutmose II died in 1504 B.C.E., he had no male heirs by Hatshepsut, who was his major queen. The throne was passed to Thutmose III, a ten-year-old boy by a minor wife, and Hatshepsut was named regent. In the second year of Thutmose III's regency, Hatshepsut boldly took the kingship herself and became the dominant ruling party. She pursued a pacifist policy during her reign. Much of her statuary and relief art depicts her as male. When Thutmose assumed sole rule upon her death, he launched a more aggressive, warlike policy. Later in his reign, an effort was made to erase the memory and defile the name of Hatshepsut. McQuary first learned about her from a book by Barbara Corcoran, *Child of the Morning*:

> *When I started reading it, the descriptions, plus all the descriptions of her felt very, very familiar, especially the description of her as a child and the way she started to grow into a young woman. I felt there was every possibility that I may have been her. She was a pharaoh at sixteen and ruled very well.*

The running theme has emerged in various ways in McQuary's past lives, but usually with a stressful or unhappy end: she fled her home in the Orient with the infant boy, ran away from her kidnappers in China, fled her troubles in Spain by taking shelter in a monastery, and ran away from responsibility as the English prostitute. Her unorthodox occupation as a female Indian runner allowed her to run emotionally from a young suitor. McQuary applies her insights from these experiences to her present relationships:

> *The lesson is certainly not to get into destructive relationships to begin with, but if you are in one, you don't run from it, you learn from it and work it out before you move on...*
>
> *I recently remarried [for the third time] and now I have a marvelous husband. I know I knew him in the 1800s in the early West perhaps in southern California or parts of Nevada. I was an Indian [perhaps Apache] and he was a trapper. He still has a love for every-*

thing about the Old West. He's from Reno, Nevada, so that's probably part of it, but I can picture him in that past life. He even looks the part of a trapper: he has a beard and rugged appearance.

McQuary said she has had more lives as a man than as a woman, yet her lessons have come primarily from her female lifetimes, including the present. From them she has learned about the use and abuse of power, and about taking responsibility:

> *This lifetime is the one that I've learned the most from about being a woman, and being a complete woman. I think what women need is recognition without sacrifice and love without compromise. It's taken me all of these lifetimes to learn that, and in this lifetime, to stand up to it. I've learned how to be a man, but I never learned how to be a woman. That's the gift of being able to see my past lives.*
>
> *The lessons for me are stand up and be my own person and not be afraid of my own power, which involves the ability see myself through my own eyes, not someone else's eyes; also, to tap into my male side in order to be a strong, assertive female, not aggressive. Everyone has male and female energies, and needs to balance the two.*

The emptiness of materialism

One of Ian Stevenson's cases concerned a young man who learned, from remembering his previous life, that indulging oneself in possessions and sensual pleasures does not bring happiness.

In turn of the century India, Laxmi Narain was an arrogant young man with fine taste in beautiful women, good food and liquor, and expensive silk clothing. As a wealthy member of the Kayastha caste in Pilibhit, he devoted himself to spending his money in pursuit of these pleasures. He didn't need to work; his inheritance left by his father, Har Narain, spared him that drudgery. He quarreled with his relatives over family property, sued for it, and won. He lived in fine style.

Narain was not without some redeeming qualities, however. He gave much money and food to the poor. He was devoutly religious, though he had a strange way of worshipping. At the start of every month, he sequestered himself in the shrine room of his house for ten to fifteen days, meditating and praying, and taking all his meals there. The rest of the month, he threw fabulous parties with great feasts of meat, *rohu* fish and wine, accompanied by dancing girls and much singing. Narain often played the *tablas*, a kind of drum which requires a great deal of discipline. For another diversion, he liked to fly kites with a neighbor friend, Sunder Lal.

As a child, Narain had recalled a previous life as a rajah's son. It was never verified, as his parents were fearful of harmful publicity.

He never applied himself to his studies, and lagged far behind his classmates. By age seventeen or eighteen, he had completed the studies of a twelve-year-old. He dropped out of school when his father died.

Though Narain had many women, his favorite was a prostitute named Padma, whom he considered exclusively his. Padma did not share this enthusiasm. One day, Narain spied another man coming out of her apartment, and exploded in rage. He grabbed a gun that his servant always carried, raced up to the rival and shot him dead.

Narain fled to the sanctuary of his house, where he isolated himself. With his money and influence, he got away with the crime. He felt it would be best to move, so he did, to Shajahanpur. He had no remorse about killing his rival, and was happy not to have been held accountable for it.

But the law of karma was about to catch up with him.

In 1918, not long after his crime, Narain fell ill with fever and lung trouble. He suffered for five months and died on December 15 of that year, at the age of thirty-two. His freewheeling, rich days were over. For a lifetime, at least.

Another case investigated by Stevenson was that of Bishen Chand. The subject was four years old when his father, B. Ram Ghulam Kapoor, took him and his older brother to a wedding party in Golda, India. They travelled by train from their home in Bareilly. On the return trip, the train stopped in Pilibhit, which is about fifty kilometers from Bareilly. Much to the surprise of his father, Bishen Chand demanded to get off, saying he used to live in Pilibhit. His father denied him, and Bishen Chand cried all the way home.

Bishen Chand was born on February 7, 1921, and from the age of ten months, he had muttered about "Pilvit" or "Pilivit." As he grew older and learned more words, he said he had lived before as Laxmi Narain. He had an "uncle" named Har Narain. His family ignored him, out of superstition that children who speak of previous lives will die early.

B. Ram Ghulam worked as a railway clerk and barely managed to support his family. They were members of the Khsatriya caste, much lower than the caste to which Laxmi Narain had belonged. They were vegetarians and drank no alcohol.

This lifestyle did not suit little Bishen Chand at all. He criticized his father for being poor and not being able to build a house. He ripped off his cheap cotton clothes and demanded silk garments. Without being taught, he skillfully played the *tablas*. Around the age of five, he demanded to eat meat and drink alcohol. He told his parents that even his servants would not eat the vegetarian food served in the house. When he couldn't get meat at home, he went to neighbors and ate it in secret. Once his family once bought some brandy for medicinal use. It began "evaporating;" Bishen Chand's sister caught him drinking it. The haughty boy said he was "used" to drinking.

At about the same time, Bishen Chand astonished his father by asking him why the older man did not keep a mistress, for he would derive great pleasure from her, enjoying the fragrance of her hair and joy from her company.

Word of Bishen Chand reached K.K.N. Sahay, a lawyer who was investigating the past-life memories of his own son. Sahay visited Bishen Chand

and persuaded the boy's father to let him verify the story. He recorded twenty-one statements about the life of Laxmi Narain as recalled by Bishen Chand.

In August 1926, Sahay took Bishen Chand on two visits to Pilibhit. The boy did not recognize his old school—not surprising, in view of Laxmi Narain's attitude toward education—but did recognize the ruins of his former home. Narain had spent so much of his inheritance that, after his death, his mother and relatives were destitute, and the house was allowed to disintegrate to a heap of bricks and mud. Significantly, Bishen Chand knew the layout of the house when it had existed in better shape, and pointed to the correct spot where the staircase had been located. He cried over the ruins, and that fact that the house had not been maintained.

He was handed a photograph of Har Narain and Laxmi Narain, and he correctly identified them.

The Pilhibit police superintendent casually asked Bishen Chand to tell about Narain's wife and children. The boy replied in first person, saying he had no children because he had been too steeped in wine and women to consider marrying.

Of the twenty-one statements recorded by Sahay, fourteen were verified as correct. In all, forty-eight statements were made. Nearly all were correct. Only two were incorrect: Bishen Chand's identification of Har Narain as his former uncle, and his assertion that Laxmi Narain had died at age twenty, not thirty-two.

Bishen Chand showed a great deal of affection to Laxmi Narain's mother, preferring her to his own. He even implored his father to allow his former mother to live with them; however, to his sorrow, she moved to another town.

He remembered the murder very clearly, and spoke of it often to his siblings. Like Narain, he had no remorse over it. He displayed a bad temper, and was quarrelsome with some of Laxmi Narain's relatives—perhaps a holdover of the old lawsuit.

Unlike Laxmi, he never showed an interest in kite flying. But he did recognize the gate of his late friend, Sunder Lal.

Padma came to visit when the boy was about six. He still carried a torch for her, but she pointed out to him that he was but a small child while she was "old" (probably in her mid-thirties).

By age seven, the only memories Bishen Chand retained of Laxmi Narain were the murder and his attachment to Padma. He quit playing the tablas at age eight, and gradually accepted the poverty of his family which relegated him to cheap cotton clothes. He completed his education and went to work for the government, earning a meager living as an excise officer.

In 1944, Bishen Chand saw Padma again by accident. He recognized her, even though she was by now about fifty-two and he had not seen her for nearly twenty years. He hugged her and fainted. That night, he bought a bottle of wine and went to her house. She threw him out and told him to go away. "You lost everything in your previous life," she said. "Now you want to lose everything again."

Two years later, at age twenty-five, Bishen Chand married a girl who, like his parents, was vegetarian and would allow no meat or fish in the house. His small income limited them to simple clothes and a modest lifestyle; he felt he should be giving away money to help others, but had no money to give. His was a far cry from the exotic, luxurious life of Laxmi Narain, and it made him feel bitter.

To his credit, he changed over time. Stevenson visited with Bishen Chand in 1969, when he was forty-eight. He still remembered the murder in vivid detail. He felt he had learned from his experiences. He reflected that he was now suffering poverty because of his spoiled behavior and the murder he committed in his previous life.

Stevenson observed that Bishen Chand was a person "who had learned that material goods and carnal pleasures do not bring happiness." In his next life, were he to have one, Bishen Chand desired not wealth but superior intelligence and mental qualities that would help him achieve something of significance.

Unfinished business

Some persons are born with an innate sense of purpose; others find it. In either case, past-life recall can sharpen one's focus or steer one back on track. Kerry (a pseudonym), is a West Coast writer with a lifelong interest in metaphysics and the occult. As she grew older, she felt the influence of past lives:

> *From the time I was small, I've been a compulsive writer. As a kid, I wrote stories, even little books, which I wrote out by hand or typed on this old typewriter, and then bound in cardboard. Most of all, I was a recorder of sorts. I had journals and record books on all kinds of subjects. I started neighborhood and school newspapers. I was fascinated by mythology, especially classical mythology.*
>
> *I also felt very old, even when I was a child. I once wrote in one of my diaries that I felt like 'an old, old woman who's cried a thousand times a thousand tears and lived a thousand lives a thousand years.' That's a little nonsensical, but I think I was tapping into the feeling of having lived many lives. I've believed in reincarnation for a long time. When I was a teenager, I rejected Christian teachings about one life on earth and then heaven or hell for eternity. It made no sense, especially in light of the incredible inequities of life experienced on this planet...*
>
> *I feel it's important to use my abilities as a writer to spread knowledge about the hidden side of things. In my research, I feel like I've clicked into things that I've known before. Sometimes I feel like a hollow straw, drawing up stuff from some unknown reservoir. I feel guided. There's this presence around me, a being I perceive as female. I have seen her in dreams. There are others as well, but she seems to be the key one.*
>
> *I went through a past-life regression once to see if I could find out*

the sources of my writing ability and sense of purpose. It was a light hypnosis. Even though I believe in reincarnation, I was a little skeptical about really seeing a past life and not something conjured up out of my imagination. Out of all the things I might have imagined, what I saw wasn't any of them.

When I stepped out of the tunnel, I found myself in some town or village that seemed to be medieval. The streets were very narrow. I was surprised at who I was—I was a man, small, thin and homely. I had a big nose and close-set, almost beady eyes. Everything about me was plain—plain brown hair, plain brown clothes, a sort of tunic outfit with brown shoes. Very drab. I knew I lived alone. It came to me that I was some sort of tradesman. I could see myself delivering big bundles that I carried on my shoulder to monks who lived in a monastery. I saw things in little vignettes, almost like freeze frames, except there was motion within the frame. It was like looking at a series of snapshots which became animated.

Everything about me, who I was and what I did for a living, felt small and unimportant, but somehow I had gotten an education. There was no explanation given as to how a lowly tradesman came to be educated. Anyway, I saw myself attending a lecture, sitting on a small bench listening to a learned man talk. I don't know who he was, but he was a Paracelsus type, an alchemist. I was very absorbed in what he had to say. I had the feeling I went to lectures often. It came to me that I was convinced that 'the monks had gotten it all wrong' about certain spiritual truths.

Then I jumped to the next frame, where I saw myself sitting in my little room—I think I lived over a tavern or something—I was on a wooden bench at a table, and I was writing on paper. It was difficult for me. I felt I was writing the Truth, recording it, preserving it. I had no idea what would happen to the writings, but whether or not they would ever be published was not the point. In the regression, I could see my iridescent spirit guide standing over me while I labored away, like she was showing me this scene in particular.

All of a sudden I felt a sharp pain in my right eye, and it almost jarred me out of the regression. It was like a nail or needle was being stabbed straight through it, and I lost the picture of me sitting there writing. I said, 'Oh, the monks have ruined my eye!' It came to me in a flash that my writings had been discovered and I had been tortured for heresy. Probably killed, but I didn't see my death. I was so unprepared for this that I did not go back into [the regression] and find out.

What hit home for me was that when I was about eight [in the present life], it was discovered that I suffered from amblyopia in my right eye. It's where the eye muscles are weak and result in 'lazy eye.' The eye is near-sighted and sometimes turns inward to become cross-eyed. I wasn't cross-eyed, but my right eye was extremely near-sighted, while I had perfect vision in my left eye. For years, I wore glasses with plain glass in the left eye. When I switched to contacts, I only had to wear one, in my right eye. When I got into my twenties, my left eye began to go near-sighted, but my right eye is still far worse. I haven't thought about the amblyopia in years. It struck me that this condition is a lingering trace of this past life.

I feel I am writing now what I didn't finish then, drawing up material from that and other past lives in which I was a keeper of knowledge. I have a sense that I have had at least several past lives where I have been involved in arcane arts and knowledge, and in ritual. In this life I am spreading the same knowledge in a different way, through books and articles. It's my theory that many persons who are involved in the New Age area—and I'm not talking about the fads—had past lives in which they were holy men and women, healers, magicians and the like. They have reincarnated in the present to help others reunite with spirit. That's one of the main reasons why I'm here.

16

A Pagan Priestess Finds Her Roots

FROM AN EARLY AGE, Selena Fox has had a sense of mission, a distinct feeling that she is here to help make some changes for the better on Planet Earth. Her mission has manifested in the form of a planetary healing ministry and Circle Sanctuary, a Wiccan church located on a nature preserve and herb farm between Mt. Horeb and Barneveld, Wisconsin. Circle Sanctuary focuses on communion with the Divine through Nature. As high priestess of Circle, Selena, along with her husband, Dennis Carpenter, directs a wide range of spiritual, environmental, healing, personal growth, and networking activities for national and international Nature religions groups. They also devote much effort to defending religious freedom rights for Wiccans and Pagans.

Meeting Selena is to be touched by a warm and loving presence. "Earth Mother" is a term that springs to mind. She is deeply connected to Nature, and radiates an aura of harmony with the elemental forces and the psychic vibrations of the planet. She is also deeply connected to the Goddess. Over the years, Selena has come to recognize that her skills, knowledge and mission in this life have been developed over a series of lifetimes. She told me:

> *My earliest recollection of past life material came to me as a child, especially during my teen years. I found I had a very strong affinity with ancient Rome, in particular the time of Caesar Augustus. I became immersed in Roman mythology. I had been raised a Southern Baptist, and as I was drawn to the study of classical Latin, it completely surprised my parents. I picked up Latin very easily and won awards in junior high and high school, and I went on to become president of the classics honor society in college. I feel part of myself in this life is rooted in ancient Rome. In terms of any historical figures I've felt an affinity with, it is Caesar Augustus' daughter, Julia. Whether I was her or just connected with her in some way, I don't know, but I have been intrigued by her ever since I began my studies of ancient Rome.*

From childhood, Selena has had psychic and mystical visions, and has experienced out-of-body travel. Such experiences, coupled with her interest in classics, led her to Wicca and Paganism. She conducted her first Pagan ritual at age twenty-one, as president of Eta Sigma Phi, the classics honor society, at the College of William and Mary in Virginia. She graduated *cum laude* with a bachelor of science degree in psychology. Following college, she was initiated into several Wiccan traditions, which are comparable to denominations in Christianity.

In 1974, not long after moving to Wisconsin, Selena was inspired in a meditation to found Circle Sanctuary. With her partner at the time, Jim Alan, and a group of friends, she formed the beginnings of Circle Sanctuary, which was incorporated as a Wiccan church in 1978. The same year, Selena devoted herself full time to her ministry. In 1983, Circle purchased a 200-acre nature preserve, where it is presently located.

Despite the growth and success of Circle, and Selena's personal feelings of accomplishment and contribution concerning her mission, the path has been strewn with obstacles. Chief among those are the misconceptions of non-Pagans, who equate Wicca and Paganism with devil-worship—a problem rooted in past lives, Selena has discovered.

Some of Selena's most meaningful past life information has come to her in dreams. Her past-life dreams are always unusual: highly vivid, intense, often lucid. They occur spontaneously, and are harbingers of events to come which enable her to integrate past-life memories or experiences into her present life. The information sheds much light on who she is and her present mission as a Pagan priestess. "Whenever I have a dream like this, which some people would call a lucid dream, or high dream, or big dream, I spend considerable time in my waking life reflecting as to why I had it and what is the message," Selena said.

She has also experienced past-life recollections in flashbacks. She had a strong flashback in 1986, during a prolonged legal controversy over the zoning of the Circle Sanctuary land, an issue that had the potential to affect the ability of Circle to operate as a church. When the zoning issues were raised by local government, Selena and Dennis were required to secure legal help. The issue was clouded by mistaken local sentiment that Circle was a satanic group, and Selena and Dennis attended numerous hearings and public meetings to set the record straight and defend their rights. The hearings were dubbed "the Witch Trials of Barneveld" in the media. Selena described what happened one night:

> *I walked into the hearing room, which was packed with people. There was a line of older white men sitting behind a table in the front. Feelings came up within me about me being on trial—being tried as a Witch in the Middle Ages. It was a very stressful and trying experience for me. I was interrogated by people in the audience and by government officials, and I did my best to answer their questions about me and my religious practices. It certainly was nothing compared to what went on in the Middle Ages, but I felt myself reliving*

something that I had been through before. Over the years, I've had dreams about dying as a Witch. There were Witch trials and intense persecution, and I saw myself being burned.

I think part of the reason why I'm such a strong activist for the Wiccan religion is not just because of what has been done to me personally and to Circle Sanctuary as Wiccan church, but because I feel that I've come back in this life to help revive Nature religions.

I also believe some of the knowledge I have about working with herbs and doing meditations with nature are a result of having been a Witch in another life, and now that knowledge has come back in this life. I have a very strong affinity with certain plants, such as lemon balm, mint and mugwort, which I think goes beyond this life. When I am out picking herbs or walking in nature, things come to me intuitively.

The following are Selena's accounts of three startling past-life experiences, all of which began with dreams. The first occurred in the summer of 1973, within a year of her move to Madison, Wisconsin. Selena was unfamiliar with the state and its history and geography; Circle Sanctuary had yet to be born.

Life #1: The Mound Builders

I had only been in Madison for a short while. I was enrolled at a technical school, studying commercial art and photography, and I was involved in creative development. I mention this because it is my theory that people who make creative work part of their day-to-day activities are more likely to trigger "peak experiences" within themselves.

One night, I had this very, very vivid dream. I saw myself as a young boy, an adolescent about age twelve, and I was wearing some kind of light-colored, loose garment. It was summer solstice. I was looking out over a grassy plain at a long, serpentine procession of people. The whole tribe marching in ceremony, with drumming and chanting, and approaching a gigantic earthen step pyramid that rose up out of the ground to about twenty feet in height. It was called the Temple of the Sun or the Mound of the Sun. I could see another pyramid mound, the Temple of the Moon, off in the distance and then another one, the Temple of the Earth. At first, I felt myself part of the procession. Then I went up to the top of the mound with what appeared to be a priest. There was a fire there—I felt it was an eternal solar fire, kept going all the time—and some kind of altar. I was playing a role in the ceremony, rather like an altar boy. I felt like I was there, yet part of me was watching myself as I was reliving this experience.

I saw myself looking out over the procession. The sun was high in the sky. The people wore feathered headdresses, not like Plains Indians, but more like Aztecs or Maya. They had shiny breastplates perhaps made out of gold, copper or some brass-like metal. The breastplates just gleamed and glittered in the sun—they were radiant. The chanting stopped. In the silence, offerings were made—herbs were put into the fire, and the incense was very sweet. As the perfume rose in the air, the chanting began again. I looked down at the wave of people. Suddenly I found myself leaving my body from this scene and traveling rapidly through time and space, and then I felt myself back in the present.

It was a lucid dream, almost like an astral projection. I was aware of what was going on; I was even aware that I was dreaming. Throughout it, I was in a very high spiritual state. As I was coming back into my body in the here and now, I felt myself ask, "Where is this place, where is this place?" I had never heard of anything like earthen pyramid mounds existing in Wisconsin. Then flashing before my mind's eye, I saw a map of Wisconsin, and a forefinger pointing to a spot about midway between Madison and Milwaukee. I saw no other names on the map, just a straight line, like a road, and a finger pointing to this spot. Then I woke up. I was so taken by the experience that the first thing I did before writing the dream down was to get a Wisconsin map. I moved my finger along the map and saw there was an interstate highway between Madison and Milwaukee. I moved my hand along and came to a point that approximated the point on the map in my dreams. I saw the word "Aztalan" and chills ran up and down my spine. I knew that was it. Instant recognition! And I knew I had to visit that place, though I did not own a vehicle at the time and had no transportation.

For the next several weeks, I asked various people about Aztalan. I had been a student of ancient Greek and Roman cultures, but knew practically nothing about ancient Paganism in America. I found out that the spot I saw on the map was now a park, but had once been the site of an ancient Indian village and pyramid mounds. It had been known to Indian tribes for centuries, though it had not been settled by tribes native to the area. In fact, it was taboo to the Woodlands Indians.

I was part of a mystical group, and a few of us decided to take a field trip to Aztalan. None of us had ever been to the park, but we found it easily, relying on extrasensory perception whenever we hit an unmarked fork in the road. When we arrived, I saw two of the three mounds in my dream and had a feeling of great recognition and excitement. I said, "Here they are! Here they are!" They didn't look exactly like the ones in my dream, but were very similar—things obviously have changed—with the exception that only two of the three mounds exist in the here and now. There were no signs of a village.

I went up to the larger mound, which I recognized as the Temple of the Sun. The Temple of the Moon was the smaller of the two mounds. The Temple of the Earth was not visible—the site was flat and had trees growing on it. The vibrations were very strong. I felt a real sense of bonding with the place—that I had lived there before and had come home. My friends and I spent the day there, recharging our energies from the spiritual vibrations of this place. We had a feast, and then went up to the top of the mounds and meditated on their mystery. I felt very protective of the place, and still do. I feel there are many mysteries connected with the site that are buried somewhere in my psyche, and over the years I have had a quest to find out more about Aztalan.

I went to the state historical society and talked with a woman that who had worked on an archaeological dig there. She told me there had been a third mound, but her findings weren't published. She seemed amazed that I knew about the third mound.

I found that the site was discovered by whites in 1835. A man named Nathaniel Hyer named it "Aztalan," which means "near water," because it seemed to match a site from an ancient Aztec legend. According to the legend, the Aztecs' homeland, "Aztalan," was somewhere far north of Mexico. Hyer believed that they had once lived in Wisconsin, and that the "near water" referred to the Crawfish River in Wisconsin, or to the Great Lakes. A map was drawn of the place in 1855. Hyer and some others tried to preserve the site, but in the late 1800s, it was sold for farmland for twenty-two dollars and a lot of it was plowed under. Dirt from the mounds was hauled out to fill potholes in roads, and artifacts were carted out by the truckload. As a white settlement, Aztalan was a bustling community for awhile, but the railroad passed it by and it turned into a ghost town. I believe that really had something to do with the fact that the sacred site was desecrated—a causal effect.

Fortunately, in the 1900s there was a greater awareness about these ancient sites and the need to preserve them. A scientific study was made in 1919, and in 1921, the site was turned into the Aztalan Mound Park and was presented to the Wisconsin Archaeological Society. In 1952, it was made a state park, and the two remaining mounds were restored to as close to their former state as possible. Also, archaeologists believed that the site had once been surrounded by a stockade, and a replica of part of the stockade was erected. The park became a National Historical Landmark in 1964.

Nobody really knows who the original builders of Aztalan were, or why their civilization died. Archaeologists believe it was occupied between about 1100 and 1300 by a people who were very different *from the surrounding Woodlands tribes, and had a much more complex society, closer to that of tribes in the southeastern United States or Mexico. The village seems to have been large, but no burial grounds have been found. The remains of what appear to be an Indian princess were found in 1920, in a place that was then named "Princess Mound." She had been wrapped in belts of clam or oyster shells.*

The pyramids clearly were built for religious ceremonial purposes. Remains of a fire were found on top of "Old Smokey," which is what archaeologists call the largest one, which I call the Temple of the Sun. That certainly checks out with my dream. The remains of what appear to be tree underwater stone pyramids have been found at the bottom of Rock Lake, which is nearby.

Finding this place awakened a deep part of myself, and was a very powerful experience. In subsequent years, I've gone there and taken photographs and meditated. I've tried to bring recognition and honor to the Indians who once were there. Some of the archaeological reports call them cannibals, and I'm really disturbed by that. I don't feel that is accurate at all. There have been other archaeological theories that just haven't felt right to me. But, I'm relying on an intuitive sense about the place.

I felt I was guided to Aztalan as a way of connecting with part of my spiritual heritage. At the time, I was becoming more seriously involved in Paganism. I was beginning to allow my intuitive self more of a priority in my day-to-day life. This helped usher me into my Pagan priestess work, as well as help me achieve a balance within my own self. In college, I'd gotten a bachelor of science degree in psychology rather than a bachelor of arts. Part of me is very skeptical, and needs to be convinced about experiences which can't be explained logically. This experience made me aware how rich consciousness can be, and how it is possible to get information through our own dreams, imagination and psyche, as well as through the intellectual route of studying books. The world has a lot more mys-

teries than it appears.

What I also got from this is that there is an inner impulse guiding me along the path of my Pagan priestesshood, to look at mystery religions and explore the unknown. Since then, as I have walked on the land here at Circle Sanctuary, I have literally had artifacts rise up out of the land to me, and I have felt a real affinity with Native American Indian ways. At times, I've been told that in rituals, when I'm chanting or doing healing work, I actually look like a Native American. I do have a bit of American Indian blood in me, but I also have a sense that I did live as one at least once previously.

Life #2: Egypt

The same year, in December 1973, near the winter solstice, I visited my parents, who at the time were living near Washington, D.C. One night, I had this dream in which I saw myself in this life connecting ceremonial objects and statutes of deities, which it seemed, I had once used in ancient Egypt. The feeling I had in the dream was that I had been a priestess in a temple, or possibly a priest, and that I had once cared for these or similar objects. I had a very strong feeling that I needed to find them, connect with them again. In the dream, I saw myself going through the halls of the Smithsonian's Museum of Natural History, and going down into the basement and through a set of doors. I found these Egyptian objects in the basement. As I held them in my hands, I felt connections with the past resurrecting within myself. I could feel memories and feelings coming from these objects, which rekindled some of the spiritual work I had done at that time, and brought it up into my consciousness.

Upon awakening, I was seized with a very strong feeling to go to the Smithsonian to see if indeed these objects were there. The dream was so vivid, and had such clear colors and intense feelings, that I regarded it as a very special dream of guidance. There was some important link in my past that this dream was speaking about.

I was so convinced that the objects were at the Smithsonian that I called up a friend of mine, who has a master's degree in anthropology and was visiting the area at that time. I said, "Let's go to the Egyptian exhibit at the Smithsonian." He said, "What Egyptian exhibit?" There wasn't one at that time! But I knew I would find these things there. He agreed to meet me at the museum.

I arrived a little early. I went up to the information desk and asked for the Egyptian exhibit. I was told the museum didn't have one, only a sarcophagus mummy that was on display. I said I was there to see some Egyptian artifacts that I believed were kept in the museum. The woman seemed a little puzzled by that but called one of the curators of the museum. Evidently somebody was in charge of Egyptian artifacts. It was arranged for me to immediately see this person, which must have been unusual, as I had not gone through the customary protocol of writing in advance to get a pass to a nonpublic area.

My friend arrived, and we met this curator, a very nice, very dignified, tall, black man who wore a big gold ankh around his neck and had a air of mystery about him, like an aura of being a guardian priest. He didn't say much, just "Come with me." It was almost as though he thought I'd been sent. He took us down to the basement of the museum and through a pair of doorways—just like I had done in my dream—and into this room where there were cabinets with drawers full of artifacts.

I was allowed to go through the drawers, looking at the artifacts and handling them. After several hours, I hadn't found the things I had seen in my dreams. Then I opened up the last drawer, and there they were! Statues of various Egyptian deities—Osiris, Isis and Bast, the cat goddess. I was particularly drawn to the cat goddess statues, and there were several of those. Some were about six inches tall and clearly were statues intended to be put on altars. There were amulets which were a few inches high.

I was so elated. It's hard to put my feelings into words. As I handled these and the other objects, I felt shivers go up and down my spine and surges of electricity go through me. I was so excited—it was so wonderful to reconnect with these objects. I don't know if these were the same objects from another life or only similar, but finding them had a dramatic impact on me spiritually. I felt power coming from the objects and passing into myself, as if I had reclaimed a spiritual heritage. A part of me connected with something very, very old, and it seemed to be an aspect of myself, a part of my soul. I felt this in both my body and my heart. My friend was amazed, and we both continued to be in a high spiritual state for the rest of the day, long after we left the museum.

This experience proved to be the turning point in my spiritual leadership work as a priestess in this life. Shortly after this happened, I became a priestess of a ceremonial magic group. I worked with a man, a priest of the group, who was very interested and involved in the study of ancient Egypt. The group itself delved more into the Egyptian mysteries. There was a synchronicity involved, a feeling among all of us that we had been in ancient Egypt together, though I don't know during which dynasty.

Other synchronistic things happened. Once, I was in a shopping mall and had the intuitive urge to go in a book store. There I found a statute of Bast, which I purchased and still have to this day. Over the years, I have connected with still other people interested in studying about the ancient Egyptian religion.

Life #3: Maya in the Yucatan

In 1986, on Beltane [May Day], I had a dream in which I saw myself in a Mayan jungle in the Yucatan questing for the remains of a temple that I had once served in, in a past life. It was a very short dream that seemed to be in the present, but kept flashing back and forth between the present and the past. The colors were very vivid. The name "Temple of the Jaguar" came to me. Part of the dream seemed symbolic and part of it was like I was actually in the jungle. I love cats, and they have played a very important part in my life as friends and as spiritual symbols.

When I came out of the dream, I knew I needed to find somebody in the Yucatan who was on an archaeological dig and share this dream. I didn't know much about the Maya at all, and I've never been to Mexico in this life or had I talked to anybody who was steeped in Mayan mythology.

It just so happened that a friend had recently met some people from Florida who were on a dig in the Yucatan at the time. He told me about them when I shared my experience with him. So I wrote to them and shared the dream. I mailed the letter on the first of May. These people were scheduled to leave the dig on the fifteenth of May. Postal officials told me that my letter could take two to three weeks to get there, and I thought, oh, great. I put a rush on it, but they didn't give me much hope for it getting there any faster. Well, it got there in four days! Here's another example of things falling into place and doors opening when a positive spiritual force is in motion. The people on the dig told me they had never gotten a letter so fast. I think there was a Divine force at work.

Shortly after my letter arrived, these people uncovered a chamber in a pyramid mound where there was a "jaguar priestess," whose body was found with a jaguar claws amulet around her neck. I was just elated. I felt the reason I had this dream was I had once been connected with this temple, and that the woman whose body was found was a priestess of the Mayan religion. I feel I was closely associated with her and that place.

Selena summed up the impact of these recollections on her life:

What these past-life dream recollections have in common is that they all involve an aspect of myself which was involved in spiritual work. I don't believe that in every lifetime I was serving in a ministerial capacity. I feel I've had these particular recollections because I am doing ministerial work in this life. One of the reasons why I look at *the dreams as past-life recollections is that it seems to be the best way of accounting for them and putting them into context with my life in terms of who I am, what I'm doing, and what I'm about.*

I don't have dreams like these very often. When they happen, I feel like I've dived into the collective unconscious and the inner workings of my own soul. I don't view reincarnation as a personality that survives from life to life—I view it more as a recycling process. I feel that when one dies, one moves into an energy pool or energy bank, dips into it, merges with the Light, and then re-emerges again and takes on another life. The soul is more of an impulse that goes from life to life through many different personality types and experiences, as a way of getting a well rounded education.

16

The Healer Within

Edgar Cayce once said that the ability to heal is both a gift and a talent developed in past lives. All of us seem to possess the gift to some extent, and can develop healing skill by training in one of the various energy transfer disciplines such as Reiki or Therapeutic Touch. Some individuals possess a great healing ability—developed over a series of lifetimes—and find their way into the traditional medical establishment, or become alternative healers.

The following is a story about a man who discovered healing after looking at past lives. Not only did he awaken new healing abilities within himself, he experienced a spiritual healing of himself:

Joe P. once enjoyed a life of wealth and material pleasure that many people would envy. An orthodontist with a thriving practice in Houston, Joe's income enabled him to indulge himself in possessions. A bachelor, he lived in a 3,000-square-foot house and filled it with art. He drove both a Jaguar and a Mercedes. He wore expensive clothes. He judged everything and everyone around him by appearances. He drank too much, but all in all, he was very happy. Or so he thought.

In 1983, at age forty-three, his life took a radical and drastic downward turn, leading eventually to a series of past-life regressions. Looking into the past opened the door to a transformation of his life.

The genesis of Joe's transformation was a near-fatal car accident in 1983 that sent him sailing through his windshield. The accident occurred when another car turned abruptly in front of Joe's car and collided with it. Immediately after impact, Joe felt himself floating about eight to ten feet above his body, watching the occupants of the other car, who were not seriously injured, attempt to revive him with cardiopulmonary resuscitation. He felt no pain.

As the men worked on his body, Joe's attention was drawn to a brilliant white light. It was unbelievably brilliant, yet it didn't hurt his eyes. A wonderful sense of well-being permeated him, unlike anything he had ever experienced before. He realized he was moving toward the light, and noticed that there were other persons around him moving in the same direction.

Then the frantic attempts of the men to save his life succeeded, and Joe found himself back in his body with a jolt. The sense of well-being was replaced with intense pain. He was keenly disappointed not to reach the light.

Joe suffered a severe concussion, two fractures in his neck and one fracture in his back. He was hospitalized, endured a lot of pain and took a lot of medication. He wore a neck collar for twenty-six months. As a result of his near-death experience, Joe looked upon life with new appreciation, yet his lifestyle remained largely unchanged.

About two years later, he contracted chronic mononucleosis from one of his young patients, and spent sixteen months in bed. He was forced to sell his practice. He was pumped full of medication, not only for the mononucleosis, but for the lingering effects of the car accident—he had four different doctors treating him. Disorientation and a severe depression set in, and Joe contemplated suicide. He'd always had a strong belief in God, but it was not strong enough to counter his despair.

He tried three times to kill himself. He took thirty-five tablets of an over-the-counter pain medication, far more than a lethal dose, and woke up the following morning without so much as a headache. A few days later, he took forty-five tablets. Nothing happened. The third time, he took fifty-five tablets. To his dismay, he woke up the following morning feeling no ill effects.

Frustrated, Joe cried out loud, "Why can't I do this?"

A voice in his head answered, "This is not open to you."

A few days after his third attempt to kill himself, Joe's sister, aware of his despondency, gave him the telephone number of hypnotherapist Sandee Mac. Joe appreciated his sister's concern but did not intend to call. A few weeks later, he found himself dialing Mac's number, adamant that he see her the next day.

When he had seated himself in her office, Mac asked, "Why are you interested in past-life regression?"

"I'm not," Joe replied. "I really don't know why I'm here."

"What's going on in your life?" she asked.

Joe told her. Mac asked him if he believed in reincarnation. He replied that he had once read a book on Bridey Murphy, and added, "I don't know if I believe in it or not. If that's the way God wants to run things, that's fine. I don't really care one way or the other."

After some discussion, Mac suggested, "Why don't we regress you and see what comes up?"

Joe considered it. "Okay," he agreed, "but I have a very strong belief in God, and if this is going to interfere with that, I don't want to do it."

Mac smiled. "It shouldn't interfere at all. In fact, I think it will surprise you."

Joe underwent weekly sessions for months, and in each session viewed several past lives. He described several which made the greatest impact upon his beliefs and attitudes, and how he changed his life as a result:

> The first regression took me back to what I believe was Atlantis. I saw an old man who had the most incredible eyes I had ever seen. They had purity. He was a man who had no deception in his life, no negativity, like I did in my present life. People came to him for help with their problems. He had a strong belief in God and felt his purpose was to help others. I didn't know it at first, but this man was me.
>
> At the end of the regression, my present self was introduced to my past self so that I could learn from the past life. The old man said to me, 'There are a lot of truths, and what is true for one person is not necessarily true for someone else. You have to tell people what is the truth for you and let them determine how it applies to their own lives. You don't make decisions about what you think is true for someone else.' I realized that I didn't let people discover their own truths. I was busy deciding what other people needed to know and then telling them that... I thought, 'If that's the way I was once, there's no reason why I can't be the same way now.'
>
> In my second regression, I was a young woman, again in Atlantis. She had been born blind and with severely deformed limbs, and was treated with healing techniques that we don't have now. Bowls and vats were lined with amethyst or citrine crystals and were filled with water. For treatment, people immersed parts of their bodies in the water.
>
> When I saw the woman, she was in her middle twenties and her limbs had been healed. Even though the power existed to heal her sight, she had chosen to remain blind. She said, 'I don't need sight because this way I can see people's souls. I don't need to see their bodies.' She was a healer and worked in a circular room divided into areas, each with a different type of bath. She played a musical instrument similar to a harp. Instead of strings, it had crystalline-like structures. When people stood near it, she moved her hands up and down these crystalline columns, making musical sounds. I could feel the

vibration in my hands as her hands moved up and down the prisms.

She said to me, 'I've been waiting for you to come back. The most important lesson you need to learn now is that you spend too much time looking at people's physical bodies and making instant decisions. If you can learn to look past the physical body to see the soul, then you will see people as they truly are.' I wanted to know how the crystals healed, but she said that was not the important lesson.

Since that session, I look at people differently. I don't pay nearly as much attention to their physical form—I listen to what they say and try to understand what they feel.

Some of the regressions Joe underwent were with others in groups. In a group session, the regressions were directed to a general theme, such as a life in a specific period of history. During one group regression to find the most powerful past life, Joe found himself once again in Atlantis:

My father was the ruler of a region and I was the second in line to succeed him. I had gotten to know a shaman, a wise man, who lived on the outskirts of town in a cave. He told me, 'Every person has every resource they need within themselves. It takes the right person with the right know-how and talent to bring it out.' I said, 'I don't understand.' He said, 'You will at the right time depending on what you choose to do.'

He said, 'You have two choices: follow your father in succession and have the power of ruling people, or else allow me give you the ability not only to heal people, but to teach them that they have the power they need within themselves to do whatever they need to do.' I decided the latter was much more important to me. I didn't care about ruling people, I wanted to help them be rulers of their own lives.

That life helped me see the value in helping others.

In another group session, the theme was to find two past lives, one's poorest and one's richest. Joe found both in the same past life:

> *I was an American Indian, a young man. At birth I had been given some gifts which made my father, who was the chief of the tribe, jealous. My mother left him in order to protect me. She ran off with a white man who was in love with her. The three of us were ostracized from our respective groups and were very poor. There was no food and no place to stay, and we were hunted and chased wherever we went. The day I died—I was in my teens—we were caught in a little cabin that was on fire because it was besieged by Indians.*
>
> *It dawned on me right at the last moment of that life that it was also my richest life. I had a mother who had left everything she knew because of me, and a white man stepfather who loved both of us so much that he had given up everything he had for us.*
>
> *The Indian boy said to me, 'I knew you were coming back to meet me, so that I could tell you that in one life, you had both the poorest and richest life you could imagine.' The lesson I learned was in that life I had everything I needed, even though I didn't have a lot of material things. I had the things that were important. I was extremely happy. Afterwards, I couldn't even talk about it. It was overwhelming.*

The lesson of self-sufficiency and richness of life without materialism was presented again to Joe with the help of an animal. The group session's theme was to identity one's tonal, or animal guardian spirit. In Indian and shamanic cultures, it is believed that everyone has such a guardian spirit, which can be drawn upon for its strengths and attributes. For the shaman, the spirit also functions as a power animal that protects and serves him and becomes a virtual alter ego. Animal guardian spirits usually are acquired in vision quests, in which an individual undertakes a lone vigil in the wilderness.

Joe's tonal appeared to him as a white polar bear. He was able to go inside the bear and look out through its eyes. The bear's lesson for him was that the bear had everything it needed within itself for sustenance and happiness.

The inner energies and forces released by past-life regressions brought about improvements in Joe's life. His attitudes toward materialism changed, and he awakened to an interest in helping others.

> *In looking back over these regressions, I could see how they all tied together. Our Higher Consciousness picks out the lives we see for a certain reason. I saw how extremely materialistic I'd been yet I still wasn't happy. So, I began to get rid of what I thought I didn't need. Now I have a small, comfortable apartment. I have plants instead of a Mercedes. In fact, I don't even own a car. I'm infinitely more happy than I ever have been in my entire life. I still have some art on the walls, but I don't have to constantly buy things and clothes that I don't need.*
>
> *I also became very interesting in healing. In a lot of other lives, I was involved in medicine or some kind of healing. In a couple of lives, I healed by putting my hands on people. That really intrigued me. I'd heard about laying on of hands but thought it was church talk. Then I found out about Reiki, which is a hands-on healing technique in which you channel energy. I went through that training and learned how to do it.*
>
> *I've also learned two other methods of healing, which have involved extensive training. I became a Mahikari master. Mahikari is a healing system based on a divine revelation given to a Japanese man around 1959, and it is widely used in some parts of the world. It's similar in principle to Reiki, in that divine light is directed by your hands. The other system is Omega Shakti, which has nine levels of expertise and is taught by only two people in the world, one in California and one in Tibet.*
>
> *I get a good feeling from doing touch healing that was different from my orthodontics practice. I don't charge for it.*

With his orthodontics practice gone, Joe decided to return to school rather than spend an estimated three years that it would take to restart another dental practice. He began work on a doctorate in genetic engineering, a subject he studied in dental school. He also began studying the reputed healing powers of music, and psychotherapy techniques. His life, he said, "just gets better and better, especially when I am helping someone else."

Another transformation for Joe was his discovery and development of his own psychic powers: he learned to astral project his consciousness out-of-body, and to see clairvoyantly.

After he learned how to astral project, Mac hypnotized him once and suggested he go to the lower astral plane, where it is believed that suicide victims go upon death. She told him, "You came close to that, and I want you to see what it was like." Joe was horrified by what he encountered:

> *It was creepy, it was just terrible. It was worse than anything I could imagine. I grew up in small towns hearing about the fiery brimstone of hell and that was bad enough, but this was worse. There was this murky, thick, gray fog I could actually touch—it was like a gel. Big, ugly 'things' kept bumping into me. The more agitated I got, the more these big, creepy 'things' bumped into me. It seemed that my agitation attracted them. There was no way out. It just got worse and worse. It was a sensation that I can't really describe. I kept saying, 'Can I please leave?' I had only been there a few seconds, but there's no sense of time there. In a few seconds I felt like I'd been there a hundred years.*
>
> *I've been told that suicide victims stay in this place for as long as they would have lived on earth. I was very thankful I had not succeeded in committing suicide.*

The lesson that suicide is counter to divine law was reinforced again when Mac asked Joe to attend a therapy session involving the soul of a suicide victim. A woman had come to Mac, concerned that a friend of hers who had killed herself had not crossed over into the divine light but was stuck somewhere. The woman was anxious to help her friend's soul find peace. Mac hypnotized the woman to leave her body so that the soul of the friend could enter, and Mac could talk to her. This was what Joe witnessed:

> *As the woman went into trance, I could see a beautiful blue aura surrounding her. Sandee said, 'I want you to move up and out of your body.' I thought the aura would then go away, but it didn't. It raised up about ten or twelve inches from the body and stayed there. Sandee said, 'Now I want your friend who committed suicide to come into your body.' The minute that soul entered the body and answered, 'I'm here,' I saw the same thick, gray, gel-like fog all over the woman's body. I got goosebumps and almost jumped out of my skin! Sandee talked to the soul and explained how she should go toward the light. The instant the soul found the light, the gray fog disappeared. The other woman came back into her body and the blue aura returned. I couldn't talk about that for a couple of days. I think God allowed me to see it for a reason, to show me once again that suicide is not acceptable.*

Joe's former ambivalence about past-life regression was replaced by a firm conviction in its value:

> *I still have a lot of questions about reincarnation, but now there's no doubt in my mind that it's true. I have a vivid imagination, but I couldn't make up things I saw and the feelings I had. My experiences have been too real not to be real.*
>
> *Each time I go to another regression, I know there's a lesson waiting to be learned. I'm excited about it, because I want to learn and grow. The car accident and suicide attempts evidently had a purpose in getting me to where I am now...*
>
> *I found an astrology chart that a woman did for me in 1980, when I still had a problem with alcohol. She said that my life would take a complete, positive turnaround if I changed direction, especially between the ages of forty-two and forty-six. I was forty-six when I*

began past-life regression. Since then, I've consulted several psychic readers who didn't know about the car accident. They told me that I had been in a near-fatal collision because I had been following the wrong path, and my guides had tried unsuccessfully to get my attention. The accident apparently was the only way to get it. I did change and started appreciating life more, but I drifted back to the old path, and then I came down with mono...

I don't push anyone about the benefits of past-life regression. When I meet people who are interested, I tell them what it's done for me. It can be a positive building force in one's life.

18

New Horizons in Reincarnation Research

We have been looking at reincarnation from many perspectives, and there is one more that deserves consideration: what do the dead themselves have to say on the subject? The living have always been in contact with the dead through mediums, dreams, apparitions, mysterious events, and technology. Are there messages from people who have died about whether or not they will have the opportunity to reincarnate? Reliable spirit communications could give us the lowdown on reincarnation.

Techno talking to the dead
The dead have delivered many messages about the afterlife. Messages delivered through mediums, while compelling, still pass through a human filter. There are various scenarios of the afterlife, many of which do not conform to religious teachings, and some of which do. Since the early twentieth century, technology has been used increasingly in attempts to better and more verifiable spirit communications. Nothing yet passes the

muster of science, but, like other kinds of anecdotal evidence, messages from the dead delivered over radios, televisions, tape recorders and other devices are often difficult, if not impossible to explain away.

The most common means of talking to the dead involves a method call Electronic Voice Phenomena, or EVP. When telegraphy, radio, the phonograph and magnetic recorders were developed, researchers noticed that stray, unexplained voices sometimes manifested, and sometimes the voices gave meaningful messages. By the 1960s, researchers discovered that a tape recorder left running might yield mystery voices. If questions were asked, and a few seconds left for answers, the mystery voices might leave answers in the blank spaces. Usually the voices were not heard in real-time, but only on playback.

Researchers developed a variety of techniques for collecting EVP. Some involved passive collection, using recorders to capture voices heard on playback. Other methods involved real-time collection, the ability to hear the mystery voices as they spoke. Most real-time methods use a noise background generated by white noise, radio static, fans, running water, crowd babble and so on. The mystery voices talk on top of the noise.

Sarah Estep, the founder of the American Association for Electronic Voice Phenomena (now the Association for TransCommunication), collected tens of thousands of passive EVPs during the course of her research from the 1970s to her death in 2008. During part of the time I lived in Maryland (1993–2009), Estep was a neighbor, and I was able to get to know her and even do some experiments with her on her recording equipment. She had made an amazing transformation from someone who had no belief in an afterlife – death was oblivion – to a believer in survival and an afterlife, and also reincarnation. "I know I have lived in this world many, many times," she told me.

After becoming active in spirit communications, Estep made three trips to Egypt, certain she had lived there long ago as other personalities, as long as 2,000 years ago. She taped some of her most startling EVP messages that indicated she had indeed lived in Egypt in ancient times. Estep taped everywhere she went, and collected about one hundred messages. At a desert site of thousands of Coptic tombs, she walked around, stopping at various tombs and inviting someone to speak. At one tomb, a female voice told her, "I buried you." Estep took a photo of the tomb, and in the ensuing years often wondered if she had been buried right there at that spot. She had the deep feeling that she had lived several times in ancient Egypt.

She had a moving experience at a small tomb by the pyramids in Cairo. She sat on a stone floor by a statue of a small boy and inexplicably became overwhelmed with grief. She taped many messages, including one that said, "I am back with you." Her daughter, Becky, taped as well, and got the message, "My mother." The voice sounded as though it belonged to an adolescent boy. They wondered if Estep had once been related to the boy of the statue.

Estep was called by name inside the Great Pyramid in Cairo. There, she also recorded a conversation among communicators about her. Voices asked if she could be trusted, and other voices answered, "Yes, she is a good person."

The EVPs convinced Estep that she had experienced past lives, and was able to reconnect with them through EVP.

In the mid-1980s, a couple in Luxembourg, Maggy Harsh-Fischbach and her husband Jules Harsh, began experimenting in EVP and got astounding results. They formed a research organization, Cercle d'Etudes sure la Transcommunication (CETL), and collected EVPs over radio, television, fax, computer, telephone answering machine and recording devices. Some of the messages eventually were live and real-time, like a two-way conversation.

CETL established contact with a group of high-level beings called The Rainbow People, who said they are interested in assisting human beings make a communications bridge to the afterlife and to other realms. The

Rainbow People are of such a high frequency that they have never been in physical form; we might liken them to our concept of angels, although they are not angels. Their point of contact with CETL is a being who calls himself "Technician." The name is more a description of his duties to aid the communication process.

Technician affirmed reincarnation in response to a question posed during a session. According to Technician, human beings require multiple lifetimes in order to mature spiritually. We do not regress, but we do pay prices for choices, and sometimes we actually choose suffering. Technician said:

> *Reincarnation exists. There are parallel worlds! Mankind evolves in a forever moving wheel of life. Some have arrived at a point of development that allows them a better understanding. Reincarnation means progression forward, not backward. Animals too are subject to the cycle of incarnation. A human being does not reincarnate in an animal body. Important Earth personalities are being born again as simple people if they used their previous life only to exploit others. There is a purpose for sickness and infirmity. Do not judge the fate of other people... Many of those individuals have selected a life of suffering for their incarnation.*

One technique of collecting EVP has become increasingly popular among paranormal researchers, and I use it myself in my investigations. It is a form of radio sweep, which augments the possibility for real-time, two-way exchanges. The sweep devices are called by different names, such as "ghost box," "Minibox" and "Frank's Box," depending on who designed them. Basically, they play a form of sweep in which the AM radio band is scanned very rapidly, moving from station to station every second or two. The result is a jumble of noise that seems to enable spirit voices to come through in real time, talking on top of the radio. It seems possible to hold brief exchanges. For more details on radio sweep, as well as the history and potential of high-tech spirit communications, I refer you to my book *Talking to the Dead*, co-authored with George Noory, the host of *Coast To Coast AM*.

Empirical evidence
In 2009, I became involved in some intriguing experiments using radio sweep and other, new methods of researching reincarnation.

In 2003, a medical doctor, Walter Semkiw, published a book entitled *Return of the Revolutionaries: The Case for Reincarnation and Soul Groups Reunited*. Semkiw had become interested in reincarnation in 1984 when he had been told by a medium that he had been John Adams, one of the founding fathers of the United States in the Revolutionary War and a signer of the Declaration of Independence.

At first Semkiw thought he had wasted his money on the reading, for it seemed like a preposterous idea. But years later, he was prompted by a voice in his head to study the life of John Adams. He did so, and found he had an astonishing match to Adams.

Return of the Revolutionaries documents matches of present-day persons to famous figures from history. According to Semkiw, such things as measurable facial characteristics, personalities, writing styles, interests, professional choices, attractions to certain geographic areas, memories, symbols and so on are barometers for the case for reincarnation. By comparing a past and present life, significant matches can be made. The evidence, of course, depends on availability from the past. Famous figures are more likely to have sufficient data recorded about them in order to make comparisons possible. A cluster of personalities involved in the birth of America comprise a soul group, many of whose members have reincarnated in the present, he says.

Semkiw's work was among many inspirations in the reincarnation research of Paul Von Ward, an interdisciplinary cosmologist in Georgia who focuses on the psycho-physical evidence for past lives. Von Ward says that reincarnation is provable by empirical data. Channeled information, dreams, and intuitive feelings are helpful, but not as good as biological data, which he used to develop a model for a "Reincarnation Experiment." In his book *The Soul Genome: Science and Reincarnation* (2008) he presents cases that are hard to explain away as chance. His model of the "soul genome" involves comparisons of physical and psychological factors that are independent of parental influences in the present life and possible past life. Von Ward told me in an interview:

> *Reincarnation is the natural process of the evolution of consciousness. History does not repeat itself but it rhymes, and that also may apply to reincarnation. We do not exactly repeat a life, but the legacy of a past life rhymes with a present life. The data I've collected in the Reincarnation Experiment suggests that each of us inherits a psychophysical legacy from a unrelated deceased individual. The inheritance appears to shape biometric factors such as facial geometry, ear forms, body types, hand and finger proportions, and hair patterns. Certain chromosomes and mitrochondrial DNA, eye iris patterns, and other genotype features may also correspond. Memories from specific lifetimes can also be verified, as they were in the 2,000-plus Stevenson cases.*
>
> *This past-life legacy also appears to influence one's personality development, including unique mental capacities, dominant emotional states, interpersonal styles of behavior, and creative interests and talents. Knowledge and skills that cannot have been acquired in this lifetime are also linked to one or more lifetimes. For example, if you are athletic in one lifetime and if you carry ability forward, you are likely to have a capability of being athletic in another lifetime. You may not necessarily have a career in athletics in both lifetimes. Instead, you may build on the legacy you inherited in order to evolve. Fame will not carry forward but what you learn will. It is important for us to know that our inclinations have genuine roots in the past. The biggest advantage of knowing about past lives may not be for the*

individual but for parents and teachers in guiding children.

Von Ward takes into consideration subjective past-life recall data, such as dreams, intuition, spontaneous recall and visions, hypnosis, and channeled material from the dead, spirits and the Akashic Records, the cosmic repository of everything in existence. All of these can provide corroboration, but they are vulnerable to being affected by a person's thoughts and wishes, he said.

I approached Paul about designing some experiments to try to obtain yet another form of independent validation of past life cases through real-time EVP with a ghost box. Could blind tests be set up that would provide supporting evidence? Von Ward was intrigued. He thought the information obtained via EVP and ITC might be similar to intuitive, psychic, and channeled material, but without the subjectivity found in popular reincarnation research. "The use EVP and ITC may also lead to presently unrecognized areas of evidence that would help test reincarnation theory," he told me.

Von Ward designed a set of experiments for me to carry out with one of my radio sweep devices called the Minibox. The purpose was to identify possible new past-life matches and corroborate evidence for cases now under evaluation in von Ward's Reincarnation Experiment. If the results were promising, EVP and ITC could help scientists eliminate some of the subject and researcher bias in analyzing "cases of the reincarnation type," as Stevenson liked to describe them.

According to the protocols established for the data collection, two types of reincarnation subjects were used: One with the name and case number of the present subject known to me and the "Spirit Voice," and another with the name in a sealed envelope not known to me, but identified as only a case number. None of the subjects were known personally to me. Each subject's form had a question about the identity of a past life or about information on events/activities in the past life.

I posed the questions during recorded EVP sessions, and noted responses, which were sent back to von Ward for analysis. In our first round, we had no significant hits, but some responses were intriguing. As of this writing, we have gone back to the drawing board to redesign the experiments. We both believe that real-time EVP has promise as a reincarnation research tool, and results will improve as does the technology.

Do your own past-life EVP research
Meanwhile, anyone can do simple EVP at home to ask questions about past lives. Get a recorder and, during a quiet time, ask some questions about who you were in a previous life, where you lived, what you did, and how you can find evidence to support the information. Leave about ten seconds blank after every question. Record for about ten to fifteen minutes, and play back your recording. You may have mystery voices answering your questions!

Some people like to leave a recorder running for a long period of time. You can experiment with that, too. Ask a few questions, and then leave the recorder running unattended.

It is important to ask for ways to verify the information you may get – the hard data is always the clincher.

In conclusion
In the course of this book, we've looked at different ways that people remember other lives, and how they have been helped by those memories. The benefits of recalling other lives can be demonstrated only through personal experience. Sometimes the benefits are difficult to explain to others – they are an intuitive "knowing" or new inner wisdom that comes to light. If you've had glimpses of other lives, allow yourself to follow the threads and see where they lead. You are much more than this present life.

Recalling past lives can have tremendous healing power. Past-life recall is not an instant fix for life's difficulties, nor does it instantly change personality and character. However, it can open awareness and can provide inspiration toward change for the better.

About the Author

Rosemary Ellen Guiley is a leading expert on paranormal and spiritual topics and is the author of more than fifty books and hundreds of articles on a wide range of topics. She has had a life-long interest in the paranormal, and has worked full-time in the field as a researcher, investigator and author since the early 1980s. She conducts her own original field investigations and research. She conducts past-life regression workshops.

Her books include nine single-volume encyclopedias. She does frequent media and public lecture appearances. You can find out more about her and her work on her main website, Visionary Living, at *www.visionaryliving.com*.

Bibliography

The following titles have been grouped according to topic or dominant theme. Some of the titles may fall into two or more categories.

General and Overview; Reincarnation in Religions

Cranston, Sylvia and Carey Williams. *Reincarnation: A New Horizon in Science, Religion, and Society.* New York: Julian Press, 1984.

Fisher, Joe. *The Case for Reincarnation.* New York: Bantam Books, 1985.

Gallup, George, Jr., with William Proctor. *Adventures in Immortality.* New York: McGraw-Hill Book Co., 1982.

Gyatso, Tenzin, His Holiness the Fourteenth Dalai Lama. *Kindness, Clarity, and Insight.* Ithaca, NY: Snow Lion Publications, 1984.

Hall, Manly Palmer. *Reincarnation: The Cycle of Necessity.* Los Angeles: The Philosophical Research Society, 1956.

Hanson, Virginia and Rosemarie Stewart (eds). *Karma: The Universal Law of Harmony.* 2nd ed., Wheaton, IL: Theosophical Publishing House, 1981.

Head, Joseph and S.L. Cranston (compilers and editors). *Reincarnation: The Phoenix Fire Mystery.* New York: Julian Press, 1977.

_____. *Reincarnation: An East-West Anthology.* Wheaton, IL: The Theosophical Publishing House, 1985.

His Holiness the Dalai Lama of Tibet. *My Land and My People: Memoirs of the Dalai Lama of Tibet.* New York: Potala Corp., 1977.

Hultkrantz, Ake. *The Religions of the American Indians*. Berkeley: University of California Press, 1967.

Kim, Yong Choon. *Oriental Thought*. Totowa, NJ: Rowman and Littlefield, 1973.

MacGregor, Geddes. *Reincarnation in Christianity*. Wheaton, IL: The Theosophical Publishing House, 1978.

Moore, Marcia and Mark Douglas. *Reincarnation, Key To Immortality*. York Cliffs, ME: Arcane Publications, 1968.

Moore, Marcia. *Hypersentience*. New York: Bantam Books, 1977.

Sen, K.M. *Hinduism*. Harmondsworth, Middlesex, England: Penguin Books, 1961.

Story, Francis. *Rebirth as Doctrine and Experience*. Kandy, Sri Lanka: Buddhist Publication Society, 1975.

Scientific Investigations of Reincarnation and Related Phenomena

Stevenson, Ian. *Cases of the Reincarnation Type*, Vols. I-IV. Charlottesville, VA: University Press of Virginia, 1975-1983.

_____. *Children Who Remember Previous Lives*. Charlottesville, VA: University Press of Virgina, 1987.

_____. *Twenty Cases Suggestive of Reincarnation*. 2nd ed. Charlottesville, VA: University Press of Virginia, 1974.

_____. *Unlearned Language: New Studies in Xenoglossy*. Charlottesville, VA: University Press of Virginia, 1984.

_____. *Xenoglossy*. Charlottesville, VA: University Press of Virginia, 1974.

Past-Life Discovery, Recall, Regression and Therapy

Avery, Jeanne. *Astrology and Your Past Lives.* New York: Fireside Books, 1987.

Bowman, Carol. *Childrens Past Lives: How Past Life Memories Affect Your Child.* New York: Bantam Books, 1997.

Evans, Jane A. *Twelve Doors to the Soul: Astrology of the Inner Self.* Wheaton, IL: The Theosophical Publishing House, 1979.

Fiore, Edith. *You Have Been Here Before.* New York: Ballantine Books, 1978.

Gershom, Yonassan. *Jewish Tales of Reincarnation.* Lanham, MD: Jason Aronson, Inc., 2000.

_____. *Beyond the Ashes: Cases of Reincarnation from the Holocaust.* Virginia Beach, VA: ARE Press, 1992.

Glaskin, G.M. *Windows of the Mind.* New York: Delacourt Press, 1974.

Goldberg, Bruce. *Past Lives Future Lives.* New York: Ballantine Books, 1982.

Kelsey, Denys and Joan Grant. *Many Lifetimes.* Garden City, NY: Doubleday, 1967.

Netherton, Morris and Nancy Shiffrin. *Past Lives Therapy.* New York: Ace Books, 1978.

Semkiw, Walter. *Return of the Revolutionaries: The Case for Reincarnation and Soul Groups Reunited.* Virginia Beach, VA: Hampton Roads, 2003.

Talbot, Michael. *Your Past Lives: A Reincarnation Handbook.* New York: Harmony Books, 1987.

Von Ward, Paul. *The Soul Genome: Science and Reincarnation.* Fenestra Books, 2008.

Wambach, Helen. *Life Before Life*. New York: Bantam Books, 1979.

———. *Reliving Past Lives*. New York: Harper & Row, 1978.

Weiss, Brian L. *Many Lives, Many Masters*. New York: Fireside Books, 1988.

Williston, Glenn and Judith Johnstone. *Discovering Your Past Lives*. Wellingborough, England: The Aquarian Press, 1988.

Woolger, Roger. *Other Lives, Other Selves*. Garden City, NY: Doubleday & Co., 1987.

Past-Life Accounts

Banerjee, H.N. *Americans Who Have Been Reincarnated*. New York: Macmillan, 1980.

Bernstein, Morey. *The Search for Bridey Murphy*. Revised ed. New York: Avon, 1975.

Clow, Barbara. *The Mind Chronicles: A Visionary Guide into Past Lives*. Rochester, VT: Bear & Company, 2007.

Cooke, Grace. *The Illumined Ones*. New Lands, England: White Eagle Publishing Trust, 1966.

Cott, Jonathan. *The Search for Omm Sety*. Garden City, NY: Doubleday & Co., 1987.

Ebon, Martin (ed.). *Reincarnation in the Twentieth Century*. New York: The World Publishing Co., 1969.

Grant, Joan. *Far Memory*. New York: Harper & Row, 1956.

Guirdham, Arthur. *The Cathars and Reincarnation.* London: Neville Spearman, 1970.

Jay, Reverend Carroll E. *Gretchen, I Am.* New York: Wyden Books, 1977.

Lenz, Frederick. *Lifetimes: True Accounts of Reincarnation.* New York: Fawcett Crest, 1977.

Leonardi, Dell. *The Reincarnation of John Wilkes Booth.* Old Greenwich, CT: The Devin-Adair Co., 1975.

MacLaine, Shirley. *Out On A Limb.* New York: Bantam Books, 1983.

_____. *Dancing in the Light.* New York: Bantam Books, 1985.

Randles, Jenny. *Beyond Explanation?* New York: Bantam Books, 1987.

Stearn, Jess. *The Search for A Soul: Taylor Caldwell's Psychic Lives.* Garden City, NY: Doubleday & Co., 1972.

_____. *The Search for the Girl With the Blue Eyes.* Garden City, NY: 1968.

_____. *Yoga, Youth, and Reincarnation.* Garden City, NY: Doubleday & Co., 1965.

_____. *Soul Mates.* New York: Bantam Books, 1984.

Sutphen, Dick. *You Were Born Again To Be Together.* New York: Pocket Books, 1976.

_____. *Past Lives, Future Loves.* New York: Pocket Books, 1978.

Edgar Cayce Readings, Interpretations and Perspective

Cerminara, Gina. *Many Mansions.* New York: Signet/New American Library, 1978. First published 1950.

_____. *Many Lives, Many Loves.* New York: William Sloane Assoc., 1963.

Church, W.H. *Many Happy Returns: The Lives of Edgar Cayce.* San Francisco: Harper & Row, 1984.

Langley, Noel. *Edgar Cayce on Reincarnation.* New York: Castle Books, 1967.

Sparrow, Lynn Elwell. *Reincarnation: Claiming Your Past, Creating Your Future.* San Francisco: Harper & Row, 1988.

Van Auken, John. *Past Lives and Present Relationships.* Virginia Beach, VA: Inner Vision, 1984.

Woodward, Mary Ann. *Edgar Cayce's Story of Karma.* New York: Coward, McCann & Geoghegan, 1971.

Between-Lives States

Evans-Wentz, W.Y. (ed.) *The Tibetan Book of the Dead.* 3rd ed. London: Oxford University Press, 1960.

Whitton, Joel L. and Joe Fisher. *Life Between Life.* Garden City, NY: Dolphin/Doubleday, 1986.

Atlantis

Cayce, Edgar Evans. *Edgar Cayce on Atlantis.* New York: Warner Books, 1968.

Donnelly, Ignatius. *Atlantis: The Antediluvian World.* New York: Gramercy Publishing, 1985.

Michell, John. *The New View Over Atlantis.* San Francisco: Harper & Row, 1988.

Spence, Lewis. *The History of Atlantis.* Secaucus, NJ: The Citadel Press, 1968.

Westwood, Jennifer (ed.). *The Atlas of Mysterious Places.* New York: Weidenfeld & Nicholson, 1987.

www.ingramcontent.com/pod-product-compliance
Lightning Source LLC
Chambersburg PA
CBHW020646300426
44112CB00007B/254